WHO

CARES

WHO CARES

NICOLAS STACEY

WHO CARES

ANTHONY BLOND

First published 1971 by Anthony Blond Ltd
56 Doughty Street, London WC1
© Copyright 1971 by Nicolas Stacey
SBN 218 51147 7
Made and printed in Great Britain by
The Anchor Press Ltd
and bound by
Wm. Brendon & Son Ltd
both of Tiptree, Essex

TO ANNE
for being so understanding and patient

TO MY MOTHER AND FATHER
for being so generous

Hitherto I have never understood why authors found it necessary to thank so many people for helping them to write their books. I wondered why they could not write them on their own without making so much fuss. Now I know differently. But for the help and encouragement of a host of good friends this book would never have been completed. My first thanks are to an ex-team mate of Woolwich, the Reverend Jeremy Hurst, for working through the first rough draft. To other members of the Woolwich team, particularly the Reverend Robert Hughes, the Reverend Brian Cooper, and the Reverend Paul Jobson, I am grateful for checking the facts and making suggestions. The emphasises and the opinions are mine. Much of the story was made possible by them and by my other colleagues. To Bishop John Robinson and Mr. John Grigg my gratitude for reading the manuscript and making comments. Over the years no man has been better served by his secretaries than I have. To Hazel Crawford, who lived through it all at Woolwich, a heartfelt thank-you. To Valerie Belton, for typing and retyping the manuscript without losing her sanity, her patience or her good humour, I can never be thankful enough.

Acknowledgement is made to the following for their kind permission to reprint material: Leslie Frewin Publishers Ltd. Faith Under Fire and G. P. Putnam's Sons First Four Minutes.

One

ON THE FACE OF IT, THERE IS LITTLE in my background and even less in my personality which makes me an obvious candidate for Holy Orders. My mother and father were members of that gay and restless London set of the 1920s recovering from the carnage of the 1914–18 war. My father, a staunch member, and one-time Chairman of White's Club, worked in the City. He was on a ship to America when the great crash of 1929 occurred. He had left England as a comparatively rich man and by the time he had docked in New York he had lost most of his money. But by the time I could sit up and take notice his financial situation had recovered, and since then my parents have lived comfortably. I sometimes wonder if my comparatively privileged background has made me insensitive to the needs, aspirations and insecurities of working-class people, who I have spent most of my sixteen years as a parson trying to serve. I hope not.

Many people and many experiences contributed to the development of the faith which made me resign my commission from the Royal Navy in order to seek ordination. Among the influences was my nanny, who was a deeply religious woman. She had been my mother's nanny and brought up my twin sister, my brother and myself. In all, she was with our family for over sixty years.

I do not recall learning much about the Christian faith at my prep school from which I was scheduled to go to Eton. But at the last moment I expressed a keen desire to join the Navy as a cadet and go to the Royal Naval College at Dartmouth. I suspect my main reason for this was that there was no quicker way to fighting in the war. Dartmouth boys went to sea as midshipmen at seventeen. Public-school boys were eighteen before they could fight. My life might have taken quite a different course had I gone to Eton, as my parents wanted, before joining the Navy. As a result of going to Dartmouth, two things happened both of which made a profound impression on me and which were, I believe, partly responsible for my ordination. Neither would have happened had I gone to Eton. First, I met the Reverend Geoffrey Tiarks, who was Chaplain of the Naval College, and is now Bishop of Maidstone and Senior Chaplain to the Archbishop of Canterbury, and secondly, I did just get to sea in the closing stages of the war, was in the first ship that went into Hong Kong after the Japanese surrendered and visited Hiroshima shortly after the atomic bomb was dropped.

I loved Dartmouth and thrived on it. It was highly competitive, athletically orientated, fast-moving and reasonably tough—very different from what is now reckoned to make a good educational establishment. My critics accuse me of being impatient. My colleagues tell me that I require things done yesterday. In the most formative years of my life it was drilled into me that when one is ordered to move 'one doesn't walk, one doesn't run, but one flies'. For four terms, I was at the Naval College overlooking the Dart. Then the college was bombed. It was a brilliantly conceived and well-executed mid-morning raid in a period when air raid routines were at their least well organized —timed for the moment when the cadets would be changing classrooms. What the German intelligence did not know was that for some unlikely reason we had been given an extra week's leave and the college was empty when the raid took place. Had we been there it was estimated that one-third of the 500 cadets would have been killed.

After a term at Müllers' formidable orphanage at Bristol, which we shared with American Negro soldiers, the college was transferred to Eaton Hall near Chester, the home of the Duke of Westminster. It was here that Geoffrey Tiarks joined the staff as Chaplain. He was, and remains, an impressive figure who was able to develop deep, yet uncomplicated, relationships with many of the cadets. Even in wartime when the best officers were required for manning the ships, the house officers at the college were of a high standard. But Geoffrey Tiarks stood out. To me, aged fifteen or so, he was a man among men. My pragmatic mind thought that there must be something in the Christian faith if it could capture the imagination, conviction and commitment of such a man. One of the greatest advantages of the boarding system of education is that it gives better opportunities than are possible at a day school for boys to get to know members of the staff. Certainly I spent many hours discussing with Geoffrey Tiarks the things that concerned and interested me. Perhaps we cadets were a conformist and uncritical lot, for as I recall, we accepted the Christian faith and the compulsory chapel-going that went with it without much questioning or protest. Except on one occasion: a Bible-punching politician who had some political office with the Navy ranted at us from the pulpit and we all started laughing. Mass beatings followed this episode. By and large we took the view that young Naval officers and gentlemen subscribed in general terms to the Christian faith, without getting over-involved; we did not think it was all that important or relevant. We knew that when we went to sea, the moment to which we were all looking forward, it was expected that officers would go to church as a good example to the sailors. When I was Chief Cadet Captain, out of loyalty to the Chaplain and to set a good example to the junior cadets, I used to make a point of going to early Communion. Today it might sound strangely pious and unctuous, but it was not considered so twenty-five years ago.

At the time, I was not too conscious of the effect Geoffrey Tiarks had upon me except that he had personal characteristics that I wished to emulate. It was a few months later, when, as a seventeen-year-old midshipman, I came face to face with the ghastly aftermath of war, and used to lie night after night in my hammock wondering what had gone wrong with the world and whether there was any meaning in life at all, that many of the things the Chaplain had said to me in our discussions began to fall into place.

On leaving Dartmouth I was posted to HMS *Anson*, a mighty King George V class of battleship. She was being commissioned in Plymouth but was not immediately ready for midshipmen, and so to fill the time I was sent to a fearful 1914–18 war destroyer called HMS *Vanquisher*. I was given a cabin in the bowels of this beastly thing next door to the oil tank which leaked. The all-pervading smell was overwhelming. No sooner had I joined the ship at Sheerness in January than we set out to sea to escort some merchant ships into the Atlantic where other and more robust vessels were to convoy them to America. For years I had dreamt about giving orders, inspiring sailors, killing Germans, sinking ships, shooting down aircraft and picking up survivors. And here was the moment of truth.

I was to report to the bridge for a watch from midnight to 4.00 am. My duties were to make cocoa and do other odd jobs for the officer of the watch. This was the moment for which we had spent four years preparing. What a yawning gap there is between fantasy and reality. There was a storm in the Channel and the waves were green when they broke over the ship. I tried to sleep for an hour before my watch but the combination of excitement and seasickness made it impossible. We had been trained never to walk along the deck at sea without holding on to a lifeline, and as I lay waiting for my time to go to the bridge I worked out how I would get there. I had to climb a vertical ladder and, at the top, open a hatch which was flush with the deck. I would get to the hatch, wait for a wave to break over the deck above and give me a few seconds to open it and get on deck, shut the hatch and grab a lifeline before the next wave broke. Alas, it did not work out that way. My oilskins caught in the hatch handle, the next wave broke before I could disentangle myself, and I was swept down the deck; saved from being dragged overboard only by the ship's railings. I staggered to the bridge soaked to the skin, cold, bruised, frightened and still feeling desperately seasick. That was the start of my active sea-going career as a keen and ambitious Naval officer. So much for one's dreams.

For five ghastly days of Channel and Atlantic storm, seasick I remained. I used to creep from my cabin to the bridge and back again praying for death. One of the ships in the convoy was sunk. How envious I was of its crew. I prayed the German submarine would get us next. Death by drowning seemed infinitely more desirable than a life of seasickness. A few weeks later when HMS *Anson* sailed on her first voyage from Plymouth to Scapa Flow we had to go to action stations in the Irish Channel. Only half the ship's company, many of whom had never been to sea before, ever reached their stations. The other half lay groaning and spewing on their mess decks. How I sympathized with them.

We were in Malta when the German war ended, and in Sydney when the Japanese surrendered. We sailed immediately for Hong Kong and, as there were no British soldiers in the area, it was decided that a Naval detachment from HMS *Anson* should occupy the island. The ship's gunnery officer, to whom I was 'doggy', was appointed second-in-command of the occupation force, and I went ashore with him. It was to be a thrilling experience. We had no idea what we were going to find or what we were going to do. My first job was to commandeer, which meant steal, all the transport I could find and go to the prisoner-of-war camps to release the service and civilian prisoners and get the sickest of them to the hospital ship which followed us in. We set up our headquarters at Hong Kong Police Station. It was my job to act as a kind of troubleshooter. Calls used to come in saying there was looting going on; a Japanese soldier was thought to be in hiding; I would collect a few sailors and try to sort it out. Only a very few Europeans (mostly those married to Chinese girls) who were particularly susceptible to pressures had collaborated with the Japanese. We had to find them and imprison them. One of my jobs was to visit them last thing at night to see they were all right, which I found horrible as there was something particularly pathetic and vulnerable about them.

We spent about six weeks ashore in Hong Kong before the soldiers arrived and took over. We then moved on to Hiroshima for a few days. It was on the bright cloudless morning of 6 August 1945 at 8.15 am that the first atomic bomb had been dropped. First came the flash and about 100,000 died. Then came the blast and the city of over 300,000 inhabitants was virtually destroyed. This was followed by the mushroom cloud and, as one eye witness described it to me, the living dead cried out for water, and the rubbery human faces sloughed off like masks.

When we got there even after two months, it still stank of death and decay. Most of the corpses had been disposed of —still, there were a few bones protruding from the rubble. The piteous remnants of the population squatted in a pathetic shanty-town of squalid huts tending their burns. The five square miles of 'total destruction' was flat, derelict and desolate. Little groups of orphan children picked their way around the ruins. I saw the bridge where the heat flash had roasted nine pedestrians and had clearly engraved their white shadows in the roadway. There was nothing but death in Hiroshima and we were discouraged from visiting it. But it lured me as it had a macabre and ghastly fascination. I used to go off alone and clamber over the rubble, and wonder and worry. I suppose I wanted to understand it and soak in the horror of it. It had a special poignancy for us because we realized that it was probably as a result of that hell that we were alive.

Had the atomic bombs not been dropped the war would have continued for some months and *Anson* would have been involved in the forthcoming attack on some of the Pacific islands occupied by the Japanese. Heavy casualties were expected in the operation, especially among ships, because of the effectiveness of the Japanese suicide planes which the pilots used to fly straight into the ships they were attacking. If things had worked out just that very little differently I would probably be dead. The war, the Far East and Hiroshima were traumatic experiences for me at seventeen.

My activities in the months that followed gave me time to digest my experience and evaluate it, for after visiting Hiroshima we did a showing-the-flag trip round the ports of Australia. We midshipmen were required to hold our liquor, which we did not always succeed in doing, and charm the teenage daughters of the local 'society', which was money for old rope, at a series of dances given in our honour. Girls are a push-over if you are seventeen and have three or four campaign medals banging on your chest. After this circus I was posted to a trawler whose task it was to lay buoys to guide minesweepers. Unfortunately no one knew where this worthy little vessel was and for two months I hitch-hiked around the Pacific looking for it. Eventually after travelling about 10,000 miles and visiting many islands in the Pacific I found it in Hong Kong.

I never really could enjoy any of the superb meals we used to have at the water-front restaurants there because I knew that we would have to climb over a knot of starving beggars too weak to stand, lying on the pavements outside. So much of what I saw appalled and depressed me. I had seen suffering on the grand scale, from the desolation of Hiroshima to the poverty and hunger of Hong Kong. What was the cause of these futile wars? Why was it that people had to be roasted to death in atomic explosions, and die in the gutters from starvation? Why did pregnant Chinese women have to earn their living humping sacks of coal from junk to jetty in the heat of the midday sun? Why did thousands have to eke out some kind of existence living in sampans? Why did an educated Naval officer spend his evening chasing imaginary black spiders up the wardroom wall? Why was the main recreation of so many of our sailors the bars and the brothels? And if this is all there is in this life of futility—is there anything beyond?

Such then were some of my experiences at eighteen which led me to resign from the Navy in order to be ordained. Basically I think my reasoning was simple although, no doubt, there are other factors involved of which I am unaware. I recalled the classical Christian teaching I had been given at Dartmouth. My own naïve and over-simplified interpretation and explanation for the horror, the inequality and the bestiality of so much human existence, was sin. Today, I am not quite so sure what I mean by the word. In those days hormones, heredity and environment were vague scientific terms; Freud and Marx and Einstein were little more than names to me. To an eighteen-year-old, the answer seemed simple: Man had misused God's precious gift of free will. He had fouled up God's good world.

Suddenly it all seemed obvious. God had sent His Son, not only to show us how to live, but to break the barriers of sin and give us the strength to live a new kind of life which would bring happiness for ourselves as well as for our neighbours. And furthermore God is not mocked; nor is He defeated. If men do not respond to His love and His call and so delay the coming of the Kingdom of God on Earth, then there is the life beyond when the inequalities of this sort will be sorted out. This explained things: it gave priorities and a programme for the present and hope for the future.

Clearly the really crucial job was not, after all, to become an admiral, but to become a parson and be in the front line against all evil, the fundamental cause of so much human misery; to dedicate one's life to trying to show people the possibilities, the relevance, and the truth of the Christian way. Any other job would seem pointless compared to this all-important one. The place then for me was not the bridge of the ship but the pulpit of the church.

Moreover, if being a parson made me as good a man as my friend Geoffrey Tiarks then indeed it would be the right choice.

When I announced my intention of leaving the Navy and to become ordained to make the world a better place many of my Naval officer friends and contemporaries were surprised and suggested that politics would be a more effective way of doing this. Perhaps they were as starry-eyed about the possibilities of political action as I was about Christian action. Perhaps it was the call of God.

My vision as a midshipman was, I think, compounded of some real insights and some considerable conceit. Both have been dulled by the years. Neither is wholly extinguished. But in 1946 as I used to pace the broad quarter-deck of HMS *Anson* on bright Pacific nights, it all seemed so obvious, so clear and so exciting. Christ was the Hope of the World. I must sign on in His Army. I must try and offer my life to Him, to receive the strength and power that He promised and be used to bring lots of people into fellowship and communion with Him so that together we might build a better world. The job of a priest, I was convinced, would be tremendously challenging, demanding and worthwhile. I think—but I am not sure—that I had a real and deep spiritual experience on those star-strung nights. Although my prayers were spasmodic and disorganized, there were times then, as there are now, when Jesus was extremely real. When I became a senior midshipman I had a minute cabin—the size of a cupboard. It was many decks below. My social life during our showing-the-flag cruise did not make heavy demands and I used to repair to my little cabin in the intervals between beach and cocktail parties and dances, and read C. S. Lewis and other popular works of theology. I used to relive the horrors of Hiroshima and Hong Kong and on my knees plan the things that one might do to build a better and happier world.

I wrote to my parents explaining that I was going to resign from the Navy and become a parson. Their initial reaction was one of disappointment. I had been quite successful in the Navy: it seemed to them to be a pity to throw away what might have been a promising career. Why should I start all over again in a field with which they were not over-familiar?

Yet, from the moment they were convinced that this was what I wanted to do, they gave me all the support in cash and kind to make it possible.

The Admiralty was to prove a tougher nut to crack. A good deal of public money had been spent on my training. As an ex-Chief-Cadet-Captain and winner of the King's telescope,* I was to some extent a marked man and at first the Navy refused to accept my resignation. Admirals had fatherly chats with me about the possibilities of Christian service as an officer in the Royal Navy. Others suggested kindly that many young men went through a religious phase which happily they grew out of. There is a tendency for senior Naval officers to patronize padres and judge them on whether they run the ship's comfort fund and tombola efficiently, and so it would have been inappropriate and priggish for me to suggest that at the end of the day the Gospel of Christ might be a more powerful weapon than the 15 inch guns they commanded. With uncharacteristic reticence I held my peace until it really looked as though they might insist that I stay in the Navy as, to be fair, they were perfectly entitled to do. Consequently at one interview I explained that all I had to do was punch an Admiral in the face and they would have to court-martial me and throw me out. This had the effect of making them realize that I really was in earnest and it was eventually decided that after completing my sub-lieutenant's courses I should be allowed to leave. These courses involved six months at the Royal Naval College at Greenwich for a mini-university course during which I alternated between God and the London Season, followed by a few weeks at the different Naval establishments where we learnt about gunnery, torpedoes, signalling and so on. I was never very interested in technical subjects and as I was going to leave the Navy shortly in any case

* The Navy's equivalent of the Sword of Honour at Sandhurst.

W.C.—B

I found it difficult to get worked up about the inside of a torpedo.

But I did pass out top of the course in HMS *Excellent*, the gunnery school, though it was always said about that admirable establishment that it was flannel rather than knowledge that was required to do well there.

While I was learning to fly a Tiger Moth aeroplane during the air course in the summer of 1947 an event occurred which was to have considerable influence on my life during the next few years. Towards the end of one guest night the station sports officer came up to me to ask why I had not put my name down for any event in the sports to be held the following day. He told me that all junior officers on course were expected to compete in at least two events. It was a good guest night and we had had plenty to drink. I asked him to put me down for the two events which made the minimum physical demands. So the next afternoon, having borrowed somebody else's gym shoes and a pair of rugger shorts which came down to my knees, I found myself running the 100 and 220 yards with a hangover. I won both events. This meant that I had to represent the station in the Southern Area Air Command Championships. These, after an absolutely minimal amount of training, I won as well. They led to the Naval Air Championship, which again I won. For the good name of the station, as the sports officer called it, I would have to compete in the Royal Navy Championships. To my amazement I won these too. I have a vague recollection that I may have even broken the Naval record into the bargain. All this happened in a period of about six weeks during which I tried to drink and smoke a little less, bought a pair of spiked shoes and a pair of those flimsy shorts which athletes wear. So there I was, the Naval Sprint Champion. My name started appearing in small print in tucked-away corners of the sports pages which, I recall, delighted me, as I thought it was the height of fame. It was all very surprising.

I had been a useful school sportsman and got into the first eleven at most sports at Dartmouth as well as being in a number of athletics finals. My ambitions, whatever they may have been in other directions, never included being a running champion. But by the end of summer 1947, I had become an Olympic 'possible' and was allocated to Mr. Sandy Duncan, Britain's top sprint coach, for special training and preparation for the Olympic Games to be held at Wembley in 1948. I also got extra meat from a sports-loving butcher.

Shortly after my twentieth birthday at the end of 1947, I finally left the Navy. It was a great wrench. Seven years of my life had been completely absorbed in it and I had few real friends outside. During the holidays in the war we only saw people within cycling distance and even after it, with severe petrol and food rationing, our social life was very circumscribed. I went straight to my father's farm to work as a farmhand for a few weeks so that I should not have time to feel depressed. Once I got over the shock of being separated from the ordered pattern of a young Naval officer's existence with its security, discipline and well-established pecking order, in which everybody knew exactly where he was, I never had any real regrets about my decision. In fact, I think I should have left the Navy later—as most of my contemporaries have now done—even if I had not wanted to be ordained. The Navy after the war had too many able men chasing too few worthwhile jobs. It saddens me to hear of my old shipmates in their early forties with little likelihood of ever going to sea again, pushing pens in Whitehall, preparing plans made redundant as soon as they are written because of changes in the political situation.

When, a few months later, I went to Oxford, I discovered that the average Naval officer with whom I had been trained was of a higher calibre than most undergraduates (although I should admit the handful of real high-fliers at Oxford were abler than the brightest Naval officers). I owe an enormous debt of gratitude to the Royal Navy. The concepts of loyalty, discipline, keenness, *esprit de corps* and quick thinking which I learnt in it have not been eroded by time. The slogan of the Petty Officer who taught us drill on the parade ground at Dartmouth, 'them that are keen get fell-in previous', is unforgettable.

Two

I SPENT THE SIX MONTHS BEFORE GOING TO Oxford training for the 1948 Olympic Games, working at a boys' club in Stepney, and learning New Testament Greek through a correspondence course. The latter was the greatest bore of all time.

Working at Stepney under Peter Booth, its Rector, now Archdeacon of Lewes, was my first introduction to parish work. What little I knew of the work of the Church was confined to ships and attending big services to hear some famous figure preach. In Stepney I saw traditional parochial work being done at its best and most imaginative. The Rector had gathered round him a team of able and dedicated curates and together they injected a great deal of love and care into that colourful place.

Nobody would wish to seek the clock put back, but there is no doubt that riverside East London was a more romantic and more tolerant place in the late forties than it is today. I welcome, and rejoice at, the new-found comfort and money, the better housing and schooling, the highly competent welfare services that have transformed the conditions of life for the people of East London. But something seems to have been lost on the way. The quick-wittedness, the humour, the resilience, the courage in adversity are still there, but some of the neighbourliness and the interdependence have gone. Part of the reason may be that the mean streets of terraced houses, where people could sit on chairs on the pavement and watch the children play, have been turned on end by the building of tower block flats. The social revolution of the last twenty-five years seems to have resulted in the working classes acquiring many of the acquisitive and isolationist attitudes of suburbia without the sense of responsibility that often goes with them.

Stepney was to remain an anchor to me for many years.

My social life at Oxford, which centred around two clubs, Vincent's and the Gridiron, was sophisticated, and my athletic life with its frequent trips abroad for international and university athletic meetings was fairly glamorous. My vacation visits to Stepney and the hopfields, where I assisted with the welfare services at the Guinness hop farms throughout my time at Oxford, helped me to keep my feet on the ground and not to lose completely the vision of my vocation.

The religion at Oxford did not on the whole impress me, although I accept this is more a criticism of me than of it. There was a high-church group centred round Pusey House which seemed to be precious and pious and full of ecclesiastical tittle-tattle and gossip about the Bishop of this and that and what dear Father so-and-so was doing. Many of the members of this group seemed to be expert on the ecclesiastical form book about which I was wholly ignorant. The low-church group was however even less attractive. For the most part they struck me as being intense, humourless and world-rejecting with their constant harping on 'sin'. But I could not help but admire their dedication. My obvious lack of it made me feel guilty, yet I thought then as I think now, that there is something warped, unnatural and ungracious and even fundamentally unloving about their attitudes. I suspect

they were working out their own deep problems and insecurities by battening on the guilt feelings of others whom
they were determined to 'convert'. No doubt there was
another group of undergraduates trying to work out what
it meant to be a Christian. If there was I never found it;
but then I did not look very hard.

Stepney, Communion at my College Chapel and a warm
friendship with its principal, Canon John Kelly, meant
that I never lost touch with the faith.

The convictions and the vision which seemed so real
when I was swinging in my hammock in the Pacific
would never be repudiated; but Oxford was so invigorating and stimulating and opened up so many new avenues
to me that I was prepared to wait until I went to my
theological college before becoming an ecclesiastic. For
one who had lived the intellectually sheltered life of a
Naval officer there seemed so much going on at Oxford
that prayer meetings, Bible Study Groups and Nescafé
parties could wait. And wait they did. Apart from a few
close personal friends who were also planning to be
ordained I found many of my fellow ordinands a little
uninspiring. I suspect they found me conceited, arrogant
and worldly.

I have one deep regret about Oxford. Academically, I
largely wasted my time there. I was the despair of my
gentle and patient Irish tutor, Mr. George Ramsey, who
at one time understandably nearly washed his hands of
me. He thought I did not work because I spent too much
time running. Certainly I did spend most of one term in
New Zealand competing for England in the Empire
Games and part of another in America, racing for Oxford
and Cambridge against Yale and Harvard. I was also Secretary, and later President, of the Oxford University
Athletic Club which were time-consuming activities. But
athletics alone was not the fundamental reason for failing

to get down to any real study at Oxford. As a result of finishing schooling at sixteen I missed that vital sixth-form period when one learns to read in depth on one's own. Perhaps I am making excuses for myself because there used to be many boys who left school at sixteen and then went on to university later. But they all had to do intensive night-school work in order to get there. I did not as I slid into St. Edmund Hall, Oxford through the back-door. The fact that I only got a third-class honours degree in modern history has not given me a chip on my shoulder, but it does sadden me that I lack the background of reading in which in a busy life I can never now catch up.

Cramming for finals at Oxford had its lighter side. Donald Carr, who captained Oxford at cricket, and who is now Assistant Secretary to the MCC, found himself in a situation almost as desperate as mine. We bought the essays of a brilliant soccer Blue, summarized them on cards, and swotted them up. We also discovered some remarkable little booklets called *Edwards' History Helps*, which, if I recall rightly, were sent under plain cover from a grim North Country town. The author asked and then aswered in potted form a series of questions. Was Queen Elizabeth a good Queen? Yes, and he gave six points. No, and he gave a further six.

After dining at Vincent's, Donald and I used to repair to my digs in the High Street and quiz each other on the noble Queen's good and bad points. While I am grateful to Mr. Edwards and his notes for getting me through finals it is no good pretending they educated me.

There is a tendency for everybody to think their time at university was a vintage period. Unquestionably, athletically 1948-51 were vintage years at Oxford. Roger Bannister was President of Oxford Athletics a year or so before I was, and Christopher Chataway a year or so afterwards.

In one respect Oxford athletics was too good. There were three international sprinters up with me and as only two qualified to represent Oxford against Cambridge and three were selected to run for Britain against other countries in international matches, it was harder to get a Blue than an international vest. Fortunately I succeeded in doing both. My athletic ability remains a mystery to me. I was an unnatural athlete who never rejoiced in physical fitness. I was unwilling to give up smoking and drinking. I found training an uncongenial activity. Indeed it would have been intolerable had there not been a number of extremely amusing men in the Oxford Athletics Team with whom to work-out daily at the Iffley Road running track.

I was an international athlete for five years and although I was never world-class, I was at one period probably the best 200 metres runner in Europe. But as my athletic career coincided with that of the world-beating West Indian sprinter, Macdonald Bailey, I never won any major championships in Britain. There was something discouraging about running behind a superbly proportioned black panther Saturday after Saturday knowing that, however hard one tried or however well one did, he would always be that tantalizing three or four yards ahead at the tape.

I learnt a lot from athletics. I discovered that human ambition is insatiable. When, inadvertently, I started on the athletic rat-race I thought that being Naval Champion would be the height of my ambitions. In fact all it did was to whet my appetite and I was soon casting my eye at running for England. This achieved, it was representing Britain that mattered. But Britain was such a small island and merely running for one's country was clearly not enough. Champion of Europe was a worthier goal. When this was within my grasp it was increasingly obvious that it was the world which was the real challenge.

In my last athletics contest, the 1952 Olympic Games at

Helsinki, I got into the semi-final. I was the last European to be eliminated and according to Mr. Harold Abrahams, the great expert on athletics, I ran faster than any Englishman had ever run over 200 metres in any Olympic Games. My ambitions were not fulfilled: I knew that I had got as far as my legs were capable of getting me, and I retired.

What was true of athletics applies to my professional life. I frequently think that if only I had some other and more important job than the one I have, how much happier and more fulfilled I might be. Yet I know this is not the case, because no sooner has one summit been conquered than another appears on the horizon stimulating once more the glands that shoot the adrenalin round the body. Happiness, contentment and satisfaction, or the lack of these things, spring from within and are only partly affected by the job one is doing and the success one is achieving.

Athletics also taught me how to rise to the occasion. I suspect the secret of success in sprinting is a combination of natural ability and the capacity to generate the maximum amount of nervous energy, which one can control sufficiently to expend totally in the few seconds of the race. If one squanders it the night before lying in bed in apprehension or if anything is left at the end of the race one does not win.

Prior to the Olympic Games I took up the quarter-mile as an insurance policy so that if I did not get selected for the 200 metres I might get chosen for the 4 by 400 metres relay. I found the cruel training programme for the quarter-mile more arduous than I could really bear so I never got properly fit for it. In view of this I decided to run the absolute minimum of these killing races but enough to establish my claim for selection over the distance. I used to pretend to myself that it was really 220 yards, rely on the momentum I had gathered to take me from the 220

yard mark to the 330 yard mark and on nervous energy
for that last ghastly 110 yards. It is amazing what nervous
energy and intense dislike of being beaten can do.

Only those who have themselves experienced the nervous strain of international sport can fully appreciate the
flavour of the tensions. Roger Bannister in his book, *First
Four Minutes*, captured something of the feeling when he
described the atmosphere of the room we shared with Alan
Dick and Christopher Chataway during the Olympic
Games in Helsinki.

Bannister wrote, 'Ours must have been the untidiest
room in the Olympic village, strewn with open suitcases,
empty milk bottles, and half-opened packets of patent
medicines for every imagined ailment. We spent most of
the day just lying on our unmade beds, reading books and
talking. It was not that we lacked the energy to make
our beds or tidy the room. We simply existed in a state of
complete suspension, in which nothing seemed important
until our races were over. We were thinking all the time
about the precious fractions of seconds that would make
us champions or failures.

'With our divided minds we would talk lightly, read
escapist books, or even discuss serious subjects. Then quite
suddenly the façade would break down and the underlying
current of our thoughts would surge upwards. We would
admit our intolerable anxiety, talk of our chances for a
moment, and swear that when the Olympics were over we
would never set foot on a running track again.

'Having relieved the tension a little we would go on
hiding our feelings for another interval. We rose from our
beds carefully, fearing we might pull a muscle—the last
disgrace. At night we crawled wearily back, not expect-
ing to sleep.

'It was well that there were moments of light relief,
which usually came from Nick Stacey. Once he stood up

saying, "I'd better rehearse that victory ceremony, just in case . . ." The rest of us burst out laughing our chances seemed so hopeless. He stood at the end of his bed, on a piece of Finnish box-like furniture that was a fair replica of the winner's rostrum in the Olympic stadium. Alan and Chris pretended to have come second and third, and stood on either side of him. He bowed his head as he received the imaginary gold medal, murmuring modestly, "I'm so glad, sir—for my country." I was just beginning an imitation of the victory fanfare when the illusion broke down, and we collapsed laughing on our beds.

'There was a knock on the door and a team mate sauntered in. He did not want anything except the comfort and relief that no one could give him. In a wretched climax of self-centredness he was attempting to lose himself for a moment—as it was very easy for him to do in the untidiness of our room. We developed a reputation for being insane humorists. Our room became a sanctuary sought by those confined in rooms where the tension was even greater.'

Yet it was the very pressure and hell of it which enabled us to drag the most out of our bodies. I get the same feelings of sickness, listlessness and sense of doom and disaster before an important speech or television programme as I did before races. Before every race I was convinced that I was going to fall flat on my face, yet in practice the moment the starting gun went my mind and body were immediately mobilized for intense concentration and effort.

Now, before every speech that I am really concerned about I am convinced that my tongue will cleave to the roof of my mouth, and yet the moment my name is called something stirs within me and my mind becomes clear.

This ability to generate and control nervous energy can be a mixed blessing. I find that I operate most effectively under pressure and as soon as it is relaxed, life loses its savour and I become bored.

I learnt, too, that 'fame', even at the inconsequential level of a lesser sport like athletics, is a drug as addictive as heroin. I am sure this is why well-known sportsmen often find it hard to reorientate their lives when they retire. The public memory is short and they are soon forgotten, but during their time at the top they become accustomed to being in the public eye. They did not have to be introduced at parties, heads turned when they entered a room, the press used to telephone them for quotes, they got the best tables at restaurants and little boys asked for their autographs. Politicians or parsons, sportsmen or television stars, however much they pretend it's all an awful bore, the vast majority love it and are lost without it. I am convinced this is the reason why politicians and sportsmen, who should be prepared to quit, cling on although their powers are fading. It is also why some ex-sportsmen take to drink and others hang around Henley or Twickenham or Lord's or White City wearing their international ties and university scarves hoping somebody will come up to them and remember what they 'did'.

I was fortunate because as soon as I retired from athletics all my energy and enthusiasms were concentrated on preparation for ordination, so giving it up did not leave a gap. I was the last but one athlete to come off the track at the Helsinki Olympic Games. The final event was the 4 by 400 metres relay in which I ran the last leg and Britain was fifth in the final of six. I gave my spiked shoes to a youth in the crowd and from that day to this have never put on a track suit, let alone run in a race. To continue in athletics after one has reached one's peak, in a state of semi-fitness, not really caring whether one wins or loses, would have been a hopeless anti-climax for me. With cricket, golf, tennis, indeed with most other sports except boxing, it is different. The ex-international can get enjoyment from his sport by playing it at club standards. In athletics it is all or nothing. And for five years it had my all and that was enough.

Athletics taught me another lesson. I believe that many people's lives become twisted and warped through envy. They feel they are missing out, or worse, that they have been cheated because they have never experienced the glamorous life they think to be the lot of those who reach the top. I have no doubt that I, who have lived a mundane existence in recent years, would feel the same if I had not in a small degree experienced the so-called glamour associated with international sport. I learnt how superficial an existence it is. There is a dreary sameness about city-centre hotel bedrooms, international airports, embassy cocktail parties and banquets. The public are also inclined to think that people whose names appear regularly in the newspapers must have particularly exciting and dynamic personalities. Hence the hero worship they receive from the public. Having been for a few years on the outer fringe of this world, but close enough to observe, I learnt that many of our public figures are rather more vulnerable, insecure and mixed-up than a good many of us. Some are deeply disturbed personalities and a few the most fearful bounders. There is little connection between the public's adulation and a man's actual worth, and even less between public popularity and personal happiness. I think the pole to the top is so greasy and the effort required to hold on, once one has got there, so great, that one needs to have a fundamentally discontented personality to make the sacrifices, often of one's own integrity, which are involved. Perhaps this is why so many people in public life seem to be deeply sad.

Men who win Blues at universities are often accused of getting jobs as a result of their athletic ability. Employers show a greater shrewdness than their critics, for they are doing more than cashing in on the Englishman's athletic snobbery. They realize that the lessons learnt in the harsh school of international sport, lessons of application, ruthlessness, determination, self-sacrifice, single-mindedness and an ability to respond under intense pressure, can very easily be applied to a man's professional life provided he has the intellect to go with them. These qualities do not necessarily make a man a very attractive personality, but they can help to make him an effective one. Disguise it as he may, any man who is an international sportsman must be fundamentally ambitious.

The ordained ministry of the Church of England is not the natural habitat of the aggressive personality. One of the Gospel texts which the Church has taken most to heart is 'They that are first shall be last and the last shall be first' although in practice it often becomes a shield for laziness, incompetence and ineffectiveness. Anyone who entered a race with that attitude of mind would not do very well, but, equally, anyone who enters the Church with a ruthless 'over my dead body do you beat me' Olympic-final attitude does not do very well either. In industry and commerce competitive people may not be liked but they are accepted and, in the most progressive companies, encouraged. In the Church they are the objects of intense suspicion. It is extremely difficult for any organization to achieve a right balance, but I believe that the cosy, complacent ethos of the Church is as alien to the Gospel as the abrasiveness and thrust of the ambitious. The Church has a number of ways of dealing with those who do not fit into its established pattern or who lack the traditional image. It gives them a great deal of rope in the hope that they will hang themselves. It promotes them in the confident expectation (usually fulfilled) that the poacher will then turn game-keeper. Or puts it about that they are really very good and able men but unfortunately, and fatally, unreliable or lacking in judgement. All these techniques have been used on me. Even if one avoids or can counter these traps, which the Establishment has had long experience in laying, one is faced with a further hazard which, in my experience, is the most disarming of all. The Church Establishment is honest and well-meaning. Its secret weapon (which I am sure it uses unconsciously) is courtesy. Its members may be pompous and even patronizing, but basically they are gentlemen. If bishops were a band of go-getting scoundrels feathering their own nests, and experts at in-fighting, one would have fewer qualms about attacking them. As it is, most of them are able but limited men who work like galley-slaves, desperately trying to keep their dioceses ticking over without the resources in either men or money to do the job properly.

Sadly, the advice I would feel bound to give to any young man who thinks he must reach the top of the Church or any large well-established institution regardless of cost to his own integrity, is to support the leadership. The more wrong it is—and it is often very wrong—the more loyally one supports it the better one is likely to do. This is why in some circles it is considered that I cannot be ambitious or else I would not be so tactless as consistently to attack conventional Church wisdom. People who take this view misunderstand the nature of my ambition. I believe deeply that in certain limited fields—communication, deployment and use of resources to serve the community, parson-management and parochial and diocesan administrative structures—I see fairly clearly what the Church needs to do, and to do urgently. I was unashamedly ambitious to influence the life of the Church in these fields, although I am the first to admit they are secondary to the complex theological issues on which I am ill-qualified to lay down the law and indeed have been very careful never to do so.

One of the difficulties of influencing the life of the Church of England is that power is divided between so many people and bodies that there are no obvious citadels to conquer, and to my mind it becomes increasingly doubtful whether the somewhat tarnished gilt of the diocesan bishop's cage is the best perch from which to try and influence events. Most bishops are so submerged by day-to-day administrative and pastoral responsibilities that they have neither the energy nor the time to question where the Church is going and what it is achieving. And if they did realize that the ecclesiastical machine they are endeavouring to run is no longer effective, individually, at least, they are powerless to do anything about it. I learnt this during two somewhat frustrating years as a bishop's chaplain.

For my contemporaries in secular professions there seems to be a ladder of promotion, and the steps to the highest offices are well sign-posted. Once they have arrived at their goal they often find that their room for manœuvre is less than they imagined. I find that most of my friends in the Church are as confused as I am as to where and how one can best be used to help revitalize its life. In the Church today the only thing that is clear is that nothing is clear, and any man whose psychological make-up is such that he needs (as to some extent I do) a clearly defined career structure, would be well advised to find ways of serving God other than in the ordained ministry.

THREE YEARS AS AN OXFORD UNDER-graduate were enough and I looked forward to going to Cuddesdon Theological College—that 'hill of vision' seven miles from Oxford. It was founded nearly a hundred years previously and had a magnificent tradition for training faithful and devoted priests of the Anglo-Catholic persuasion. Many hundreds of men serving Christ all over the world look upon it as their spiritual home where the foundations of their priestly ministry were well laid.

I went there determined to let it work its 'magic' on me as it had done so successfully on so many before me. Having no ecclesiastical background, having read history rather than theology at Oxford and having had only a most tenuous connection with the Church while I was an undergraduate, I desperately needed what Cuddesdon set out to provide. This was a training in the spiritual life, teaching in theology and an introduction to the skills of the priestly and pastoral ministry.

It was done within the setting of a tightly-knit and disciplined community, living in a rabbit warren of a Victorian monstrosity in a typical Oxfordshire village. Each student had a sparsely furnished little room with an iron bedstead, a table and a chair. The linoleum on the floor, like the varnished pitch-pine, was dark brown. We had to be in chapel by 7.00 each morning for one and a half hours of prayer. Lectures on the Old and New Testaments, Christian Ethics, the Prayer Book and Doctrine started at 9.00 and continued for the rest of the morning. In the afternoon we had two hours off during which the more learned students browsed round the religious sections of the bookshops in Oxford to make sure they were abreast with the latest theological developments. We had to be back by 4.00 for a cup of tea which was followed by Evensong. The periods before and after supper were devoted to study and the day finished with a service called Compline in which the student taking the service would remind us that we must be sober and vigilant 'because the devil as a roaring lion walketh about seeking whom he may devour'. In practice we did not have much opportunity for being anything but sober as the local pubs were out of bounds and we were only allowed college beer at lunch-time on Sundays. I used to hide a bottle of sherry in my chest of drawers among my underclothes and a few of the bolder students would sneak into my room for a quick glass before supper. After Compline we were not allowed to talk until breakfast the next day, although we were permitted to say 'Please pass me the soap' if we met in the communal washrooms before going to bed. We were allowed out on Saturday evenings but had to be back by 9.00 for the inevitable Compline. Huddled together in the college chapel it was all too easy to know who had been drinking and I became accustomed to sideways glances from my more pious colleagues on Saturday nights.

Keen as I was to absorb its Christian atmosphere and learn what it had to teach me I did not take easily to the life. The contrast between the freedom of Oxford and the gay and colourful friends I had made there and the monastic routine of Cuddesdon was very marked. The college had a tendency towards preciousness, cosiness, and introversion, which gave some of the young men too great an opportunity for worrying about themselves and their fellows. I guess I fulfilled a useful purpose by giving some of the more intense of my fellow students plenty to worry about. From time to time I would overhear whispered conversations about whether Nick was finding the place a strain and how we must all pray even harder for him. I once went to a meeting of the Chapel Committee at which the best way of laying out the robes was discussed —a necessary activity no doubt, but far removed from what I thought the Church was really about.

Mercifully, however, the immaturity, intensity and lack of sophistication of some of the men was balanced by having a few older students. I owe an enormous debt of gratitude to two men who were contemporaries, Charles Young, the headmaster of Rossell School, who had taken sabbatical leave to train for the ministry, and John Habgood, now Principal of Queen's Theological College, Birmingham, an ex-Scientific Fellow of King's College, Cambridge. I used to go for walks with them when I would let off steam and they would explain to me the subtler points of theological lectures.

In retrospect I am critical of the pseudo-country gentleman's ethos of Cuddesdon with its croquet, lawn tennis, and scouting in the woods of the Bishop of Oxford's palace across the road. Such an environment was more suitable for training the younger sons of the upper classes for the country ministry in the nineteenth century than for the ex-grammar school boys of the 1950s reared in suburbia whose priestly lot was likely to be cast among the industrial workers in new municipal housing estates.

The strain and tensions were aggravated for me because during my first year at Cuddesdon I was also training for the Olympic Games. This involved dashing from college retreats, where we were kept silent for five days at a time, to the hubbub and excitement of international athletic meetings in European capitals. Had it not been for the understanding and humanity of the Principal, the Reverend Kenneth Riches, now Bishop of Lincoln, there were times when I wondered whether I should get through the first year of the two-year course. I am convinced that part of the training for the priesthood should involve cutting oneself off from one's normal environment; but today I doubt whether Cuddesdon was the right place to do it. Perhaps a better method of training would be to have one's theological study within the context of the university and intersperse it with practical field work in a down-town area, where there are plenty of people who could benefit from the pent-up compassion of young ordinands. Periods of real isolation could be arranged in some holy, remote and austere monastery where one is left alone with God, oneself and the stars.

It is now fashionable for self-consciously progressive ordinands to deny the validity of the spiritual disciplines imposed by theological colleges, but I found the daily two hours of compulsory prayer, meditation and worship a great help. I rebelled against the details of it with the dreary Old Testament lessons and incomprehensible Psalms but it gave me an opportunity of laying what I hope were spiritual foundations. The discipline of having to get up in the early morning and the practice of silent meditation, much as one's mind wandered, did have a cumulative effect. There were times when the power of the Spirit of Christ was real and vivid. I longed to be absorbed into the sinless life of Christ, to offer myself without reserve, to be used in His service and be able to cry out 'Not my will but Thine O Lord be done'. Slowly, almost imperceptibly, and often painfully, I think my life was changed. I came to know myself better and my priorities and motives were, to some extent, purged and reorientated. My attitude and approach to theology was simple, and probably naïve, which made me a willing and humble pupil. I was deeply concerned to become an effective and competent priest. I had decided to go to Cuddesdon because, of the priests I knew, the ones whose spiritual and theological beliefs and attitudes to the world appealed to me most, and those who seemed best able to articulate the faith within them, were those who had been trained in the Anglo-Catholic tradition. I argued to myself that Cuddesdon had had very considerable experience in training priests and I was prepared to learn and accept what they taught me without much questioning or heart-searching. Today this may seem unbelievable and possibly intellectually immoral. But my attitude, far from being unusual, was, I think, typical of most ordinands of the early 1950s.

Before I went to Cuddesdon I was deeply convinced of the truth of the fundamentals of the Christian faith, and so what I required of my theological training was to give me a clearer and deeper understanding of these and help build a doctrinal superstructure upon them. Frankly, I thought then, and am even more convinced now, that much of this theological superstructure is irrelevant. Nevertheless, when I was at Cuddesdon I wanted to learn what it was because I thought that a properly trained priest should know the answers. Consequently I swotted away at learning all the various theories of the Atonement and their connection with the Old Testament views of sacrifice. I struggled with all those heresies (whose names I found so difficult to pronounce) about the nature of God and the person of Jesus in the history of the early Church. I felt guilty that I could not get very interested about them, and wondered at times whether there was something theologically unnatural about me, as I could raise so little enthusiasm for supper-time conversations on the merits of Monophysitism against Apollinarianism. We were taught that it really was most important to know about these matters, and many other equally abstruse ones; otherwise we could never understand the present day nor meet the deeper needs of some members of the congregations which one day we would be committed to serve.

As I had never been a regular member of any congregation, had never, up to this point in my life, as far as I can recall, actually met a Sunday School teacher, I was in no position to question the validity of our teachers' claims. And so, apart from occasional outbursts of exasperation and considerable feelings of guilt, I was an eager theological student who did his best to eat up all that was put on his plate. To be fair there was quite a lot of mainstream Anglo-Catholic doctrine which seemed true for me at that time. It had a logic, a solidarity and a simplicity about it. In any case, I was in a believing mood.

Our training in the practical pastoral work of a parish priest really was very thin. Alumni vicars who were making successes of their parishes would drop in for an evening's lecture to tell us how they did it. Devoted ladies from the Church of England Sunday School headquarters would descend for a day or two to put us on the inside track of Sunday School teaching, and then we had the odd session on subjects such as developments in modern psychiatric methods. Occasionally we preached in neighbouring village churches and visited wards in Oxford hospitals. We each preached one sermon before our fellow students after which there was a general discussion on it.

While I was only half aware of the irrelevance of much of the theological training, at the time I was very conscious of the inadequacies of the practical training for the priesthood. As an ex-Naval officer and international athlete, I felt I knew quite a lot about life, leadership and simple administration. While I was at Cuddesdon I never questioned the 1000-year-old tradition of the parochial ministry with its full-time vicar, parish church and fixed orders of service, but many of my friends and I were highly critical of actual parochial performance with dull sermons, badly edited parish magazines and poorly conducted Parochial Church Council meetings. We were not so worried about the 'know-what of belief' as about the 'know-how of communication', and I felt that many of the parishes which I had seen on occasional visits and missions were run with extraordinarily little imagination, conviction, panache, efficiency or drive.

I know that I wanted to see the Church recapture those great pre-1914–18 war days in Portsea, where Cyril Garbett, later to be Archbishop of York, was vicar and where men of similar calibre surrounded by able and dedicated curates served, and, to a considerable extent, dominated, every large city in Britain. It never occurred to me that, given the right men, the traditional Gospel and Church life could not be made to live in the hearts of men and in the life of the community. Whatever they may say now, in trying to be wise after the event, most of my contemporaries believed the same. We put the weakness of the Church and the apparent ineffectiveness of the Gospel down mainly to what we arrogantly considered to be the indifferent calibre of many of the men who were ordained between the two great wars. In the early 1950s there was some evidence that our analysis of the situation was right. Able men, of widely differing gifts, like Mervyn Stockwood among the working classes at St. Matthew Moorfields, Bristol; George Reindorp among middle-class young nurses at St. Stephen's, Rochester Row, Westminster; and Edward Henderson with the upper classes at St. Paul's, Knightsbridge, all had full and lively churches. They are now the Bishops of Southwark, Guildford and Bath and Wells respectively.

Nothing at Cuddesdon prepared us for a future in which, however hard one worked or prayed, there would be virtually no visible results. I doubt if the college staff saw such a situation themselves, and if they had done so most of us would not have believed them. It took twelve years of hard work and much anguish to work out of my system the conviction that the Gospel vividly presented with clarity and power would not lead to changed lives and full churches. Had I known on the eve of my ordination what I know now, going through with it would have taken very much more courage than it did. In some ways the very inadequacy of Cuddesdon in the field of practical pastoral training, far from undermining my sense of vocation and desire to be a priest, positively increased it by adding to my belief that if only the clergy were trained to perform better, the Church could be revitalized. Whatever Cuddesdon's failings may have been, when I went there I would have been quite unsuitable for ordination, but by the time I left I had imbibed sufficient of the ethos of the Church of England to cope with most of the demands of the ordained ministry. That it should have achieved this is no mean tribute to the place.

In fact I was so convinced of the importance and relevance of the priesthood, and the need to recruit more and abler men to its ranks, that I used a three-month break in the middle of my time at Cuddesdon to visit fifty public and grammar schools to put before sixth formers the claims of the ordained ministry.

I had put before the recruitment committee of the Central Advisory Council for the Training for the Ministry the suggestion that they should sponsor me on a tour of sixth forms at no cost to the Church, as I could at the same time lecture and show a film on the Olympic Games for which I would charge a fee. The committee of leading churchmen who considered my suggestion took an attitude which shocked me at the time but to which I have now become well accustomed in Anglican circles. They would not sponsor me, but would not stop me either, and suggested that I endeavour to arrange the trip myself. The Archbishop of York, Dr. Cyril Garbett, and the Bishop of Coventry, Dr. Neville Gorton, were made of sterner and more decisive stuff and within a few days of my approaching them they had written to leading schools in their dioceses and the tour was on. Once I had started, the educational bush telegraph got working and I was soon inundated with far more invitations than I could cope with, and I drew the line at fifty schools.

Assessing success in Christian work is almost always misleading, but if it can be said that helping young men find a vocation to ordination is a plus, it was one of the most successful operations I have ever undertaken. Today, whenever I lecture to a large group of junior clergy, a member of the audience invariably comes up to me afterwards to tell me that I had first started him thinking about the possibility of ordination. The report I made to the Chairman of the Central Advisory Council for the Training of the Ministry at the end of my tour is such a masterpiece of modesty and understatement that Edward Knapp-Fisher, now Bishop of Pretoria, who succeeded Kenneth Riches as Principal of Cuddesdon for my last year, must have had a hand with the drafting. The report said:

'The real value of this experiment is suggested by the following considerations:

'1. The attentiveness of the boys and the interest shown was exemplified by the quality and the quantity of the questions and discussions which followed each talk. Headmasters and chaplains said that they rarely recall a sixth form lecturer having to deal with so many questions. The fact that 100 to 150 sixth form boys can discuss freely and frankly the question of vocation, the shortage of clergy and the work of the ministry cannot be without value. Questions ranged over a wide field but the many criticisms of the church were sensitive, constructive and pertinent. It seems fair to hope that boys went away with a clearer conception of the opportunities before the clergy as well as some of the difficulties confronting them. Boys from day schools asked as many questions but they tended to be more concerned with Christian apologetics.

'2. Many chaplains felt that the talk had assisted them in their work and wished that further lectures of this nature should be given by people outside the school—preferably laymen.

'3. The very encouraging letters from headmasters, and reports received from other sources suggested that schools were not dissatisfied.'

So great have been the changes in attitudes towards the Church and the ministry in the last fifteen years, I doubt if a similar tour today would be possible or acceptable.

Four

MY FIRST CURACY WAS TO HAVE BEEN at Hull, but the vicar to whom I was to go for training left to become an Army Chaplain. Instead I went to St. Mark's, Portsea, a well-known training parish in the Portsmouth Diocese whose vicar, the Reverend Christopher Pepys, now the Bishop of Buckingham, ran the parish in the best pre-war Anglo-Catholic tradition. There were about half a dozen curates who did exactly as they were told by the vicar, and the atmosphere of this considerable parish, with its mother church and two daughter churches, was like an extension of Cuddesdon. All of us, including the vicar, worked extraordinarily hard, starting at 7.00 am in church for meditation, and finishing at 10.30 pm, having spent the afternoon and evening in house-to-house visiting, each curate having his own area. We did not run the various organizations attached to the church but acted as chaplains to them. As curates we were allowed to preach once a month in the evening—after reading our sermon to the vicar on the Thursday before—but were never allowed to preach at the main parish Communion service because this was the vicar's prerogative.

Because the church was hopelessly over-stretched financially we were abominably paid and appallingly housed. I lived in one large icy room which my mother visited before I was ordained. She was so horrified by the condition of the bedding and most of the furniture that she flung it out of the window and burnt it in the garden. I was afraid she might have overstepped the mark, so concerned was I that the vicar should not think I was worldly. The clergy-house housekeeper was a young married woman who had been given the flat at the top of the house in exchange for cooking for the unmarried clergy. Unfortunately she could not cook, and in any case we could only afford to give her a few shillings a week for food. In my first winter I got pneumonia which the doctor put down to undernourishment. Later I saw to it that the large number of curates I employed benefited from my experience at Portsea; I always ensured that they were properly housed, heated and fed.

It may seem smug, but we were so devoted to our work and keen on the job that it never occurred to us to complain. We admired and were enormously fond of the vicar, who remains one of my closest friends. There was a great sense of *esprit de corps*. We prayed, worked, loved and laughed, and the response from the parish in churchgoing terms was such that our whole strategy very nearly worked. The ugly red-brick Victorian parish church was nearly full, and 100 or so confirmation candidates appeared each year via the Scouts and Girl Guides and the various youth organizations. We prepared them with the greatest care and kept them together in youth clubs; even so most of them had lapsed within a year of their confirmation. Adult confirmation candidates were occasionally recruited through baptism and marriage interviews. We clergy were so absorbed in our church activities and in caring for the skilled working-class people who made up most of the parish, that we had little time or concern for the state schools, the community centre and secular organizations in the area. It is difficult to be sure what contribution the church really made to the life of the community. I suspect it was considerable. The church was in touch with eighty per cent of the people living in the parish. Some ten per cent were churchgoers or belonged to one of the many organizations attached to the church. Although the congregation was elderly, and drawn from the better-class roads where the school teachers and white-collar workers tended to live, and unquestionably some used it as a prop and some as a club, I believe lives were changed, vision widened, faith stimulated and love generated. It certainly did not occur to me at this time that, provided we prayed hard and worked imaginatively, the traditional Church could not be made to live and meet real needs of many people.

I did sit loosely to what I considered to be some of the more old-fashioned Anglo-Catholic attitudes of the vicar, but otherwise I questioned neither the relevance nor the importance of what we were doing and the way we were doing it. It did, however, occur to me that our methods of communicating the Gospel and presenting the life of the Church to those who were not members were inadequate and that if only we could find some medium which would capture people's imagination we should have no difficulty in increasing the congregation. Consequently I started a tabloid parish newspaper to replace the conventional magazine, a move which started me on the road to journalism. In terms of circulation, it was a great success and over 120 distributors sold it to eighty per cent of the 6000 or so houses in the parish. I so enjoyed playing with this toy that I could not admit that it failed to recruit many new members; I satisfied myself with the fact that it did create a lot of local interest and ensured that church members were calling on four-fifths of the homes in the parish for a monthly chat.

After I had been in Portsmouth for eighteen months, I

married Anne Bridgeman. For many years I had been going on an annual skiing holiday with a group of Oxford friends. The party got smaller each year as a result of one of us marrying one of the girls who came with us. In fact it took two skiing holidays with Anne for me to realize she was the girl I wanted as my wife. My parents had always warned that girls looked different in the champagne atmosphere of the mountain skiing resort, so I held back from proposing until we had been in the sobering lowland atmosphere of an English February for a fortnight. Another Oxford friend was pressing Anne to marry him, and I had an anxious few weeks while she made up her mind. Anne had recently completed reading for a degree in Agriculture at Reading University, where she had been sent by her father so that she might manage the home farm and help him run his estate in Shropshire. I am afraid my father-in-law did not get his money's worth. Within two years of graduating she was married and living in a little gardenless terraced house in a street known as 'Lav Av', because the tiles of most of the houses in the road were the same as those used in public lavatories. She claims I married her because I could not stand the non-cooking in the clergy house, and I maintain it was to save her from being a cowgirl. In fact I married into what must be one of the most dedicated families in Britain in which my wife runs true to family form. My father-in-law, as well as putting on its feet his impoverished estate on the Welsh borders, was Lord Lieutenant of Shropshire, took an active part in the House of Lords and earned his living in the City. I would guess he is almost the only Lord Lieutenant in the history of Britain who would think nothing of sitting up all night in a milk-train after a hard week's work in the City, in order to be back in his county on Saturday morning to present the prizes at the Police Cadets' Sports. My mother-in-law, who is the niece of the late Lord

Halifax, was brought up in the strictest Anglo-Catholic tradition.

My wife's upbringing, in which public duty and Anglo-Catholic piety over-rode all other considerations, was in contrast to the more permissive and relaxed atmosphere of my own home. Apart from Anne's unselfishness, I am sure the secret of our marriage is that we are opposites. She is shy, gentle and cautious. I am gregarious, aggressive and a gambler. She enjoys a quiet life while I thrive on controversies. As the years pass by I find myself drawing more and more on the power provided by a relaxed peaceful marriage and family life and a well-ordered home.

We have three children. Caroline, now aged fourteen, was born when we were working in Portsmouth; David, who is twelve, when we were in Birmingham; and nine-year-old Mary in Woolwich. Some clergy children are said to grow up as deprived children. They have to share their father with hundreds of parishioners while their mother is so busy helping her husband in the parish that she is prevented from giving them sufficient care. My children have had too little attention from me but Anne has always maintained that her first loyalty is to the home. Neither of us believe that one is setting a Christian example if the parson's wife is so involved helping with the Mothers' Union that her own children become neglected.

I suppose it is true of all great institutions that those who would try to bring about changes and introduce new ideas and attitudes, find progress frustrating and sometimes heartbreakingly slow. The temptation for the parson to contract out and play it quietly is particularly strong. It is amazing to me that the Church orders its affairs in a way which positively encourages the clergy to do the minimum. It speaks well for their sense of vocation that more do not succumb. For most men, the harder and more imaginatively they work, the more paid help they are given and the better able they are to support their families; the opposite is true for the priest. In most cases he himself has to pay the secretaries, personal assistants and office expenses, which I have found essential to deal with the volume of work which I took on.

For more than four years I was curate at St. Mark's, Portsea, learning the trade of a traditional parish priest the hard way, and I do not regret a day of it. No curate could have had a more understanding and long-suffering vicar who took infinite pains teaching what he considered the art of priesthood. I arrived at Portsmouth an awkward amateur and left a professional priest, confident in the assured role of the Church. Today, I question how much professionalism in the priesthood is really possible, and see the primary qualifications as a large heart and a sense of humour; but nevertheless I am glad to have been trained in the norm from which I now deviate.

It was in my next job as Domestic Chaplain to the Bishop of Birmingham, Dr. Leonard Wilson, that I became convinced that many radical changes were needed in the life and organization of the church. The contrast between the church in Portsmouth and what I found in Birmingham was very marked. In Portsmouth the traditional pattern of church life worked adequately wherever a parish was led by a confident and competent vicar assisted by loyal and hardworking curates. In Birmingham, while there were able and devoted men doing outstanding work, the quality of the clergy and church life was much more uneven. I did not fully realize it at the time, but to compare the two dioceses was unfair. Portsmouth is a tightly-knit island community dominated ecclesiastically for many years by the great St. Mary's, made famous by Archbishops Lang and Garbett, and more recently by St. Mark's, under the Reverend Gerald Ellison, now Bishop of

w.c.—D

Chester, and the Reverend Christopher Pepys. The Portsmouth churches were able to draw on the financial resources of the rich parishes in the Hampshire hinterland to pay large numbers of curates to work in the city, which has been as consistently well-served by the Church as any other city in Britain. For a young clergyman it was an ideal place to start his ministry. It is a genuine city with all the social challenges and problems which this involves and many churches with great traditions and outstanding vicars. Portsmouth itself, close to the Isle of Wight and the lovely Hampshire countryside, was a delightful place to live. On top of all that, in my day, it had a Bishop, Dr. Fleming, now Bishop of Norwich, who for many years had been a Cambridge don: he was in close touch with the theological colleges and eager to snap up the best ordinands as they emerged from their training.

The traditionally non-conformist and brassy city of Birmingham had endured eccentric non-leadership for many years under the episcopacy of Dr. Barnes, who not only held unorthodox beliefs, which put off many of the sincerest clergy from serving in the diocese, but also was more of a scholar than a pastor and a leader. Thus, when the stocky and lion-hearted Leonard Wilson, an ex-Dean of Hong Kong, Bishop of Singapore, and Dean of Manchester, succeeded Dr. Barnes he found the diocese run down, the clergy's morale low, weaknesses in diocesan administration, and a chronic shortage of curates. At the same time, an exploding population was being rehoused in massive new estates in which churches had to be built and clergy recruited. Before I became his chaplain, Dr. Wilson had been in Birmingham for four years during which he had gone a long way to restoring confidence. He had made a profound impact on the city whose leaders are more impressed by personality and performance than by philosophical ideas. He appeared as a man of integrity, depth, power and vision. He was much sought after as a speaker at civic functions and dinners. He had raised a massive sum of money to build churches in the new areas and increased the number of curates serving in the diocese. But like all bishops in the Church of England, he lacked the legal powers to make radical changes in personnel in key positions and to rationalize the Church's resources, as the situation demanded.

By the time I joined him he was a somewhat frustrated man still suffering from the aftermath of the terrible tortures he had received at the hands of the Japanese during the war. I was the wrong man for the post because, instead of being a soothing influence helping him come to terms with the severe limitations of his position, I was much more exasperated than he by the lack of powers he had to reorganize the diocese. Throughout his distinguished ministry Dr. Wilson had been consistently ahead of his time, but neither his fellow bishops, who in the late 1950s sat mutely under the schoolmaster discipline of Dr. Fisher, the Archbishop of Canterbury, nor his own diocesan staff, gave him the support his ideas deserved. Frequently in public life one sees lesser men with a flair for showmanship and a good public relations sense having a greater influence than those of wider vision and deeper thought whose very integrity holds them back. Dr. Wilson is a classic example of the latter, and the tensions between the conservatives and radicals in the Church today spring, in part, from the failure of his superiors to heed his liberal voice in the 1950s.

His death in the summer of 1970, a few months after his retirement, has left a gap in the lives of his countless friends and admirers. Leonard Wilson was one of the most underestimated bishops on the bench. Perhaps this was because he was a reluctant ecclesiastic who felt more at ease in the secular world than he ever did in the episcopal one. Gatherings of churchmen and the things they talked about tended to bore him. He was not always able to disguise his impatience with their concern for ecclesiastical trivia. But if the Church never listened to him as attentively as it should have done, ordinary people did. He had an unrivalled ability of talking about God to non-Churchmen in a way that gave them hope. They understood and appreciated his sanctified common sense and his liberal attitudes in theology, morality and politics. Big in mind, large in heart, Leonard was a great and good man.

The Bishop had not had a full-time domestic chaplain before me. This had the disadvantage that, to start with, the hard-pressed parochial clergy were suspicious of me and wondered whether I was really necessary. The further difficulty was that there was nowhere for my wife and family to live: so for a few months I had a bachelor existence sharing a house with the other-worldly and austere Suffragan Bishop of Aston and his quaint Irish housekeeper. Eventually the Bishop of Aston, now Bishop of Bradford, who had spent his life in Birmingham, kindly gave up his own house which was too large for his needs so that my wife and children were able to move in. A great advantage of having no predecessor was that I was spared the chores of being an ecclesiastical valet and was largely able to create the job for myself. Apart from acting as an advisor, gadfly and devil's advocate on the many problems with which the Bishop was confronted daily, my main responsibilities were looking after the junior clergy and helping the vicars in the intractable downtown areas where church life was often at a very low ebb.

I thought it might increase the vitality of church life in these areas if we produced an ecclesiastical tabloid with a *Daily Mirror* format and slip editions for each parish. So, on an overdraft of £100, I started the *Birmingham Christian*

News: it was soon selling over 35,000 copies a month and proved so successful that we launched a national edition a year later. Both of these, nearly twelve years later, are still going strong. The paper aimed to show that the Church cared, was alive and militant as well as removing erroneous ideas about its aims and activities. Through the parochially produced section of the paper, parish priests were able to speak to the thousands who never went to church, while by house-to-house visiting, the committed Christians who distributed it were brought in touch with the people of the parish. In tabloid form, and easy to read, it was meant to be the spearhead of a permanent mission in each participating parish.

Monica Furlong, in an article in the *Spectator* commenting on a typical issue, described it 'as the wildest beast caught alive on a recent safari, with concerns a long way from the difference between a cope and a chasuble, but most of it excitingly close to everyday life. It deals with the kind of moral problems with which people with little or no doctrinal knowledge battle in everyday life and it is on their loving solution that the efficacy of English Christianity stands or falls. The virtue of the *Christian News* is that it informs thousands of ordinary people, many of whom will describe themselves as Christians though they do not go to church, what the Christian line is. It leaves them in no doubt of what love thinks of the colour-bar or corporal punishment or the death sentence or pornography. In a church as painfully inarticulate as the Church of England this is in itself a newsworthy achievement.'

The paper was born and suckled on controversy. In order to create interest and increase circulation we aimed each month to have a story or comment which the Birmingham newspapers, and often the national as well, would pick up. We very rarely failed. Sometimes it landed us in rows we did not foresee. I was determined to bring the paper out at all costs during a printing strike, and therefore sent it for printing to a 'black' firm. This caused a lot of trouble.

Another kind of difficulty came over the advertisements we carried for family planning. A number of celibate high church priests were worried about these advertisements and took the trouble to fill in the coupon to find out more. ('Please send me under plain cover a free copy of *Planned Families are Happy Families*. I am married or about to be married.') They were not very happy about the suggestions they received!

On another occasion I asked my secretary to get some pictures of pretty girls relaxing on the beach, with which to illustrate an article on the Christian attitude to holidays. The one I chose for publication was of a young film star whose sex life, unknown to me, was somewhat bizarre. The national press rang me to ask if I thought it was sexy and I replied that anybody who was excited by it was clearly in need of psychiatric treatment. They then contacted the Bishop who said he thought it was a provocative picture: they quickly reported, 'Your chaplain thinks you are in need of psychiatric treatment.' To this I later commented that the paper would pay for the treatment of all bishops so affected.

The Bishop never liked the *Birmingham Christian News* and one could almost see his blood pressure rising as each publication day came round. But it was typical of him that he never tried to censor it, never attacked it in public, and on occasions even did his best to defend it, meanwhile, I am sure, secretly praying that I would grow up, cool down and shut up! I knew that the paper was brash and on occasions cheap and vulgar, but I believed in it passionately. I wanted to use it and go on using it to help alter the image of the Church of England in industrial areas.

In my experience many people appeared to need what
the Christian Gospel and the Church sets out to provide,
and yet for some inexplicable reason the message was
failing to capture their imagination. Of course I could
understand all too readily why some clergy and congregations were failing to win the hearts of their parishioners.
But I was constantly surprised that first-class priests, and
loving outward-looking and vital congregations were
making comparatively little progress, especially in working-class areas. I suspected the reason for this was that the
whole situation was bedevilled by its image and if only
we could project the Church as a life-enhancing, loving,
sacrificial and efficient community we could expect a
breakthrough for the Gospel.

Dr. Vance Packard, in his book *The Hidden Persuaders*,
described how motivational research analysts had discovered that the prune was virtually unsaleable in
America because it had an image which burdened it with
psychological limitations. It was seen as the symbol of de-
crepitude and devitalization. It was associated with
parental authority—something that one was made to eat
as a child because it was good for one. Indeed the image of
the prune was summed up as 'that joyless puritan'. How
similar, I thought, to what many people felt about the
Church. Consequently I believed at that time that an
attempt should be made to mobilize the Church at every
level from the small country parish to Lambeth Palace to
project a simple image that would be both true to the Gospel and easily comprehended. In the *Birmingham Christian News* and later in its national edition, we attempted to
do just this. In an interview I gave to the *Daily Mail*, I said,
'Our policy is quite clear. We want to be a platform for the
prophetic voices of the country. We want to show that the
Christian faith is relevant to twentieth-century living and
that the Church is concerned with all the activities of man.'

I would not claim that we had much success but we certainly caused a stir. 'When the first copies of the *Christian News* dropped through Birmingham letterboxes with a loud bang last January a chorus of disapproval rushed round the city like a tidal wave', claimed the *Daily Mail*. 'Crucifixion as a news report—shock treatment in church newspaper', was a headline in *The Times*. I was described as a pedlar in pornography, compared with Hitler, and denounced as dragging the Church into the gutter.

But the more deeply I became involved in the life of the Church, and the more I understood the throbbing and exciting vitality of Birmingham, the more I came to realize that it was the ecclesiastical structures which were no longer viable nor effective; the parochial system with its single-handed vicar, with a minute congregation bravely struggling to maintain an enormous ecclesiastical building used for only a couple of hours a week was dying and powerless. In my opinion the Church's influence and contribution to the secular community could have been much greater if its resources were reorganized. There was a disturbing breakdown rate among the vicars in working-class areas and a deep sense of disappointment amongst the junior clergy, whom I was meant to be trying to help. This was not primarily because the Gospel was irrelevant nor because the men themselves lacked faith, courage or stamina. It was the system which was squeezing the life out of them. Exceptional men with outstanding gifts could still make it work, but no organization can run effectively if it is dependent upon nothing but top calibre men, especially at a time when the Church is recruiting fewer and fewer men of ability. I felt increasingly that the job I was meant to be doing was frustrated by the structures. So I prepared a paper for the Bishop suggesting how I thought the Church should be reorganized. In it I claimed, 'The Church of England is not at the moment organized at any level to meet a missionary problem as acute here as anywhere in the world. It is over 100 years since the start of the industrial revolution yet the clerical manpower of the Church is still deployed as though England was an agrarian community. Out of twenty-four livings that became vacant in England in the first week of November 1958, eleven have populations of less than 1000. In the Isle of Wight there is a population of 100,000 people ministered to by sixty clergy. In the rural deanery of Aston in Birmingham there is a population of 250,000 ministered to by fourteen clergymen.'

I then described the church situation in working-class areas:

1. In most of these areas there is one church, hall and vicarage to every 10,000 people or less. Each has a vicar, few have a curate. The congregations in most cases are small—between fifty and 100 and often eclectic.

2. The expenses of maintaining the plant by such a small congregation means that the energy of the priest and his congregation is almost entirely absorbed in raising money. The Church is no longer a giving society. It has to beg to keep going.

3. What little time the clergy have left after money-raising is spent on administration and keeping organizations going. Pastoral care of the non-churchgoers goes by the board. A recent article in the *Sunday Times* described the feelings of the clergy working in such areas in this way:

'They feel themselves caught in the machine they cannot get out of, an institution many of whose attitudes and activities have become wholly irrelevant, yet which somehow imposes its irrelevance upon them. Breakdowns among the clergy are so often caused by the tension of propping up devotedly an institution which, as it is now, simply doesn't work. Young men full of enthusiasm to grapple with realities are ordained to find themselves gobbled up by the insatiable machine of irrelevant church life, while outside is a world on the borders of despair.'

4. Many of the clergy are appointed to these parishes lacking both the ability and experience to cope. And while it is true that a few men of quite outstanding gifts (and they are usually able to attract curates) can make the parochial system work it is rarely possible to find another man of equal ability to replace them when they leave and the congregation sinks back into the rut from which it was recently extracted. Visitors to churches in these areas are not infrequently struck by the gloom and hopelessness that pervade both the services and the weekday activities.

5. The impact that the Church makes is almost negligible.

I then suggested a possible answer:

1. Amalgamate three or four or five of these parishes so that the new parish has a population of between 30,000 and 50,000 depending on local circumstances.

2. Pull down or convert for other uses all but one church in the new parish. Keep the vicarages of the closed churches. It costs about £3000 a year to run a church and assuming that three churches are pulled down there would be a saving of about £9000 a year plus the money received from the sale of church sites.

3. As a result of this reorganization there would be the salaries of four incumbents plus £3000 a year available for staff.

4. Appoint an incumbent at the new parish and give him a staff of three or four specialist chaplains who would live in the vicarages of the closed churches and be paid an incumbent's salary. Spend part of the £3000 on a lay parish bursar and secretary who would run the administration of the parish and co-ordinate the money-making efforts, etc. The remainder of the £3000 would go in stip-

ends to two or three assistant curates or women workers or youth leaders.

Finally, I tried to answer what I thought would be some of the criticisms—the outcry at closing churches, the problems of transferring congregations to a central church, and the judgement of the world that the wholesale closing of churches would be a retreat. I finished, 'There are at least two working-class areas in this diocese which are grossly over-churched—Smethwick and Sparkbrook. It is urged that pilot schemes be operated in both these areas as soon as possible. A really alive, well-staffed church in these areas would not only have an invigorating effect on the whole district but would be a real tonic to the entire diocese.'

The diocesan hierarchy was unsympathetic to my suggestions and the Bishop told me that however right these ideas might be in theory, Church opinion was not ready for them and in any case legal difficulties would make their implementation impossible. I asked the Bishop to select the names of twenty clergymen in the diocese whose judgement he most respected to whom I could send a copy for their comments. To his surprise they were overwhelmingly enthusiastic and we formed a small committee which included Donald Tytler, Director of Religious Education; John Morris, Vicar of Longbridge; and John Grimwade, Vicar of Londonderry, to work out a practical scheme of parochial reform in the Borough of Smethwick where the life of the Church was particularly weak. In the meantime my memorandum was published in the privately circulated *Cambridge Correspondence* of which Dr. John Robinson had recently taken over the editorship from Dr. Alec Vidler. It was clear that a number of other young clergy throughout Britain were of the same mind and we produced a statement signed by over fifty clergymen summarizing my memorandum to the Bishop which was widely circulated among young incumbents throughout England. The response was so encouraging that a conference was held at Keble College, Oxford, in May 1960, which was attended by over 130 clergy and leading laity. And so was born the Keble Conference Group which helped to organize, canalize and mobilize the forces of reform for several years until it petered out.

For six months we put a lot of work into preparing a realistic scheme of reorganization for Smethwick but it was received with no enthusiasm at diocesan level. And so, after eighteen months I sadly came to the conclusion that no significant reforms would be initiated from the top. I could not see myself aged thirty as a greaser of the cogs of a creaking diocesan ecclesiastical machine geared to maintain the *status quo* and I told the Bishop that I thought I ought to return to parochial work where I would at least have a chance of putting into practice some of the reforms for which I had been pleading. The Bishop, I suspect, was somewhat relieved, as he must have found it wearing to have an *enfant terrible* so close to him, and he recommended me for a living in the Birmingham Diocese. But before the patron offered me the job the newly appointed Bishop of Southwark, Dr. Mervyn Stockwood, invited me to become Rector of Woolwich.

Deciding whether to leave Birmingham to go to Woolwich was the first major decision in my life when I felt uncertain about what was the right thing to do. My admiration, affection and loyalty for the Bishop of Birmingham ran deep. The fifty or so diocesan clergy in the Reform Group pressed me to stay. Eventually after six weeks of indecision it was decided that I should go to Woolwich provided the Bishop of Southwark would allow me to take it up in six months' time—March 1960— which he agreed to do. I summed up two years' experience in Birmingham in a farewell sermon at Birmingham Parish Church and an article in the *Birmingham Mail*.

From the pulpit of St. Martin's in the Bullring I concentrated on the theological aspects of the new-look Church. 'It is of vital importance that we believe much more deeply and experience more really than most of us do today the fundamental beliefs of our faith. But I think we must be prepared to be reverently agnostic about some of the less fundamental beliefs which churchmen have clung to with such enthusiasm and tenacity in the past. The new-look Church instead of preaching from above a cut-and-dried, we've-got-all-the-answers faith must stand alongside the enquirer, the doubter and the scoffer and admit that while we know some of the answers there are many things that we are unsure about and confuse us.'

In the *Birmingham Mail* I said, 'I came to Birmingham a callow conformist from the South. I leave next week for South London a roaring nonconformist and unrepentant rebel. Brummies are prepared to lay aside convention and tradition and "have a go". I don't know any other city where people are more open and responsive to new ideas such as I have been hawking around the diocese like a rag-and-bone man for the last two years. We have got to face the fact that the Church in Birmingham is up against it. When the two facts of the difficulties confronting the Church and the Brummies "have a go" spirit are married, the result is that a number of people ask whether the Church does not need a new look. Reform is in the air, but not even an optimist like me believes it is round the corner. The obstacles are enormous. Some older clergy and lay people, well entrenched and in high places, find it hard to think imaginatively and courageously and are fearful of change and experiment.' I finished with an appeal to the laity : 'There are many Christians bored stiff by the Church who criticize from the touchline. To them I say for God's

sake come and join us. We know things are wrong. We
have a glimmer of an idea as to how they might be put
right, but we need your prayers, your support, your enthusiasm, your vision and your vitality, if we are to break
through the blanket of deadening conservatism and obscurantism which hangs over the Church like a cloud. Go
to it Birmingham! The Church throughout England is
watching and waiting.'

The conservative *Birmingham Post* paid me the compli-
ment of devoting its first leader to my departure and
claimed, 'The Reverend Nicolas Stacey, during his time
here, has made an impact on Church life which even those
who disagree with him can hardly ignore.'

I left Birmingham with a clear idea in my mind as to
how the life of the Church, even in the most difficult areas,
could be brought to life. At Woolwich I was to have the
opportunity of putting my theories to the test.

Five

IN THE LIGHT OF ALL THAT HAS HAPPENED
since, it may come as a surprise that the late 1950s
and early 1960s was a time of high hopes for the
Church of England in the minds of a number of us
who had been ordained since the war. I am not
ashamed to admit this although I have noticed some of my
contemporaries, who were just as enthusiastic and optimistic as I was, now claim—no doubt in an attempt to
be wise after the event—that they did not expect as much
as I did. I summed up my hopes in an open and much
publicized letter that I wrote to Dr. Ramsey when he became Archbishop of Canterbury.

I told him 'You will wish to shine a searchlight on the
entire organization of the Church from the top to the
bottom.' I suggested, 'If you do give the lead which the
Church desperately needs, you will have to turn a blow-
lamp on the human fossils so securely riveted to every part
of the creaking, ecclesiastical machine.' I begged him to
follow President Kennedy's example by gathering round
him a brilliant team of unlikely men from unlikely jobs
to advise him.

I finished my letter on a note of hope and optimism:
'If you mobilize the whole Church for concerted action
you will discover, perhaps to your surprise, the vast support you will get.

'There is an air of expectancy in the Church as we wait for you to take up the reins. We pray that God will give you the vision, courage and energy that you will need if you are to match the hour.'

We believed that if the organization, the image, the liturgy and the spirituality of the Church and its methods of communication could be refurbished, the decline could be halted and the Church could look forward to a flourishing and relevant future. And there were some signs that this could be done. New canons and new Ecclesiastical Courts were being created. Revised lectionaries, catechisms and psalters rolled out. A report on deployment of the clergy was commissioned. Christian stewardship came across the Atlantic from America and was catching on. In middle-class suburban parishes, where there was an active and imaginative minister, congregations were increasing slightly.

And so in 1960 an editorial in the *Church of England Newspaper* was echoing the thoughts of many when it announced 'A new Church of England is being born, a Church efficient, sophisticated and progressive, a Church with money enough and to spare.'

The newly appointed Bishop of Woolwich, Dr. John Robinson, said at the first confirmation he conducted in 1959 'You're coming into active membership of a Church at a time when great things are afoot. I believe, in England, that we may be at the turning of the tide. Indeed in Cambridge University, where I have recently come from, I am convinced the tide has already turned.'

The tide was flowing our way and with dynamic leadership we thought new life could be breathed into the dry old ecclesiastical bones. I, for one, believed that Prime Minister Harold Macmillan's appointment of the young radical, Dr. Mervyn Stockwood as Bishop of the sprawling South London Diocese of Southwark at the end of 1958 could herald the beginning of a new era. On the announcement of his appointment, and long before there was any question of my joining his diocese, I wrote to him. I think I echoed the thoughts of many when I said: 'You have a bigger responsibility than you know, because I suspect a great many people, myself included, are going to watch very carefully to see whether you can break through the legalism and obscurantism which, among other things, are crippling the Church of England at the moment.'

I told Mervyn Stockwood that, having been a bishop's chaplain for six months, I could see only too clearly the difficulties before him—freeholds, Church Commissioners, the Privy Council, archdeacons, sub-committees, vested interests and conservatism. I added, 'I feel for you very deeply.

'If you fail, break your heart or die of frustration, it will be the final sign that it really is impossible to make the ecclesiastical machine work in such a way as to build the Kingdom of God rather than merely to maintain the *status quo*.'

If anybody in the Church of England was capable of leading a new movement it was, in my opinion, Dr. Mervyn Stockwood. He had proven success behind him in two quite different types of parish. After nineteen years in a downtown area in Bristol where by a combination of inspired showmanship, deep pastoral care and intense hard work, he had made one of the most exciting parishes in England, he had gone to Great St. Mary's at Cambridge which had virtually no congregation. By using almost identical techniques in the vastly more sophisticated university situation he had in a year or two achieved the same remarkable results. The 8.30 pm Sunday Service at Great St. Mary's to which speakers prominent in the news were invited, was packed every Sunday with undergraduates. So

W.C.—E

successful was Dr. Stockwood's ministry, both in terms of the number of people who attended and the interest and discussion he generated, that many people were asking whether his work there might be the spearhead of some kind of religious revival.

Looking back now I realize that we had hoped too much of him. If some people are now disappointed in him, this is more a comment on their naïveté than a criticism of his inadequacies. The difficulty lies in the structure of the Church of England. In a parish, a priest with powers of leadership can have a profound effect. He is master of the local ecclesiastical 'show'—in Mervyn Stockwood's case a gifted master of ceremonies and an impresario. A parish priest can decide the policies and priorities of the local church and can choose and sack his own curates. Even if the church is generally in decline he can to some extent buck the trend by drawing a congregation from way outside the parish, often at the expense of other local churches with less gifted ministers. Provided he has the support of the parochial church council, which is usually a malleable body, there is virtually no experiment he cannot try.

A diocesan bishop, however, is in a totally different position. He is far from being master of his own house. I learnt this when I was Chaplain to the Bishop of Birmingham. How well I remember pacing up and down Leonard Wilson's study telling him how to reorganize the diocese, only to be told that each new exciting reform I was recommending with such enthusiasm was impossible because he had no power to implement it. One of the myths about the Church of England is that bishops have power. (Their Methodist opposite numbers are in a much stronger position.) But it often happens in British public life that the greater the prestige the less the power. Surprisingly, bishops still have considerable, but declining prestige. A certain amount of glamour still hangs around the episcopal office. A bishop is always good for a headline if something out of the ordinary happens, like splitting his trousers when he steps over a tombstone on the way to conduct a confirmation. Even in today's secular society a bishop can have a limited indirect influence on the local community. However, he lacks effective control over the household of God. He cannot move the clergy against their will and he is only responsible for about fifty per cent of the clerical appointments within his diocese. He has little control over the diocesan finances, while rationalization and deployment of the diocesan resources of men, buildings and money are virtually impossible. A bishop may be a colourful bird, as indeed the Bishop of Southwark is, but he is trapped in a gilded cage.

I have little doubt that Dr. Stockwood, flushed by the success of his ministry in Cambridge, was as excited and optimistic about what could be done in the rundown Diocese of Southwark as were his young admirers. Certainly no man could have worked harder or given himself more unsparingly than he has done in the last ten years in Southwark. Yet the statistics show that despite his efforts, nowhere in Britain has Church life ebbed faster than in South London.

There are few people in the Church of England for whom I feel more sympathy than Dr. Stockwood. He has always been accident prone, has worn his faults on his sleeve and has laid himself open to criticism. He is obviously and painfully torn between heart and head. Intellectually he is a Radical Socialist dedicated to the building of a fairer society with a lively concern for the underprivileged. Emotionally he is a high church Tory who finds compensation for his bachelor life in the trappings and glamour of episcopal office and the prestige of a seat in the House of Lords.

On one hand he can see through the hypocrisy and cant

of much of the Establishment, and yet on the other, he needs the security it provides. Inevitably the radicals are suspicious of his prelatical heart and the Establishment suspicious of his Socialist head. And so his is a lonely life. In view of the disappointments and frustrations of much of his work in Southwark it is to his lasting credit that he has prevented his heart from completely controlling his head. There are many occasions when Mervyn Stockwood has infuriated me and many times when I believe he has deserved criticism. But there are also times when I realize he was a scapegoat for my own frustrations.

I remember him best on the one occasion in eight years that I served under him when I desperately and urgently needed his help. Although we had one of the largest staff of curates of any parish in the Church of England, this was the only occasion in my eight-year ministry in Woolwich that we had a serious staff problem. One of the curates developed a persecution complex and spoke with a lack of discretion. His outburst happened at a time when everything we were doing at Woolwich was much in the public eye and the sad episode could easily have become a front-page national newspaper story. The situation demanded fast, firm and fair handling by the Bishop, and received it. It is in this kind of crisis that Dr. Stockwood is at his best and he shows himself in his true colours as a man of compassion, firmness and sensitivity. Whereas many clergymen in the diocese have experienced this side of his nature it is not one seen by social acquaintances, interviewing journalists and the public. Consequently, he is often judged more harshly than he deserves.

I was flattered and honoured to have been invited to become part of the Southwark scene by being offered the Rectorship of Woolwich at the early age of thirty-one. Mervyn Stockwood was anxious to bring some new faces into the diocese and was fortunate that vacancies occurred in three or four key jobs. He offered the Suffragan Bishopric of Woolwich to Dr. John Robinson, the Dean of Clare College, Cambridge, soon to achieve world fame with his book, *Honest to God*. Dr. Robinson, who at that time was almost unknown outside academic theological circles, had been a curate of Mervyn Stockwood at Bristol. The Reverend Eric James, the Chaplain of Trinity College, Cambridge, went to St. George's, Camberwell, the Trinity College mission church in the back streets. The Reverend Bill Skelton, Chaplain of Clare College, Cambridge, became Rector of Bermondsey.

Mervyn Stockwood was faced with an appalling problem in the riverside parishes from Battersea to Woolwich. Church life in these areas, which had never been strong, was at an all-time low. The picture was one of derelict churches (in Bermondsey three within half a mile), bleak-hearted clergy (vicars turn over faster than anywhere else in England) and small disheartened congregations. His plan was to appoint a few magnetic and imaginative men to key churches along the riverfront in the hope that at least some lively Christian centres would be created. It was a strategy which had my full support. Indeed it was the only possible one in such depressing circumstances.

My excitement and enthusiasm for joining the Church in South London cooled off a great deal after I had actually visited Woolwich in August 1959. It was one of the hottest days in the year and I spent the first five hours of it in the depths of the BBC working on a programme on Christian stewardship. The programme finished with a discussion between a very complacent gentleman from the Church Commissioners and myself. It was one of the very few times that I have got really cross in a broadcast and I left Broadcasting House for Woolwich feeling limp and bad-tempered. I was greeted by the Rector, the Reverend R. C. Thompson, who had been appointed a resident Canon at Southwell Cathedral. He had been in Woolwich for sixteen years, having succeeded Cuthbert Bardsley.

Dr. Bardsley, in the 1950s, was the 'glamour boy' of the Church of England : he had gone on from Woolwich to be successively Provost of Southwark, Bishop of Croydon and now Bishop of Coventry, and was likened by his fellow bishops to Tommy Steele. By all accounts he had exercised a wonderful wartime ministry in Woolwich. His Eton and Oxford charm was so great and his ex-Moral Rearmament sincerity so intense that he seemed almost too good to be true. The comfort and inspiration he gave to the people of Woolwich in the long nights spent in air raid shelters is gratefully remembered to this day. As a preacher with enthralling gifts, Dr. Bardsley had been able to build up a considerable congregation, mainly from the better-class areas outside the parish : a number of these people followed him to Southwark Cathedral when he left Woolwich. He must have been a very difficult man to succeed, especially by one whose gifts were in such sharp contrast.

But for sixteen years, Mr. Thompson had laboured, sometimes single-handed, in a parish with three churches and 12,000 people. He was a shy, saintly and scholarly man. He was also very tired. We tramped the streets of the parish together on a stifling evening. The homes were a mixture of new council houses and flats and old slums which were being rapidly acquired by the local authority to be pulled down. The parish also included the main shopping centre of the London Borough of Woolwich with the colourful Beresford Square open market, the Town Hall and other local government offices, a fast expanding Polytechnic and an equally fast declining Woolwich Arsenal. The Royal Artillery Barracks was also in the parish but was served by its own Chaplain.

Woolwich itself I took to at first meeting. It is a typical

working-class riverside area but far enough from the centre of London to have a life of its own. When General Booth did his famous survey of London at the end of the last century parts of the parish were marked with the black ink he reserved for the most notorious sin spots; and up until quite recently policemen had patrolled certain areas in pairs. Due largely to an enlightened and progressive Borough Council most of the sordid parts of the centre had been cleaned up by the end of the 1950s. I sensed from my very first visit that I would feel at home in the bustling, gregarious, noisy atmosphere of Woolwich; but the Church scene, which the Rector both showed and described to me, made me doubt whether I should accept.

The main Church of St. Mary Magdalen, the mother church of the Borough, stood magnificently on a hillock overlooking the Thames. It was surrounded by a garden converted from a graveyard and beautifully maintained by the Borough Council. To the east was the town's busy shopping centre and to the south and west hundreds and hundreds of families tightly packed in flats and houses. To the north was the river. The present church was built in 1735 in classical Georgian style but it is thought there had been a church on the site since the sixth century when Christianity was first introduced into that part of Kent. I noticed the list of Rectors went back for over 700 years. The view from the outside of the church with the East India docks across the river and the ceaseless stream of ships, barges and boats was of great character and even romantic.

As long as I live I shall remember the moment when I stepped into that great building. A moment earlier I had been standing in the gardens outside the church and the whole of life was around me. There were the ships and the docks; the great Tate & Lyle factory across the water;

the new tower blocks rising into the sky and the drab little slum houses which nestled at their feet. There was the Odeon cinema at the garden gate with queues of young people; opposite them were more queues as their parents collected fish and chips. There were children playing in the garden, and there were courting couples on the benches which overlooked the river. It was a marvellous scene. No church building could have been better placed.

But inside the church it was dark, dank and decaying, and depressing beyond all description. Rats and mice scurried round the unused galleries, damp patches in the ceiling told their own story of a leaking roof. The place had not been decorated for generations and the remnants of the paint were flaking off. It seated 700 and had a congregation of about fifty. Off the Vestry (where drapings from Queen Victoria's funeral still hung) there was a lavatory which, according to local tradition, had been transferred by Noah from the Ark. The building had lost even the sad dignity of an aristocratic old lady who has fallen on hard times. And to me on that sunny summer's evening the church building proclaimed that God was dead, and I began to wonder how much the Christian Church had achieved in its 1300 years in Woolwich. I looked with renewed admiration at the Rector who had stuck this for sixteen years. Certainly I did not blame him. How could a minute congregation, mainly elderly and female, raise the money that would be required to restore the building? The Rector explained that the heating system did not work properly and was inadequate. Later I was to discover that he had not exaggerated.

When I had seen the historic parish church I thought I had seen all. But further shocks were in store for me. There were two other churches in the parish which I had yet to see, even more sparsely attended than St. Mary's. One was on the market in Beresford Square by the gates of Woolwich Arsenal. Derelict it looked and derelict it was, with a small congregation that liked incense and insisted that the church be kept open although it was only half a mile from St. Mary's. As if this was not enough for one evening there was a third, a church in a further corner of the parish. This drab dual-purpose horror had been built at a time when the very poor people who lived around felt uncomfortable in, and were probably unwelcome at, St. Mary's in the presence of the middle-class people who at that time lived at Woolwich. For a time, too, it had served as a soup kitchen. Memories of humiliating queues were, I am sure, partly behind the completely negative attitude of nearby residents to this particular building.

I questioned Mr. Thompson on other aspects of the church life as we went from building to building. I discovered that the only full-time assistant he had was a sweet and gentle Church Army Sister. He did import one or two clergymen from the suburbs to assist him with the Sunday and weekday services, at the three churches. One of these priests was over eighty. There was a clergy house—a vital asset because virtually the whole parish was owned by the local authority and there were no suitable privately owned houses for sale. It was therefore essential to have somewhere to house the assistant clergy I was hoping to recruit if I accepted the job. Unfortunately, however, the large clergy house was in such a bad state of repair that only the basement flat was habitable. There was no church hall, but a fund had been started in the hope that eventually there would be enough money to build one. There was an endowment which brought in £600 a year, enough to pay an assistant curate, but as the parish did not have a curate, the diocese took the money. There were the usual organizations attached to the church, such as the Mothers' Union and Scouts but the Rector explained that it was difficult to find people to run them and that they were going through a thin period. I did not doubt it. In worldly terms the only bonus I could see was an unostentatious but comfortable modern rectory which looked from the outside like two council houses put together, but which could be made nice inside. Nobody, I thought, would be able to look at the rectory, suck their teeth and claim, 'It's all right for him'. It also had, by London standards, a reasonable garden with which I knew my wife could have fun.

The Rector's salary of about £1100 a year also came from endowments. As far as I could make out this had not altered since the beginning of the century, which made me think that either the Rector of Woolwich in 1900 was very overpaid or his successor in 1960 was somewhat underpaid. By the time the tour was over and we were back in the rectory, my spirits were very low. The resigning Rector was a man of honesty and integrity and could not disguise the extent of the 'challenge'; on the other hand he did not want to put me off. It was, he thought, time to hand over to a younger man who would bring new ideas to an old problem—how to attract working-class people into the worshipping community of the Anglican Church.

I had arranged to go on later the same evening to see the Bishop of Woolwich, who lived about four miles away in Blackheath, in order to report my reaction. It was the first time I had met John and Ruth Robinson who were later to become such close and intimate friends. I found them almost as depressed as I was; they were wondering whether they had not made a ghastly mistake by leaving Cambridge for a Suffragan Bishopric in South London which was traditionally the graveyard of so many ecclesiastical reputations. Their honesty and frankness then, and throughout the long years we worked together, was enormously refreshing and encouraging. There are few people whom my wife and I have come to admire more. John, who comes from a long line of clerics, is essentially an ecclesiastic and a scholar. Deeply secure in himself and totally lacking in personal ambition, he has never sought to shock or hurt. All his writings have been the products of an honest and inquiring mind; he has never written in order to express his personal frustrations or thwarted ambitions. He is impatient with the Establishment, because he believes deeply that it is misguided and inhibits the truth: there is no question of any disguised impatience with himself. He is shy, and this makes him more at home with ideas and words than with people. This shyness has been misunderstood as offhandedness. It also explains why, in my opinion, he is not a better judge of character —a weakness he shares with the late William Temple. His inability to be ingenuous or play to the gallery makes him a bad politician and this is probably to his credit. It was none of John's seeking that he became a notorious bishop and this is why he was much less vulnerable to criticism than his Diocesan, the Bishop of Southwark. But it was his very lack of sophistication—almost naïveté—in the ways of the world which led to the media using him rather than the other way round. The admiration he received in some circles could have made a lesser man conceited and arrogant. The abuse he has been subjected to by others would have crushed the spirit of anyone who lacked great inner resources, especially as much of the time he was in great physical pain from slipped discs in his back.

His wife, Ruth, is the intellectual equal of her husband. Coming from a less ecclesiastical background, she has fewer qualms about making sharp judgements on the Church. She shares with John the same intellectual honesty and hatred of cant and hypocrisy. She is a superb debunker and exposer of pomposity—in every way an unusual and engaging bishop's wife.

It would not be right to say that John Robinson persuaded me to accept the Rectorship of Woolwich. He did not. But my conversation with him that evening did persuade me that he was a man who understood the problems. I felt he would support me in attempting to carry out the Bishop of Southwark's mandate: 'To build up a team of clergy and for God's sake do anything to show the people of Woolwich that the Church exists.'

I returned to central London with my mind in a turmoil and spent a restless night. I was worried that I might have shown my gloom to Mr. Thompson, so I wrote off to him the next day thanking him for putting me so clearly in the picture about the parish. I said, 'I must admit by the end of last night I saw the immense difficulties of the job more clearly than the immense possibilities. This morning I think I see the whole thing in better perspective. I feel particularly, if I may say so, the privilege of serving a congregation which has been trained by you during the last years. Knowing that there is a hard core of really well-instructed Christians who will be able to teach me what the Christian faith is all about is a very strong factor.'

Eventually I accepted Woolwich with grave doubts and from mixed motives. I had been 'banging on' in Birmingham about how the Church in downtown areas should be run if it was to become alive. I had constantly said that the successful church in middle-class suburbia does not compensate for the failure of the Church in working-class conurbations. After all, at that time three-quarters of the young people in Britain were leaving secondary modern schools at fifteen and if the Church of England is to be the Church of the English people it must catch the imagination and win the allegiance of some of them. To refuse an opportunity of putting my ideas into practice in such a situation would have shown a lack of courage. Moreoever, it had been ingrained into me in the Navy that a good officer never asks a sailor to do what he is not prepared to do himself, so I was afraid I would forever suffer from a sense of guilt if I ducked this assignment. I believed, too, that with Mervyn Stockwood and John Robinson it was more likely that a breakthrough could be achieved here than in any other diocese. But I also recall saying to myself—and this is very much less laudable but no less honest—that five years in Woolwich, by which time I should be only thirty-six, should lead to bigger and better things in the Church.

Much has been said and written since about my naïveté (and, by implication, my conceit) in thinking that it would be possible to make a success in Woolwich in view of the long history of non-churchgoing and apathy towards the Church. Woolwich, of course, had this in common with all similar areas, as is now agreed by all social historians. I know that man proposes and God disposes. I know that man's ways are not often God's ways. I am aware that there is a great difference between man's ideas of success and failure and God's assessment of these things. I understand the argument that the holy and humble thing to do is to allow oneself to be guided step by step by the Holy Spirit, although I often think that this is an excuse for sloppy thinking and a refusal to make decisions. I was aware then, as I am more fully aware now, that the filling of a church is not the same as building the Kingdom of God in a community. I plead guilty to underestimating massively the depth and significance of social pressures which keep the English working class away from the worshipping community of the Church.

Nevertheless, I believe that any man undertaking a new job must have a clear idea of his target. My plan and my hope for Woolwich was that within a five-year period we would be able to build up the congregation to 300 or 400 regular worshippers. Looked at in percentage terms of the local population it was not ambitious—less than four per cent of the population of the parish and, as parish boundaries in London are meaningless, less than one per cent of those within easy reach of the church. It meant increasing the congregation six or eightfold. I hoped that by good leadership, teaching and preaching these 300 or 400 people would, as an expression of their Christian commitment, involve themselves in every aspect of life in the Borough according to their various abilities. I wanted to see people inspired by Christian concern offer them-selves to their political parties as candidates for the Borough Council and to take leading roles in the many voluntary organizations in the area. In short, to be active co-workers with Christ in the building of His Kingdom.

I do not believe that the Church in its social outreach should attempt to duplicate what is better done by the statutory social services and secular voluntary organiza-tions; therefore the Church should concentrate on closing gaps in the existing services and meet new social needs as they emerge. But because the Christian community should show a concern for all people in the parish we would aim to form a house church in every street and block of flats which would become the localized care centre reaching out to everybody in the street. In these house churches churchgoers and non-churchgoers would be able to meet together for discussions and action on common problems.

This, then, was the plan. The tactics for implementing it would have to be worked out on the ground with the con-gregation. That no such plan was working anywhere in similar areas did not deter me. From all that I had seen of the Church of England in the last ten years I was con-vinced that nowhere had the attempt been made, with the energy, drive and singlemindedness which I intended to bring to it. Perhaps I should mock myself for being so adolescent as to think that such a plan was feasible. But yet I wonder whether, if such aims are not achievable, the work of the Church has any relevance. I did not go to Woolwich to prop up a moribund ecclesiastical club, nor as a celebrant of residual tribal rites of birth, marriage and death : to have done so would have been contrary to my nature as well as being a denial of my vocation. I went there with two deeply and passionately held aims. First, to be the instrument by which men and women are helped to discover the living relationship with God through Jesus Christ—a relationship which gives a new purpose, dimension and hope to human existence. And secondly, to ensure that the Church played its part in trying to make the Borough of Woolwich more like the Kingdom of Heaven. I believed then, as I believe now, that Christians have an unavoidable responsibility to help to create a world in which all men can live in freedom and dignity, a world in which they can give full expression to their talents. For the next eight years Woolwich was the part of the world in which I was to try to work out this belief.

Six

THERE ARE SOME PAROCHIAL CLERGYMEN
who have the capacity of leading from behind. They are prepared to sit back in a parish
for many years and quietly fan any sparks of
local leadership that may appear. They are
not too concerned about results, and if nothing much happens 'because the congregation or the parish is not ready
for it' they do not get worried, impatient or bored. I am
not such a man, either by temperament or by training. So
from the moment I had accepted the Rectorship of Woolwich, I was convinced that my plans were dependent upon
recruiting a team of assistant clergymen. It was not a
question of bypassing the faithful few, which is all the
congregation consisted of, by superimposing on them a
team of high-powered professional clerics. It was a question of providing the leadership which would draw out
the best in them; it would also mobilize the potential goodwill and resources in the service of the community, of the
thousands of other parishioners who had no contact with
the church.

But, as I knew at the time, and see even more clearly
now, there are real dangers in such a policy. For generations the downtown areas, where there is very little local
indigenous leadership, have had things done for them by
people coming in from outside. The understandable tempta-

tion for the local people is to sit back and let 'them' get on with it. Some modern community development officers and sociologists believe that local voluntary organizations will not really come alive unless the leadership and the inspiration come from within the community itself. Yet waiting for this to happen can be like waiting for Godot. The political parties and the voluntary organizations in an area like Woolwich are faced with the same dilemma as the Church. They too find that the leadership comes from the better-class areas in Plumstead and Eltham, where go-ahead people can buy their own houses. Consequently the school teachers, social workers, health visitors, probation officers and local government officers working in the parish all lived outside.

The dilemma is made more acute by the creation of massive local authority housing schemes in which there are simply no houses for sale. Even up to the beginning of World War II the centre of Woolwich was a mixed community. Shopkeepers used to live above their shops; there were one or two roads where the local professional people lived and considerable numbers of modest terraced houses owned by the occupier. By the time I had arrived in Woolwich the whole parish was virtually a council estate, so that anyone who wanted to buy his own home had to leave. Inevitably it was the least ambitious, energetic and thrifty who were left behind—the very people least likely to give a lead in local affairs. Paradoxically the more energetic the local authorities are in buying up slum property and replacing it with council estates, the more acute the problem becomes. Today the vast number of people who live along the banks of the Thames from Battersea to Woolwich in council accommodation belong to one class, and the cry rings round the area 'nothing works here'.

Throughout my years at Woolwich I was a keen supporter and admirer of the progressive and enlightened Borough Council Housing Department which worked unceasingly to deal with the chronic housing shortage. Its leaders were as aware as I was of the problems that their policies were creating. It is easy for theoretical sociologists to say that some areas in local authority housing schemes should be allocated to private developers for owner occupation but private developers are very unwilling to make use of such sites because they know that the houses and flats will be hard to sell. The fact is that many school teachers and social workers like to get away from their work and live among their own kind in the suburbs. It is equally unrealistic to expect local housing authorities to provide housing for professional people who can buy their homes at market prices when there are hundreds of homeless families and thousands of slum dwellers on the council's waiting list. This is why I never asked the local authority to provide accommodation for any of my staff, although I knew that by living as well as working in the area they were contributing much to the life of the community. The only answer that I could see to the problem was to bring in the best men I could recruit, who I knew would give themselves totally to the people of Woolwich.

When I was looking after the junior clergy in the Birmingham Diocese, I was depressed by the poor working relations many of the curates seemed to have had with their vicars. This made the curates much less effective than they might have been. It also meant that they wanted to escape from the vicar/curate relationship and become vicars themselves as soon as they possibly could; this in turn often meant going to small country parishes which were the only ones they could get, where insufficient demands were made on their energies. In my opinion the Church of England gives far too much security of tenure to its vicars and far too little to its curates. A vicar has a legal freehold and without a court case it is impossible to move him against his will. A curate on the other hand can be dismissed at six months' notice at the whim of the vicar. Bishops have virtually no authority over a vicar because of his freehold, but vicars have dictatorial powers over their curates. The situation is made worse because vicars receive no training in man management. This is further aggravated by the system in which a priest will, after his first or second curacy, be promoted to become vicar of a small parish which has no curate. The young vicar working on his own for five years may then get further promotion to a larger parish which has a curate. But he will by then be so used to working single-handed that decentralization and consultation are difficult for him, and he either treats his curate like a dogsbody or allows him to go his own way so that the parish is denied cohesive leadership.

It was for these reasons that I was determined to develop a new system of working with my clerical colleagues. I wanted to run a genuine team ministry at Woolwich in which all the clerical staff would pray, plan, work and make decisions together and in which the whole team would be responsible to the Parochial Church Council. I wanted the newest curate straight from his theological college to have the same say and the same vote as I had myself in the way the parish was run. I would have no veto and once decisions had been taken, if necessary by a vote of team members, they would be binding on all, including myself. Further, each member of the team would have his own clearly defined area of responsibility for which he would be accountable to the remainder of the team. This was the basis on which I started trying to recruit men to come to Woolwich and I believe it was the reason we were able to attract some of the ablest young clergymen in the Church of England.

The first to join us was the Reverend Paul Bibby. He brought with him exceptional gifts, a wide variety of experience and an attractive wife. After Winchester he had served in the Merchant Navy and run a youth club in downtown New York. At Cambridge he won a Blue in Athletics. He was trained for the priesthood at Westcott House and had served his first curacy in Manchester, where he had been greatly loved. Bibby came from a very favoured background. His father was a well-known jobber in the London Stock Exchange and his mother one of the most distinguished looking women of her generation. Before the 1914–18 war a significant number of men like Bibby were ordained priests in the Church of England. Since then the number has drastically declined and the Church is the poorer without them. Secure and confident in their own positions, unworried by financial cares, lacking personal ambition and abrasiveness, such men had a gentleness, graciousness and easygoing tolerance in their dealings with people which it is hard to match. In our early days in Woolwich when there was so much reorganization to do and so many things to be started, I was always concerned that the congregation should not be left behind or feel overlooked, and it was Bibby who had the task of caring for them. He did it with patience, humour and love. After his stint in Woolwich, Bibby became a vicar in Manchester and is now back in South London as head of Cambridge House in Camberwell.

The other man to join us, who was already a priest was the Reverend Robert Hughes. Like Bibby he had been trained for the ministry at Westcott House, but before that had been at Trinity College, Oxford, to which he won the top scholarship from Eton. He came from a highly gifted family. His father is the distinguished novelist, Richard Hughes, the author of *High Wind in Jamaica*, and his mother an artist. For a year between gaining his degree and going to theological college, Hughes had worked on the shop floor of an aircraft works in Coventry, where he was later to be a curate. It was on the council estate in Coventry where he was working that he met his wife, Sheila, who shares with him a remarkable ability to get alongside and help drop-outs. This made them brilliant at running the branch of the Telephone Samaritans which we were to set up at Woolwich. Hughes is an outstanding priest but is not a typical product of Eton. He is totally classless, a convinced Socialist, a good theologian, uninterested in personal comfort and his appearance, which tended to be somewhat scruffy. He joined us primarily as industrial chaplain, in which role he visited local factories and organized apprentice conferences.

I think it was Hughes' integrity, straightforwardness and complete absence of pomposity or self-seeking which made him such a success in Woolwich.

I had not realized the extent of his popularity with a remarkable variety of people until he had a serious accident on his side-car motor cycle. He was due to take the 7.00 am Holy Communion service on Ascension Day. Shortly after 7.00 am I was rung up by a member of the congregation from the church and told he had not arrived. It was very unlike Hughes to oversleep, and no sooner had I put down the telephone than I got a call from the police saying that one of my staff had been involved in an accident and was now on his way to hospital. Having arranged for someone else to take the service, I rushed to the hospital to discover that Hughes' foot had almost been severed. The Casualty Officer said it would have to be amputated. I insisted that I should tell him myself, and, although dazed, the news came as no surprise to him and he asked me to tell his wife. While I was doing this, the Casualty Officer sent for the Orthopaedic Consultant to do an amputation. When the Consultant saw the foot he thought there was a chance in a thousand that he could save it. So when I returned to the hospital later with his wife, I found Hughes still with both feet. Since his father was in Greece writing a book and his mother, who had also been involved in the accident, was in the next door cubicle in a state of shock, with a broken wrist, his aunt came to Woolwich to assure herself that leaving the foot on would not be worse than removing it. Because she was lady-in-waiting to the Queen the Queen's surgeon was summoned to give a second opinion and told the orthopaedic surgeon he had done one of the most remarkable operations he had ever seen in his life. Although Hughes now has to wear a special shoe and walks with a slight limp, he can again climb the slopes of his beloved Welsh mountains. The day before the accident, Hughes had been on one of his regular visits to the machine shop of an engineering works and had mentioned that he was going to be moving house at the next weekend. Within twenty-four hours of the accident, the shop steward of that section had telephoned to offer the help of twenty men to handle the whole move.

News of the accident went round Woolwich like wildfire and such was his popularity that a special guard had to be put outside his room to keep the people away. The vast majority of people in South-East London find the Church wholly irrelevant and clergymen no longer automatically command respect. Nevertheless, people still give their affection and loyalty to priests like Bob Hughes more completely than to any man in any other profession. Like so many of the better young priests, Bob is now serving God outside the parochial ministry in an important pastoral and administrative job at Birmingham University.

The other two men who were founder members of the Woolwich team came straight from theological college. In their different ways both were outstanding. Brian Cooper, who had been the first man since 1945 to achieve three first-class honours degrees in Mods, Greats and Theology at Oxford, brought some additional theological ballast to the team. I first met Cooper when we had lunch together at Vincent's Club in Oxford. He was still at theological college—Ripon Hall on Boars Hill. I was surprised when he told me he had never heard of Vincent's, although he had spent four years at Oxford. He was tall, gangling, unsophisticated and inexperienced. But he had an intellectual humility, and a frankness and honesty about himself which immediately endeared him to me—an endearment that ripened into a close and intimate friendship as I got to know him better. When he first joined us he was remarkably innocent about the ways of the world. But I have never come across a man who learnt more quickly, and in a few months he was outstripping us all as an effective parish clergyman. The clarity and discipline of his mind were such that he never allowed us to get away with woolly thinking. The obvious disadvantage of operating a team ministry in which all members have an equal say and vote was that the younger members, if they wanted, could have thrown their weight about and attempted to lay down the law on matters on which they had little experience. This never happened, largely, I think, because from the outset, Cooper set such a magnificent example by making his contribution in fields in which his knowledge, insights and judgement were better than those of the rest of us and keeping quiet when he had nothing to say. This is a rare gift among the clergy. Cooper left Woolwich to teach theology at a theological college in Canada and has now returned to Britain as Vice-Principal of Westcott House, one of the Church of England's leading theological colleges.

Finally, there was Richard Garrard. The director of the ordination candidates in the Peterborough diocese, from which he came, and the Dean of King's College, London, where he was trained, described him as the best man they had. I found their judgement perceptive. His gifts were less dramatic and newsworthy than the other members of the team, but he became an anchor man in Woolwich for over five years. He came from an Anglo-Catholic background and was less radical than the rest of us. At team discussions he ensured that we did not depart from traditional orthodoxy unless the reasons for doing so were overwhelming. He won the respect of us all by having, what is called in the trade, 'a pastoral heart'—in fact, the largest 'pastoral heart' of any man I have ever come across. He had the grimmest and most depressing corner of the parish to look after. It was in an area in which some of the houses had been condemned as unfit for human habitation thirty years earlier. The people who lived there had had much experience of being 'done good to' by social workers of all kinds and were shrewd judges of professional do-gooders. They saw in Richard Garrard the genuine article and nicknamed him 'Richard the Lion-heart'. After going to Great St. Mary's at Cambridge, Richard has become Chaplain to a college of education.

We also asked Miss Jessie Fairham, a retired school mistress who was a member of the congregation, to join the staff in an honorary capacity. Miss Fairham was loved and respected by both the staff and congregation. This made her an exceptionally effective go-between. She constantly interpreted the congregation's attitudes to us and ours to them. She had an uncanny way of knowing what would upset the congregation, how much they could take and where we must draw the line. It was Miss Fairham who stopped us racing too far ahead of them.

A vacancy occurred in the Headship of our Church Primary School a year or so after I went to Woolwich. We were able to appoint Miss Peggy Taylor, a remarkably dedicated and lively Christian teacher as Headmistress, who was invited to become a member of the St. Mary's team. Miss Taylor quickly became one of the key figures in the team. She had more experience than any of us of Woolwich-type areas, and knew instinctively how local people would react to our various schemes. She was superbly allergic to clergy pomposity and a shrewd critic of clerical dominance. Miss Taylor ensured that we resisted the temptation of the clergy team becoming a sophisticated esoteric little group, with its 'in' jokes and private language. She was a remarkable debunker, and would fearlessly take us all on at once if she thought we were being insensitive or impatient or over-critical of Woolwich. Not only did some of the clergy staff teach at school, as is traditional, but we endeavoured to see that every venture the school undertook was supported by the church. As a result, we had a very close and happy partnership between church and school.

There was also a succession of young personal assistants on the staff. Each stayed for a year or two before going on to university. Although my car insurers were not enthusiastic about these young men, they were a great asset to the team. They turned their hands to everything from fixing the details of a Royal visit to the parish to staying by the bedside of a dying parishioner. Their work with us helped them to decide whether or not to be ordained themselves. All but one decided against it.

In addition there was the saintly Church Army Sister whom I inherited who stayed with us for a few months until, understandably, she found the pace a bit fast and left. There was also my magnificent secretary, Mrs. Crawford, who stayed with me for my entire period at Woolwich. This was the team that assembled at the parish church during 1960 and 1961. They were not all able to start with me when I was instituted by the Bishop of Southwark in March, but with the loyalty that characterized them all they appeared from all corners of Britain to be at the service.

The institution of a new Rector, especially at a civic church like Woolwich Parish Church, is always a big occasion and attended by the local leaders. The Labour Mayor of Woolwich at the time, who later became a great friend of mine, was an atheist and refused to attend, but the Town Clerk, the Leader of the Borough Council, and the MPs were present. There is a long tradition that until the new Rector is actually installed by the Bishop he must not interfere in the affairs of the church. This meant that apart from attending a rehearsal I had no say in the organization and ordering of the service. The arrangements were in the hands of the elderly cleric who was vicar of a nearby parish who had been responsible for looking after St. Mary's during the interregnum. I hoped that it would go smoothly. I thought it better not to appear until just before the service started and when I entered the church I was surprised and disappointed that there was no pre-service organ music. Congregations need music while they are waiting for services. It creates the right mood and drowns the hubbub of voices. I went into the vestry to find Dr. Stockwood with his shoulder against the lavatory door. He was trying to break it down as the organist, a delightful but nervous man, was locked inside shouting to be let out. Eventually we got the organist out and Mervyn Stockwood in and safely out. But as he explained the plug did not pull. It was I thought a symbolic little incident. 'Nothing works too well.'

The basis of the team's life was a common spiritual discipline. The team imposed the discipline upon itself and we decided to spend from 7.00 am to 8.20 am each morning with Holy Communion and Matins, followed by half an hour's meditation and intercessions for the parish. We all met together for another half-hour in the evening for prayers. It was a demanding routine because it meant being up shortly after 6.00 each morning and it was rarely possible to be in bed before midnight. We got desperately tired but we continued it for over two and a half years before switching the morning service to after breakfast. The whole of each Monday morning was spent in study and planning parochial strategy and going through lists of parishioners to ensure that everybody was being adequately cared for. Each of us tried to spend the inside of a week each year away in retreat and about twice a year we would go away somewhere for thirty-six hours, when we would attempt to make dispassionate objective assessments of the way our policy was working. At team meetings there were some moments of disagreement; we had a long argument before deciding to start bingo sessions in the church school hall in order to raise money. But we rarely found it necessary to take a vote, because we usually managed to come to a common mind.

In the whole of my eight years at Woolwich I was, I suppose, outvoted on major issues about half a dozen times. In every single case events proved that the majority was right and I was wrong. There was one occasion when I was anxious to accept the Bishop of Southwark's invitation to take over a large new LCC estate as an extension of Woolwich Parish Church. It was about three miles away and had staggered from one ecclesiastical disaster to another and was in very poor shape. The plan was that we would recruit two or three more clergymen and run the parishes together in double harness. The team was unanimous in thinking that it would be unworkable and accused me, justly I think, of empire-building. They told me not to accept the Bishop's invitation, and in retrospect, I realize how wise they were.

One of our rules was that no new member should be

recruited into the team without the agreement of all. I
insisted on this, mainly because I had a high regard for
my colleagues' judgement, but also because I knew if they
were party to the decision to appointing a new man they
would do their best to see it worked out well. There was
one man I particularly wanted them to accept, but the
team were doubtful whether he would fit in. I was outvoted and the subsequent career of the man concerned
proved them right.

There was only one occasion when we came to a complete deadlock. It was at the time when the extent and
seriousness of London's homeless became public. Some of
the staff were living in flats in the clergy house which had
cost a lot to repair and convert. The house was crucial to
us because unless we could house men we could not em-
ploy them. I also knew that every clergyman's housing
needs seemed to vary. A young priest arrives as a bachelor
and is happy with one room. He finds a wife and needs
two rooms and a kitchen, and within two or three years has
two children and wants another bedroom. Consequently,
I had arranged for the house to be converted in a way
that gave it the maximum flexibility. Bob Hughes and the
other residents worked out that by reducing their own
living space they could rearrange the accommodation so
as to provide a flat for a homeless family. It was a typical
expression of their dedication and concern for people. I
shared their feelings for the homeless and indeed later
started an association which is now housing nearly 1000
homeless families. Nevertheless, I was very wary about
bringing a homeless family into the clergy house. Once
they were there, it would be unthinkable that we could
ever turn them out, and if one of the existing staff left we
might not have adequate accommodation to offer his successor. I begged the team to temper their idealism with
realism and to balance the short-term gain—a flat for a

homeless family—against the possible long-term conse-
quences. We were divided equally on the issue and although this particular question was not the responsibility
of our church-wardens, with whom we had a wonderful
relationship, we agreed that they should be the final ar-
biters. I welcomed this decision as I thought they would
probably side with me. In fact, they backed the others and
we housed a homeless family. There were times in Woolwich when we sought publicity for what we were doing.
On this occasion we did not want to make any song and
dance about what we had done, but it leaked to the Press
and as happens from time to time something that one feels
is of little real consequence becomes a worldwide story.
I think the publicity it was given encouraged other parishes
with property to see if they could take in a homeless family. Our family were excellent tenants, and as luck would
have it, just as my forebodings were about to be proved
right they came to the top of the local authority housing
list and were offered a new council home.

I have never experienced before, and I do not ever expect to experience again in this life, the remarkable *esprit
de corps* we developed in those early days in Woolwich.
It was an enormously exciting time. We trusted and respected each other and we knew what we were trying to
do. But we did not take ourselves too seriously and I
laughed more then than I have ever laughed since. The
pace we set ourselves was gruelling, and although I tried
to be firm and insist on one whole day off a week each,
unwittingly there crept in a measure of competition as to
who could work hardest.

It is difficult to describe a typical day because it is both
a strength and weakness of a clergyman's life that his work
is so varied.

The strength is that a parson cannot complain that he is
bogged down in a soulless and repetitive routine. The

weakness is that in switching from tasks of such a widely differing nature he often has insufficient expertise in most of the things he does and is in danger of being no more than a well-meaning and enthusiastic amateur.

After an hour and a half in church in the early morning I would return to the rectory for breakfast at 8.30 am. I would aim to get through four daily newspapers by 9.15 am by which time I would be back in my office in the church. On most mornings three-quarters of an hour with my secretary would enable her to clear the mail. From 10.00 am onwards anything might happen. Perhaps I would spend an hour writing a speech or an article or preparing a sermon. Occasionally I would be able to snatch an hour's reading. This could be followed by going up to the crematorium to take a funeral. After that I might see the Town Clerk to plan some ventures for the Borough or visit the sixth form of a local school to lead a discussion. Or I might return to my office for interviews which could range from seeing the coffee bar manageress about why we were not making adequate profits on the meals to talking over an unhappy marriage with a young wife. Between times some ten to twenty telephone calls would be taken or made.

Interruptions to deal with crises were common and would disrupt my tightly packed schedule. I think we were good at decentralizing in Woolwich but it was inevitable that some people wanted to see me personally and at once. Although my secretary, Mrs. Crawford, was a champion at trying to elicit from people what they wanted to see me about in the hope that she could pass them on to somebody else or deal with the problem herself, there are limits to the probing that anyone else can do on a parson's behalf. Many were the times we rearranged an already overcrowded programme to fit someone in who wanted to see me urgently about an 'important private matter', only to discover that the matter was wholly trivial. But once they were in one's office it was not easy to dismiss them after the ninety seconds it took to deal with it without being thought abrupt.

I also learned that people often started by raising some unimportant question in order to break the ice. A little probing on my part would elicit what they had really come for.

There was one man who insisted on seeing me and after I had sat him down he asked me which organization would like his late mother-in-law's clothes. I was just about to pass him back to my secretary when, with that additional sense that I think one develops, I thought this was a cover-up question and it was not long before I discovered that he was deeply worried about an incestuous relationship he was having with one of his daughters—a more common problem in Britain than is realized.

On most days I would have a working lunch in the coffee bar.

I would spend part of most afternoons visiting people in their homes or in hospitals intermingled with more interviews in the office. We tried to keep committee meetings in the evening down to the minimum as this was the best time for doing christening, confirmation and marriage preparation or for speaking to non-Church groups in the Borough.

By 10.30 pm when the work planned for the day should have come to an end one would learn that calls had come in which required an immediate visit.

Perhaps somebody was dying or a young girl had run away from home or a boy was in trouble with the police and the parents were frantic. It could be one of a hundred things and in a large parish where we clergy were each in touch with hundreds of people and had, I hope, a reputation for caring and being helpful the demands upon us were endless.

By midnight I used to feel fairly drained. For the last five years that I was at Woolwich we were chaplains to a large hospital which meant that from time to time we had night calls. They always seemed to come around 3.00 am when I am at my lowest ebb.

The particular wards that I looked after were the neuro-surgical ones where all the patients with brain injuries were sent. Few things made heavier demands on me than trying to console the parents of an eighteen-year-old boy who has smashed his head in in some fearful motor cycle accident or—every bit as agonizing—a young child dying from a brain tumour

Looking back on it now, I think our work routine made unfair and unreasonable demands on our wives. I was for-ever ringing Anne to say that I would have to miss a meal or suggested she went to bed as I would be late. Not infre-quently I would call her to ask her to make up a bed as I was bringing some lost soul back for the night.

Even if we had had the stimulus of visible results I doubt whether it would have been possible to continue the tempo of the first four or five years. Working at the pace we did tensions were inevitable, and from time to time we would have frank discussions followed by dinner in Soho with our wives; then the air would be cleared. Few people are lucky enough to work with those whose company they really enjoy. I cared deeply for these men and shall ever be grateful to them for what they tried to give to God and to Woolwich and for what they succeeded in giving to me.

There were many disappointments in Woolwich, but I count the reality of our team ministry as one of our real achievements. At a later stage, as I shall describe, the team included members of the laity, and ministers from the Presbyterian, Baptist and Methodist churches. At the end we also had a Roman Catholic priest. None of the original team members stayed in Woolwich as long as I did. I did not expect them to. Nor would it have been right for them to have done so. They were needed by the Church in wider spheres of influence and nothing pleased me more than to see all of them go on to really important jobs where they have served with the same distinction as they did in Woolwich. It is significant that none of them is now in parochial work. They were replaced by men of equal ability and the same enormous capacity to care. But it was the first group that set the pattern and worked out, by trial and error, rules and a system for the team which remained almost unaltered throughout the years, although the size and complexity of the team were greatly increased.

If the team was a taste of Heaven, then finding the money to pay for them was continual hell. Early in his episcopate, Mervyn Stockwood had decided not to attend any diocesan committees. Having seen some of them in action I am bound to admit that I have some sympathy for his decision, although the official reason for his non-attendance was that it would give him more time for the pastoral care of the clergy. His decision, however, produced difficulties because Dr. Stockwood used to promise one thing and the committees which held the strings of the purse would decide otherwise. So although I thought I had the necessary assurances before I accepted the job that the money with which to pay the staff would be forthcoming from the diocese, I was proved wrong. I think I must take a measure of blame. Diocesan committees bored and irritated me and when I put to them my case for larger grants I never really treated them with the respect they thought they deserved. After one such encounter I told Mervyn Stockwood that it would have been more profitable for me to have gone to the monkey house at London Zoo and talked to the inmates. His reaction was to put me on one of the committees which I was complaining about and whose meetings I then endured for a number of years. John Robinson used to say to me after these meetings, 'Why don't you learn how to win friends and influence people?' Of course, he was right, the fact is that diocesan committees simply are not to my taste. I was not the favourite son amongst those who distributed the money. They were sincere and well-meaning and either argued that it was unfair that I should have a larger staff than other parishes or that if they did not meet Woolwich parish's financial requirements I would have to find the money somewhere, somehow. And find the money I did, in ways that most other clergymen might have found difficult. They were right but it was an endless struggle.

Each year my expenses of office, secretary, personal assistant and car came to more than my stipend, yet I could not possibly expect the poor congregation, already giving generously, to help with these essential expenses so they had to come out of my own pocket. On top of that I had to find money each year to bridge the gap between the real cost and what the parish and the diocese provided towards the pitifully small stipends and housing of the staff. It seemed to me that there were two ways in which I might make some money without giving too much time to it. One was to get a non-executive directorship which would involve only a monthly board meeting. At the time I was considering this idea, the Atticus column of the *Sunday Times* did a piece on 'The Hell Raisers of Southwark' which featured me among others, and through which I was able to appeal for directorships. Apparently my talents, so vividly depicted by Atticus, did not appeal to the board-rooms of Britain and I did not receive any offers. But luckily, Sir Michael Coleman, who used to visit my parents' home in East Kent when he was doing National Service at the end of the war, read the article and very kindly came up with a covenant from his family's charitable trust. Without it we should never have managed.

The other possibility was freelance journalism. I had written articles from time to time for national newspapers, but what I really needed was a regular column. I went to see Sidney Jacobson, who was editing the *Herald* at that time and for the remaining two years of its life I was a regular contributor. It was a bit of a disappointment that when the *Sun* rose I was never offered a job. However, I moved stables to the *Evening News*, which proved a splendid paper to work for. One often hears about the rat race of Fleet Street—how tough and unscrupulous it is. This has not been my experience. In eight years of freelance journalism for national newspapers I have never been asked to write an article which compromised my beliefs or principles. Perhaps some would say this may tell more about my principles than it does about Fleet Street. I must admit, however, that from time to time the headlines which sub-editors put on my articles—'I would gladly preach in my pyjamas', 'Revolution at the vicarage', 'Well, and I wicked and worldly?'—may not have been very good for my image in the Church. But I was faced with a real dilemma. I had to earn money to pay the staff. And while I never wrote anything I did not believe, I did sometimes write in a more vulgar way than I would have liked. But over-scrupulousness on my part would have meant that the staff did not get their salary cheques at the end of the month. Anyway, as a result of my journalism, Woolwich Parish Church owed much more to the press lords than it ever did to the Diocese of Southwark.

I think it is right for the Church to ask a lot of its servants, but often it expects too much. It seemed rather unreasonable when Dr. Stockwood asked me to take yet another man into the Woolwich team when I could not adequately pay the ones I already had. It did occur to me that his staff—chaplain, secretary, chauffeur and gardener —were all paid in full by the Church Commissioners.

Seven

CHURCH BUILDINGS ARE BOTH THE GLORY and the curse of the Church of England. They are part of its great heritage; their architectural wonders and the works of art that they contain have been an inspiration to men and women for centuries. Even today great modern monuments to the glory of God, like Coventry Cathedral, capture the imagination of millions. But church buildings also pose a pressing problem. There are about 18,000 Anglican churches and chapels in England alone. About £5 million a year is spent on upkeep and a further £9 million on capital expenditure. In fact, about fifty per cent of the money raised in parishes each year is spent on the church buildings, whereas just over four per cent is spent on the work of the Church overseas and one per cent on general charitable purposes inside and outside the parishes. In thousands of parishes, the building is a constant anxiety. Parochial church councils have come to dread the five-yearly survey by the architect, and in many parishes the energies of the faithful are absorbed in running bazaars and jumble sales to keep the roof on. Very few churches are in constant use during the week. On Sundays, when they are used for two or three hours in the day, the vast majority have a seating capacity massively in excess of what is needed, except on very special occasions.

Church buildings fall into four categories. First, there are those which serve a useful purpose as centres of worship and which the congregation can afford to maintain properly. Secondly, there are redundant churches, but of great historic interest. A few years ago an Archbishop's Commission on redundant churches put the number at 500, which would cost millions of pounds to repair. It would seem only sensible, if the Church is not to be dragged to the grave by the historic buildings round its neck, to deconsecrate most of them and hand them over to the State. No doubt many will survive as museums. Thirdly, there are churches that are redundant and have no historic interest: they are, therefore, expendable. Lastly, there are churches which lend themselves to adaptation to meet modern liturgical practice and pastoral needs.

In Woolwich, there were two buildings in the third category and one in the last. I was convinced that it was spiritual, pastoral and economic nonsense to keep three church buildings going, each with a minute congregation, all in an appalling state of repair and one nearly derelict. I found that some of the reasons (in fact, they were not the main ones) that people gave for not going to church were that they found the buildings dreary, depressing, cold and draughty. I could not disagree with them: indeed, I felt the same myself. So I determined to try to transform Woolwich Parish Church—the one by the river—so that at least these reasons for non-attendance would no longer be valid.

The church's architect was Mr. Alan Ford. He was the son of the founder of an architectural partnership which specialized in churches. Alan Ford himself was an expert in Georgian buildings. He was also a man of transparent honesty and integrity and he quickly won my confidence. Unlike me, he was cautious and slow to commit himself. We made a good team. I asked him to do a thorough in-

spection of the fabric and to report on exactly what needed
to be done. The more he probed, the more horrifying the
picture became. The whole building needed re-roofing
and, as water had been seeping in for years, many of the
main timbers were riddled with rot. When we eventually
uncovered them, we found that beams as thick as a man's
torso, had become as soft as butter melting in the sun. It
was a miracle that the roof had not fallen in. The key of
the plaster had gone in many places: and so the list went
on. I trusted Alan completely and knew that he would
never ask me to spend money that was not necessary, and
would get work done at the keenest price. It was largely
due to him that by the end Woolwich Parish Church
was, in my opinion, one of the most exciting and most
useful historical parish churches in Britain. He worked unceasingly for us but was always loath to send in his account, and on one occasion I told him that I did not think
he was charging us enough.

Even before I joined Woolwich, it had occurred to me
that we might seal off the galleries from the rest of the
church and turn them into offices which would bring in
some rent. I went to look at the parish church at Kenning-
ton, near the Oval, where they had done just this and were
accommodating a nursing organization which was paying
a handsome rent. I sought the advice of the local estate
agents in Woolwich to discover whether they might be
able to find a tenant and how much they would be likely
to pay. They were not very optimistic. So I decided that
we would use the space ourselves and create parochial
halls in the galleries of the church. I was opposed to the
plans I had inherited of building a conventional church
hall opposite the church school, which already had a hall
used by Scouts and Guides in the evenings. We wanted
smaller, cosier meeting rooms for adult organizations and
ad hoc meetings. Why not turn one gallery into a carpeted

lounge with comfortable chairs and gay décor, and the other into a coffee house? I was excited by the idea and was encouraged when the church-wardens saw the merits of the scheme and were ready to back it.

There were moments when I felt that my inheritance in Woolwich was pitiful. But no Rector could have inherited two more helpful and loyal church-wardens. They were Mr. Ernest Batson and Mr. Harry Attenborough. Mr. Batson's father had owned a small flower shop in Woolwich. As an eight-year-old boy young Batson used to go to Covent Garden on his own and do the buying for the shop. He left school at fourteen and joined the Stock Exchange at sixteen as an office boy. After spending the war in the Fire Service he returned to the City as a clerk, but in a few years had been made a partner in his stockbroking firm. Today, he includes many leading merchant banks amongst his personal clients. He and his wife, Effie, loved the church in Woolwich so much that they continued to live within range of it at Bexley Heath so that they could go on worshipping there. Ernest Batson was the only person in the congregation whose job was in a top executive position. His knowledge of the area, his wisdom about the world and his outstanding goodness together with his great ability made him a powerful supporter.

Harry Attenborough was the chief clerk and cashier of a small leather firm. He represented the conscience of the congregation. He had that brand of simple honesty and lack of guile which one associates with cautious and somewhat unimaginative Englishmen at their best. He was the kind of man who really is the backbone of the country, as he was of his small firm. He said his prayers and paid his taxes. He was reliable, hard-working and plodding. Such men, because they rarely make a fuss or draw attention to themselves, often go through life insufficiently rewarded and recognized. Harry Attenborough was no exception.

He died in middle age when I was still in Woolwich. My secretary rang through to me at a school where I was about to present the prizes. I got the message just before I went on the platform and it was as much as I could do to go through with the ceremony. To me both men were as gold. I do not know if the Church of England can claim any share in helping them to become the kind of people they are. If it can, it is greatly to its credit.

It was a cardinal principle of my ministry in Woolwich never to take any step without the support of the church-wardens. Both had served the church in Woolwich for many years with great loyalty and faithfulness and were much respected by the congregation. They had an uncanny way of knowing how the Parochial Church Council would react to proposals. As at this stage I barely knew the members' names, let alone their attitudes, the church-wardens' advice on how to present things was invaluable. This largely accounts for the fact that the Parochial Church Council, which can be the bane of so many vicars' lives, supported, often unanimously, every major proposal that we put up to them. Many of these were, by church standards, revolutionary.

Before I could even consider presenting my plans to the Parochial Church Council, I had to discover how much it would cost to repair the parish church and where the money would come from. Finally I could see that my only hope was to sell one of the other churches. Before I went to Woolwich there had been tentative plans to close the near-derelict church of Holy Trinity in Beresford Square, but the congregation was bitterly opposed to the idea. The plans had been put into abeyance pending my arrival in the hope that I would decide to restore and revive it. I had great sympathy for the handful of people, many of whom travelled several miles each Sunday to the church, for the Anglo-Catholic services it provided. Nevertheless,

I knew that, even if we could have raised the fortune that would have been required to restore it, it would have been impossible to build up the congregation. It was too close to St. Mary's. But once I had decided that my plans for restoring the mother church of St. Mary's hinged upon getting Holy Trinity closed and sold, I had to tread with great care. There was no great love lost between the congregations of St. Mary's and Holy Trinity, and the Holy Trinity congregation would not have been impressed by the argument that they should close their church in order that St. Mary's should benefit.

There was a further difficulty. When church sites are sold the money goes to the diocese and not to the parish. The diocese may decide to give all or part to the parish but is under no obligation to do so. In any case, as the church site was zoned for road widening and light industrial development, its value was not great. The diocese wanted to appeal to the Minister of Housing to obtain rezoning for shops and offices, a decision which would have quadrupled its value. I was opposed to this as I did not think that it had any hope of success and would just make the church look greedy. When at a later date the diocese went ahead with the appeal I asked publicly to be dissociated from it. My fears were well grounded, the appeal was rejected and the Church accused at the hearing of making a purely mercenary application which the local press was quick to pick up.

I had another and more effective plan for raising a large sum of money from the Holy Trinity site. Attached to the church were two derelict halls. They could not be pulled down without pulling down the church and vice versa. Nor could the halls be sold without the church site as well. The halls, however, were owned by the parish and any money realized by their sale could not be touched by the diocese. Moreover, because I was planning to create parochial halls inside St. Mary's church by sealing off the galleries, I was able to invoke a ruling called Rule 5 which requires a local authority acquiring church property to pay sufficient compensation to reinstate elsewhere in the parish what they are acquiring. Understandably, Borough Councils look with horror upon this rule as it can be extremely expensive for them. I negotiated with Woolwich's Town Clerk, Mr. David Jenkins, a tough Welshman who was dedicated to the interests of Woolwich. I eventually persuaded him that we were reinstating Holy Trinity church halls inside St. Mary's church, and that therefore Rule 5 applied. He agreed to put the application before the appropriate Borough Committee. It was very rare for Jenkins, who was known locally as Mr. Woolwich, to have his recommendations turned down and I considered that we were home and dry.

While these negotiations were going on, I made a personal call to every member of the Holy Trinity congregation. I explained to them individually why I felt that with the best will in the world it was impossible to restore Holy Trinity, and that sadly I must get their approval to start the lengthy procedures that are involved in closing a parish church. I hated doing it. They were sweet people who loved their old building. They had struggled for years to keep it open. They understood with their heads the logic of my case, but found it desperately difficult to accept it with their hearts. In the privacy of their homes they agreed with me, but when they got together in meetings to ratify officially the recommendation for closure their hearts reasserted control over their heads. They were like the master of a very old dog which had to be put down. The master knows that it is in everyone's interests that the dog should go but to summon the vet is more than he can bear. We had many difficult and somewhat painful meetings, but I maintained good personal relationships with the congregation throughout.

It is often the small things that please and win people over. The congregation was much attached to the incense used at the services. They knew I was unaccustomed to incense, and I soon discovered that there is much more skill than meets the eye in waving and swinging the censer about so that the thick smoke keeps puffing out of it. To people who are interested in these things, it is important how many times and in what points of the service, the altar, the servers and the congregation are censed. I took a lot of trouble to learn these things so that I did it in the proper manner and they were grateful. I also spent untold hours arranging for the high church *bric-à-brac* with which the building was furnished to be given to churches of the congregation's choosing. The congregation felt that Holy Trinity furnishings were continuing to serve God in many places, which pleased them.

But when it comes to closing churches, getting the congregation to agree is only the first of very many steps that have to be taken. The appropriate Diocesan Committee, the Archdeacon, the Bishop, the Church Commissioners also have to give their consent, and eventually after the most tedious legal procedures the scheme for closure has to lie in the House of Commons. At any time during this grisly and protracted process, people and bodies have a right to object to the church's demolition and eventually to appeal to the Privy Council. Every time I heard that strangers were snooping around Holy Trinity my heart sank, as I had visions of my old friend Mr. Ivor Bulmer-Thomas and his Friends of Friendless Churches taking up the Holy Trinity cause.

When we were eventually able to have the final service at Holy Trinity, Anglo-Catholic clergymen from the area came to join in. Paul Bibby was in charge of the ceremonies. He worked everything out with meticulous care and thought there was no detail he had overlooked, and no emergency he had not prepared for. He was wrong. In the middle of the service one of the high church clergymen slid across the sanctuary to give Bibby the 'kiss of peace'. At the same time he called out the traditional greeting in Latin, 'Pax vobiscum' to which Bibby should have replied 'Et cum spiritu tuo'. He was so taken by surprise that he responded for all to hear with 'Et tu Brute'.

Once the decision was taken I was not prepared to wait for the months and possibly years that it would take before the church and halls were finally closed and sold before pressing ahead with the conversion and restoration of St. Mary's. After I had the Town Clerk's agreement on equivalent reinstatement and the congregation's agreement to close the church, I considered that there was enough financial light at the end of the tunnel to go to St. Mary's PCC with the master plan. The cost of converting and restoring St. Mary's, putting the Clergy House in shape and building a small house for a member of staff would be around £35,000. I explained that if everything went according to plan there ought to be about £25,000 available, and that I would try and raise the remaining £10,000 from friends and from businesses in the Borough. The financial agreements were complicated, to say the least, and it was a lot for the members of the PCC to absorb. £35,000, of which £10,000 had to be conjured up, was an enormous sum and was nearly outside their comprehension. They were reassured by church-warden, Ernest Batson, whose financial acumen they respected. Our architect, Alan Ford, had produced some splendid plans which showed how the gallery floor would be levelled and the sides closed in with frosted glass to seal them off and yet to let light into the main body of the church. Lavatories would be created apparently in thin air. To people who are unaccustomed to looking at plans it was difficult to understand. When presenting important matters to the Parochial Church Council we always took as much trouble as we could—as much as is normally taken in making important decisions in the business world. So I waxed eloquent on how the church would look when it was redecorated in white and gold and blue. We tried to describe the friendly atmosphere that would be created in the coffee bar and how people would be able to sit on stools and look out across the river as they drank their coffee. I knew that I was asking a great deal of their imagination. Nevertheless the response was encouraging.

We had a long discussion about the ethics of eating in church. Some thought it would be all right to have sandwiches and coffee but not meals which required a knife and fork. Others were worried about smoking in the coffee house and lounge. The episode of Our Lord with the money changers in the temple was quoted a good deal. Noise and smells percolating from the coffee house through the glass partitions were other genuine problems. We got round that one by curtaining off the Lady Chapel so that people could pray undisturbed during week days when the coffee bar was open, and the other by an efficient air extraction system. Another difficulty that was raised was the fact that once a year there was a civic-military service at St. Mary's, to which troops were drafted to attend in sufficient numbers to fill the galleries. This was the only time in the year that the church was full. Unless the sermon was very good the wretched soldiers would play dice throughout. What would happen, I was asked, if there were no galleries for the pressganged soldiers to sit in? I explained that even if it was a good thing for soldiers to be dragooned into church to play dice, it was totally uneconomic to keep the large galleries cleaned, heated and repaired for use for one hour a year. I asked the Parochial Church

Council to think how much the goods would cost in department stores if whole floors were only opened to shoppers for one hour in a year. Our architect's quiet and gentle manner was very reassuring, and he promised the PCC that the architectural beauty of the church would be enhanced by the alterations: a view, incidentally, which was later confirmed by the Historic Buildings Trust, from whom I was to raise some money after the work had been done.

We had a long and anxious evening's discussion. But eventually the PCC agreed by a large majority to the plans. It was a great act of faith on their part. I announced our plans with a flourish to the press on the following day.

The press handout said, 'Not only will the galleries provide just what is needed for women's afternoon meetings, evening meetings, etc., it will have certain enormous advantages over a conventional type hall.

'1. After the services the congregation will only have to go upstairs for refreshments. This, we believe, will be a great help in building up the fellowship of the church.

'2. We will be able to run a crèche for babies in the galleries for mothers who would otherwise be prevented from coming to church worship below.

'3. We shall be able to run a lunch-time snack bar for shoppers and business people, many of whom already use the church gardens in the summer. They will be encouraged to come and eat their sandwiches in the coffee bar or actually have lunch there—we hope to provide omelettes, salads, etc. This will bring the church in touch with hundreds of people and will enable us to hold regular lunch-time services and encourage people to say their prayers in a church during their dinner hour. In this way the church will be able to serve the vast numbers who visit the parish to shop or work in Woolwich's magnificent new shopping centre.

'4. The coffee bar will be open throughout the day, and should prove a popular meeting place in a congenial and peaceful atmosphere.

'5. In the closed-in galleries we shall hold exhibitions, lectures, debates and discussions.'

The first four months in Woolwich had been a hectic time. The staff were only just beginning to arrive. I was still editing the *National Christian News*, which I was later able to hand over to the Reverend Timothy Beaumont, now Lord Beaumont of Whitley. I was also arranging a national conference at Keble College, Oxford, for the Church Reform Group. But I felt that we were making progress. Little did I know the troubles that were ahead in restoring and converting St. Mary's. Once the PCC had agreed to the plan, I asked the architect to get the builders in as soon as possible. I was convinced that until we had a good multi-purpose base for our operations we would not be able to make much impact in the area. A first-class building firm was recruited, but understandably its Managing Director wanted to know how we intended to pay. I explained that, provided I could get Holy Trinity closed and provided the Borough Council agreed to paying the equivalent reinstatement on the Holy Trinity halls, once the church was closed; provided that I could raise £10,000; provided the cost of restoration was not more than we thought it would be (which we could estimate once the roof had been removed and we could learn the full extent of the dry rot) I would have no difficulty whatever in meeting the cost at some time in the future. He pointed out gently but firmly that there were rather a lot of provisos. I could hardly deny this as about forty different things had to go right before we would get all the money required. Yet to wait until the money was in the kitty would have been intolerable and would have taken the steam out of the operation. I decided to underwrite the

cost from my personal capital. It absorbed every penny
I had. It was an absurd risk to take as my salary was fully
absorbed paying my secretary and other expenses, and
we lived on the interest from my capital.

No sooner had I made these arrangements than the
Town Clerk told me that his committee was unhappy
about paying equivalent reinstatement on the Holy
Trinity halls. It was a bitter blow and faced me with a
hideous dilemma. I had, of course, the right of appeal which
would have involved a public hearing and much publicity.
The church would have been seen trying to squeeze ratepayers' money from the Council on the controversial Rule
5 in order to put its own house in order. Even had I won it
would have been harmful to my relations with the
Borough Council, upon whose goodwill and cooperation I
depended. In all my dealings with councillors and chief
officers my theme had been that the Church exists to serve
the community. This would have looked very unconvinc-
ing if I was being seen to use unpopular laws to get every
penny I could out of them. I was across a barrel. Possible
bankruptcy on the one hand, and undermining everything
I was trying to do with the Borough Council on the other.
I never asked, so I do not know what eventually persuaded
the Borough Council to change its mind and agree to
Rule 5. I did not feel guilty about taking the money because I knew that if the plans for St. Mary's could go
ahead the church could make a significant contribution
to the community life of the area from which all citizens
would benefit. Anyway, they agreed, and I slept again
at night.

But not for long. Once the builders had started work we
discovered that the fabric was in worse shape than we
thought and almost daily the architect was asking me to
agree extra expenditure. I told Dr. Stockwood that he
should have appointed not an Anglican priest as Rector of

Woolwich, but Charles Clore. Under the shadow of mounting debts I launched an appeal. Woolwich is a poor borough and I knew I could expect little response from the general public. I was not much more hopeful about the business community. Many of the family-owned shops and businesses had been taken over by multiple stores. Those that had survived had moved to secondary shopping positions and were struggling. In any case none of the owners lived in the parish and if they had church connections or loyalties they were with the suburban parishes where their wives and children worshipped. That the appeal succeeded so well was due to a very large donation from the Ogilby Estates which owned part of the main shopping centre, the generosity of my family and friends, and from Jewish people. It was the open-mindedness of the Jews that amazed me. Colonel Maurice Dale and Mr. Harold Salmon, two leading businessmen in Woolwich, both of whom were Jews, worked hard and successfully on the church's behalf. As a result of their efforts many of the Jewish-owned High Street multiple stores contributed handsomely. The people of Woolwich learned that but for the generosity of Jewish people their historic mother church might never have been restored.

As the work went ahead the critics of the plan got going. A vicar in another part of the diocese wrote in his parish magazine, 'If Stacey thinks he can build the Kingdom of God by frying eggs on the altar and percolating coffee in the organ pipes he should think again.' Others climbed on the bandwagon with the inevitable jibes of coffee-bar religion. While the publicity received by our critics may have hurt the appeal for funds, it never undermined the confidence of the congregation which was really beginning to understand the theology of what we were trying to do. As luck would have it the completion of the coffee bar and lounge coincided with the diamond jubilee of the Borough. To celebrate the occasion Princess Margaret and Lord Snowdon were to visit Woolwich to open a tower block of flats and a multi-storey garage. It was agreed that the Princess and her husband should officially open the coffee house and lounge as well, if we could get them ready in time.

It was touch and go. The final nails were still being knocked in minutes before the Princess arrived. The workmen entered into the spirit magnificently. (We gave a party for them when it was all over.) There was a West Indian who was a particularly hard worker. One day he asked if I could do something for him. He had done so much for us that before I heard what he wanted I was determined to try and oblige him. He wished me to bless his football coupons. He claimed that one of his mates had got his blessed by a priest and had promptly won. He must have thought it very odd when I replied that if he wanted a present of a fiver I would happily give it him, but bless his football coupons I could not do.

We appointed the manageress a month before the Royal opening so that she should have plenty of time to make the necessary preparations. I explained to her that our way of working was to try and recruit really good staff, give them their brief and let them get on with the job without interference. I told her I wanted a simple but good tea laid on for the Princess, the VIPs, the principal donors and the congregation who would be present at the opening. Thereafter the coffee house would be open to the public from 9.00 am until 10.30 pm. As we expected the opening ceremony to attract national television and newspaper coverage she must expect many customers. Staff must be recruited and trained, menus and prices worked out. In short, everything must be ready for the great day. About a week before the opening I was having doubts about her preparations but the manageress reassured me. After the staff had finished praying on the morning of the Royal visit, they told me that as far as they could make out the catering arrangements were inadequate. Indeed they went further and said they were virtually non-existent. I could not believe it and rang the manageress who was still in bed. It was clear the staff were right. We all rushed off to the market to wait for the stalls to open in order to buy tomatoes and cucumbers for the sandwiches. The clergy wives put down their babies and poured into the coffee house to prepare the food. At one point in the day I was reduced to standing in the main street and stopping likely looking women by saying, 'Excuse me, we have got Princess Margaret coming to tea in a couple of hours. I'd be so grateful if you could come and cut some sandwiches for an hour.' They thought I was mad but I got the recruits and the visit was an enormous success.

The local press, always great allies of ours, were enthusiastic. The *Kentish Independent* proclaimed 'The church at Woolwich has got a new look and with it comes a new look for religion. Built in the staid hellfire and brimstone days of 1735 it is now being turned into a centre of social life; a coffee bar resplendent in modern contemporary decoration now fills one of the two massive galleries. In the lounge which occupies the gallery on the opposite side of the church easy chairs and low tables have replaced hard pews and stirring sermons which once boomed upwards to the back rows will be superseded by lectures on social affairs. The church has had rotten roof timbers torn out and new wood inserted. Its grey stone pillars now shine under a double coating of fresh paint, the whole décor seems as if it might have been the creation of the great Josiah Wedgwood with its white and grey and blue sheen. St. Mary's is, in fact, a new church for the new generation while at the same time does not impinge too much on the long held ideas of the elderly. The trees which now obscure the view of the river and the ships passing to and fro are to get a trimming so that one can watch while eating lunch. If one wants coffee without going into church there is an entrance up to one side of the main doorway. Signposts have been put up round the gardens pointing the direction. Mr. Stacey hopes that they might also point out to some the way back to religion.'

A few weeks later we held the Service of Thanksgiving for the restoration of the church at which the preacher was the former Rector, Cuthbert Bardsley, the Bishop of Coventry. In his sermon he was enthusiastic as only he can be about the building and reassured the handful of old people who still had their doubts. To them the words of their beloved Cuthbert were indeed the oracle of God Himself. We started the service with 'Hail thee festival day' which always sends shivers down my spine. The second verse of this great hymn describes what I wanted St. Mary's to be. 'This is the House of God, a place of peace and refreshing; Solomon here to the poor offers a treasure untold'. The bidding prayers set our sights on the next stage of our work. 'We pray that the beauty of this building may be matched by the dedication of the lives of those who worship here. We ask for God's blessing on the clergy and congregation of this parish that this church may be a great centre of worship, prayer, peace and Christian service whose influence will penetrate every corner of Woolwich.'

It was a great service. The congregation who had somewhat anxiously put their faith in me by agreeing to the scheme were obviously thrilled and elated with the way it had turned out. They could not imagine that their old building could be made so beautiful. I was happy because I believed that the barren womb I had taken over could now become the fertile mother of a large family. And in many ways this was how it worked out.

My hopes for the building were fulfilled beyond my expectations. Within a short time of its reopening, it was being used by over 1500 people a week. Hitherto I doubt whether 150 people had passed through its gloomy portals. It was opened at 6.45 each morning so that those who wished—and they were very few—could slip in and say their prayers on their way to work. The coffee house and lounge were open from 9.30 am until 10.30 pm. The lounge provided a peaceful resting place where the weary could put their feet up and nobody would bother them. The coffee house had different types of clients at different times of the day. Travelling salesmen would drop in for coffee in the morning, clerks and local government officers for lunch. Housewives returning from their shopping expeditions would come to tea and surprisingly in the evening it became a centre for mods and rockers. For many months, they treated it as their second home, and behaved impeccably until another gang arrived and trouble broke out.

We had converted the vestries into parish offices and I worked in the church instead of in the rectory. I found this a great advantage. Many people who have no church allegiance often gravitate to a church building in moments of crisis and sadness in their lives. They come to cry or to pray or to be quiet. They very often come, as I discovered, in the hope that somebody would be there to put an arm round their shoulders and listen to them. They were not disappointed when they came to St. Mary's. We made a point of always having a member of staff around who would be tipped off by our lively church cleaner if there were somebody in the church 'in a state'. This kind of pastoral care was enormously demanding and time-consuming. It made it difficult to plan one's day because one never knew when one was going to be interrupted by a crisis. But it was what people wanted and it met a real need. When life suddenly becomes overwhelming and seems hopeless one does not want to book an appointment through a secretary to see the Rector in ten days' time. One wants, one craves, to see someone immediately.

It was this experience which encouraged us to start a branch of the suicide Samaritans, whose headquarters we put in the church. We discovered that the multi-purpose nature of the building—all under one roof—had tremendous advantages. We learnt that people in trouble need several things consecutively. The new St. Mary's could provide all of them. After a talk—and a cry—with one of the clergy, they want to go to the lavatory and have a brush-up. Then they want a cup of coffee and something to eat and we would take them to the coffee house. This would often be followed by a little sit down and 'feet up' in the lounge and then a telephone call to their employer to apologize for being away from work. Our policy in the coffee house was clear-cut. No customer was ever to be preached to. We did not think people wanted Christ rammed down their throats when they were eating a ham salad.

On the other hand the coffee house staff were encouraged to be sensitive and if they were not too busy, as they were in the lunch-time rush, they should be ready to listen sympathetically to a customer who wanted to talk. This balance was difficult to achieve. We found that those coffee house staff who were good at cooking and waiting were not so good at listening. And those who were good at pastoral care were less interested in the catering side. The small-time catering trade does not often attract the most professional worker and, for a number of years, the actual management of the coffee house was a constant headache. It had to pay its way and it was vital to get the right amount of cups of coffee from a pound of beans and the right profit on each meal. This meant no fiddling—a very difficult thing to stop in a small establishment. Fortunately, however, when the coffee house was first opened Miss Doris Sayer, who I had got to know at Oxford. She joined us to run the coffee house in the evenings when there was more talk than trade. I know no other person who has a greater capacity for giving herself to other people than Doris Sayer; she it was who set the tone of humour, fun and compassion which gave it the very special atmosphere, on which sensitive visitors, who came from all over the world to inspect it, constantly commented.

On many evenings there would be eight or nine activities going on inside St. Mary's at the same time. In the Lady Chapel an evening Communion Service for a handful of people; in the coffee house fifty or sixty mods; in the lounge a discussion group; in the tower the bell ringers; in my office a marriage interview; in the Samaritan office pastoral counselling of suicide cases and in the parish office a confirmation class. For fifteen hours a day people were coming and going, laughing and praying, talking and crying. Telephones were ringing, typewriters banging, lavatory chains pulling, bells ringing, ovens roaring and hoovers humming. The church was bursting with human life. It was exhilarating and we all loved it. Everything was gay and bright and warm and clean. It spoke of the majesty and power and love of God. So often in poor areas public buildings and facilities are tatty, tawdry and vulgar. In St. Mary's we were determined to have only the best of everything. I think we succeeded. From time to time I used to go across the river at night in the Woolwich Ferry and look across at St. Mary's from the north bank of the Thames. It was a great sight. I had insisted that all the hideous pink and green ecclesiastical Victorian glass in the church be pulled out (leaving only what little good stained glass there was). We replaced it with clear glass. Unashamedly we used to spend over £120 a year having all the windows cleaned regularly. (All too often church windows are filthy.) Perched, as the church is, on a little hill on the south bank of the Thames with every light ablaze, it sparkled like a diamond. I thought it really was beginning to be the spiritual power station I was always talking about. It was complementing the great Woolwich Power Station a few hundred yards down the river. We put a little light over the Cross on the main altar which we had covered with a glorious Italian brocade cloth. Behind it hung rich blue velvet curtains. Late at night when everybody else had gone and the building was locked and I was very tired I used to sit alone in the church with that single light on and hope that what we were doing was what God wanted.

They were euphoric days for the staff at Woolwich, but there was a cloud which I only dimly perceived at the time. Perhaps that was just as well, because had I realized the full implications of it I would have found it hard to bear. When the work on the church was completed, we decided to have four special simple popular evening services. After all, hundreds of non-churchgoing parishioners had told us that it was the shabby state of the building which prevented them from going to church. Now was their chance to join in the worship. We took great pains over the preparation of the service. Every word was weighed, so as to speak to the condition of the people we expected to come. The subject and content of every sermon were hammered out by the staff with the same care as the Queen's speech at the opening of Parliament. The great Cassandra of the *Daily Mirror* could not have done better. The hymns too had to be exactly right: tunes people knew, with verses of doubtful theological credibility cut out. After the service coffee and biscuits were to be served, newcomers welcomed and introduced to regular members of the congregation. Really carefully prepared services must be supported by equally careful publicity. We banged the big drum. Every home in the parish received a leaflet. The local papers as usual rallied to the occasion. Every member of the congregation was encouraged to invite a non-churchgoing friend. Schools were informed, notices put up in factories and posters in people's front windows. Before the services I was worried that there might not be enough pews and chairs for the congregation. By closing in the galleries we had reduced the seating capacity from about 750 to 500. I had visions of some of our critics seeing the over-crowding and saying, 'I told you so'. The weather was kind to us on each of the four Sundays, never so cold and wet as to keep people indoors or so sunny as to keep them outside. There were no special television programmes competing with us. The church had received enormous national as well as local publicity and I was convinced that many people would come out of curiosity—to see what a coffee house in a church actually looks like, if for no other reason. In the early 1960s there was much women's magazine sentimental adulation of the Royal Family and we guessed that some parishioners would want to sit where Princess Margaret had sat.

And so we waited for the crowds to come. In fact, twenty or thirty additional people turned up, mostly from suburban areas outside the parish.

I told myself that we must not expect too much too soon. The staff had barely arrived and were only just beginning the intensive house-to-house visiting campaign we had planned. We knew that we had only just started on the task of raising the missionary enthusiasm of the congregation. In spite of my disappointment, I saw no reason to lower our sights or alter our targets.

Eight

THE CHURCH IS NOT THE CLERGY. NOR IS it the buildings. It is the people of God—the congregation. We could have a large staff and a fine church building, but by the standards and goals I had set myself I would judge the success or failure of our mission by this: how far we were able to deepen and widen the dedication of the existing members of the congregation as well as increase its numbers.

It is difficult for priests to be dispassionate about the congregations committed to their care. The relationship they develop with them is special, precious and, I think, without an exact parallel. It is more personal than between a doctor and his patient. It is barely less personal than between a father and his children. A father may wish his children were more intelligent than they are; that they have better jobs and marry prettier wives than they do. He may be disappointed in them in a hundred ways but he still loves them. And I believe we loved the congregation of St. Mary's. We claim no merit for this, and cared no more than thousands of priests in parishes up and down the country. It is difficult not to love those whose secrets one knows, whose sorrows one has shared and whose battles one helps to fight. We gave them Communion; we battered them and pleaded with them from the pulpit;

we coaxed them and cuddled them. We scolded them and sometimes swore at them, and laughed with them too. We prayed with them in private and did knees-up-Mother-Brown with them at parish socials in public. We visited them when they were sick and held their hands as they died. In spite of all the changes we made I can only think of about half a dozen people who gave the clergy as their reason for ceasing to worship at St. Mary's. We demanded more of them than they of us. They were usually tolerant, patient and kind. They were also sometimes short-sighted, stupid and petty. Before they got to know me they must have found me a difficult person to understand. For the sixteen previous years they had been used to a conventional Rector. I know I did not always fulfil the traditional expectations they had of the clergyman's role. I sometimes failed to disguise the fact that they often bored me, sometimes irritated me and occasionally maddened me. I rarely had time to make social calls on the congregation in their homes for a chat about the weather over a cup of tea. And when I did I was not very good at it. But I would always lay down anything that I was doing at any time if I was urgently wanted by them. This they knew and whenever they were in real trouble they came to me at once. There were times when they wanted to be relieved of me, as I did of them. They would have wished to take things at a slower pace, but the vast majority backed everything we did at Woolwich—not just with their words and votes at church meetings but with their actions.

On my first morning as Rector of Woolwich there was a deputation of ladies from the congregation to see me. They were choking back their tears. I thought this was a somewhat unpromising start, and wondered what it was all about. Very graciously they had come to resign their various jobs of running the Mothers' Union, doing the church flowers, etc., so that my wife could take over. Needless to say I was able to tell them at once that my wife had no intention of taking over anybody's job and they went away happily. This little incident made me resolve that none of the clergy staff wives should on any account run anything in the parish. They could help in menial tasks, like washing up after the parish breakfast, but the leadership must be in the hands of the members of the congregation. I am sure this was a right decision and it was fully endorsed by the clergy wives themselves. I had seen plenty of petticoat government by clergy wives at parochial level when I was in the Birmingham Diocese.

Before I could hope to make any progress with the congregation it was essential to get to know them and hopefully to win their confidence. As a start, my wife and I decided to give a series of coffee parties at the Rectory for a dozen or so members of the congregation at a time. Every church has what is known as an electoral roll. It is the equivalent of the membership roll and entitles one to vote at church elections, although theoretically everybody who is christened is a church member. There were some 250 names on this roll which was about five times as many people as seemed to appear at church services. I reckoned that attempting to draw some of those people back into active membership of the church would be a good starting point.

And so I arranged for everybody on the roll to be invited to a coffee evening. I was surprised when less than fifty per cent of those invited turned up to the first few parties. When a new Rector arrives the congregation is usually curious to know what he, his wife, children and dogs are like. One of the reasons for giving the parties in our own home was to satisfy people's curiosity and so encourage them to come.

We discovered that some half of the people on the roll

were either dead or had moved away. We had virtually
100 per cent turn out of actual church members. I discovered that nearly three-quarters of the more or less
active church members were female and elderly and half
lived outside the parish. It was painfully clear that we
were going to have to build on a very small and narrow
base. I was worried that the congregation did not seem to
be truly representative of the area. The majority of the
people living in the parish were manual workers, while
the employed members of the congregation—the majority
were housewives and old-age pensioners and did not go
out to work—tended to be white-collar workers. This
meant that the ethos generated by the congregation was
more 'refined and respectable' than that of the area. I used
to notice this difference acutely at marriages and christenings which were attended by large numbers of ordinary
parishioners. They were markedly different from the congregation. The same was not true about the Roman
Catholic congregation in Woolwich. Not only was it almost ten times larger than the Anglican congregation, but,
as they poured out of Mass on a Sunday morning, I used
to notice that the Catholics were more truly representative
of the area. The Anglican churchgoers were numerically
the odd man, or rather the odd woman, out. Less than half
of one per cent of our parishioners were regular worshippers at an Anglican church. But they were also socially
and psychologically outsiders, even if they lived inside
the parish. Indeed one of the reasons that non-churchgoers
gave for not going to church was because they claimed
that those who did were hypocrites and had a superior
attitude. I think this was an unfair and unjustifiable comment. But the typical non-churchgoing Woolwich parishioner was right in sensing that the style of the congregation
was not for him. No blame for this was attached to either
party. Neither could be other than they were. I suspect

this subtle class distinction played an important part in keeping many parishioners away from the church.

It is fashionable in some quarters to write off congregations of churches as being made up of somewhat inadequate people who have been left behind in the social revolution of the last thirty years and are using the Church as a prop—a cosy, introverted club with God as a useful appendage. As individuals they might not cut much ice in the harsh secular world. But in the religious club they are appreciated and loved, nursed along by the clergy and able to participate in the conduct of the church's affairs through membership of its multifarious committees. The world may not have treated them as individuals but the Church did. There would be a measure of truth about the congregation of St. Mary's in such an analysis. But it was by no means the whole picture. In their way, most of them were enormously sincere, and some of them deeply and genuinely dedicated, giving themselves unstintingly to the community. Their faith did seem to make a difference to their lives and they were more able to cope with the buffetings of life. The church enabled them to become more human, more disciplined and more hopeful. There really was a little bit of leavening in the lump of Woolwich. The question was how to increase the quality and size of that leavening. It was clear that Mervyn Stockwood's advice to me about getting members of the congregation to stand for the Borough Council was quite unrealistic. All but a handful would have been totally out of their depth even if they had been acceptable to the political parties.

The clergy staff gave hours of time trying to work out a cohesive strategy. Rarely can so much thought, prayer and energy have gone into an attempt to draw the best out of so few people. We decided on a six-pronged programme for the congregation. We would concentrate on the church services, the potential leadership, an educational programme, a Christian Stewardship campaign, participation in democracy, and the build-up of the Christian family spirit.

I had seen too many young and enthusiastic clergymen alienate their congregations by making alterations in church services. They ended up by getting the worst of both worlds—driving away the faithful and not attracting newcomers. In the early 1960s many of the *avant garde* clergy thought it was very important that the priest faced the people when celebrating Communion, that one had bread instead of wafers and cheap dry red Algerian wine instead of the expensive sickly wine provided by the traditional ecclesiastical wine merchants. I am glad to say none of the Woolwich team wished to impose these views on the congregation. We had heard how another of Dr. Stockwood's imported incumbents had, on his first Sunday as vicar, replaced the traditional altar in the sanctuary with a mobile table in the nave without any prior consultation with the congregation. It took him at least two years to undo the damage he had done. At Woolwich we maintained that what the congregations wanted were good sermons, services conducted in such a way that every word was audible, and sounded sincere, and hymns they could sing. Worshippers also liked to know where they are in the service and to be convinced that any changes are for the better. I was prepared to accept the majority vote of the Parochial Church Council as authority for making the most radical changes in parish administration but with church services it was different. We made no changes in these without the overwhelming support of the whole congregation. And when several years later we made some fairly drastic changes we insisted on keeping the traditional 8.00 am Holy Communion service on Sundays and in the middle of the week for those who liked the old ways.

In my time I have appeared on a number of television programmes throughout the world, I have preached at many cathedrals and have tried to speak the word of God at a number of special occasions considered important, but I am bound to say that none of these things made me as nervous as preaching at Woolwich Parish Church before a handful of South-East Londoners. The reason was that the clergy team at Woolwich was ruthlessly critical of each other's sermons and rightly so. We took enormous trouble over them. First we discussed the theme at our weekly staff meeting. We were keen to have courses of sermons so that the congregation heard the Gospel in the round. But we discovered that if we announced courses it put them off. So we gave them courses without announcing the fact. The member of staff who was due to preach—we did it in strict rotation—was required to go through his sermon with another member of staff of his own choosing. I introduced this arrangement because when I was a curate we had to read our sermons to the vicar. Much as I liked him, I thought his theological insights were limited and I did not want my colleagues to be subjected to my limitations. And then at Monday morning's staff meeting there was a 'post mortem' on the previous Sunday's sermon. It could be a humiliating experience. At the height of the *Honest to God* controversy we tried to explain to the congregation what John Robinson was saying. I forget now which part of his book I had to deal with. But I do recall having given insufficient time to the preparation of the sermon and choosing the member of staff who I thought would be most lenient with me to clear it as fit to preach. Monday morning was that moment of truth. Brian Cooper suggested in the kindest but clearest possible way that if last Sunday's performance was the best I could do I would be better employed serving in the coffee house!

None of us was happy about proclaiming the Gospel

from the pulpit—six feet above contradiction—so after the services the preacher went to the lounge where the congregation could question and disagree with us. Few came. We were equally ruthless with each other in the conduct of services. In church I tend to sound parsonical and occasionally drop my voice at the end of a sentence. I was never allowed to forget it.

The traditional services themselves we changed little. We insisted on the minimum of ceremony but what there was had to be done with dignity and without fuss. There were two problems we never solved. The size of the church was such that it needed a big choir to give an effective lead to the singing. From time to time as a result of an intense recruiting campaign in the church school we managed to increase the choir numbers but after a bit the boys would get bored and disappear. On other occasions the organist would spend weeks training them to sing an anthem for some special occasion like Easter Day. When the day came the boys would not bother to turn up. Our other problem was that on normal Sundays the congregation was not large enough to fill the church. This made it so very difficult to generate that atmosphere and sense of togetherness that makes an act of worship 'take off'. I believe that in every building there is a minimum congregational number; if fewer people than that minimum are present it is almost impossible to have a really lively service. We tried to rope off the back pews, but it did not work. On special occasions we had some magnificent services in which one really felt the presence of God. But I was never satisfied with our ordinary Sunday services. Ironically, some of the best regular Sunday services we ever had were when the church was closed for alterations and we had to move into the hall of the church primary school. It was small and intimate and the congregation filled it; which raises the whole question of whether one really needs church buildings at all for acts of Christian worship. Inadequate as our church services were in many ways, they were never dreary. Nor was their quality such that they would have put people off.

We asked twenty or so members of the congregation who showed the greatest signs of potential leadership to join a special course aimed at preparing them for becoming house church leaders. I had had experience of house churches and groups in Portsmouth and in Birmingham. In the intimacy of a small group meeting in people's homes for prayer, discussion and the planning of action, I found that it was possible to develop a depth of personal relationships, mutual understandings and commitment to Christ which is harder to achieve in the larger group meeting for worship in church. In a church service one can sit back playing very little part and giving very little of oneself. In a small group one has to contribute. At a church service, one probably is not greatly missed if one is not there, but in a group of half a dozen people one's absence is felt at once. Such groups also gave their leaders a sense of responsibility and helped them to become less dependent on the clergy. I had also been particularly impressed in Portsmouth by the way that a prayer group of this kind appeared to be able to achieve very remarkable results. I can recall many instances when a chronically sick person for whom the group was praying actually appeared to get better. A sceptic may say it was a coincidence but there were so many coincidences that it has made me wonder.

We asked one of the diocesan missioners, Miss Cecilia Goodenough, to take the course for potential leaders. We were not training a group of people to give Tupperware parties or sell cosmetics to housewives. We were attempting to develop some tough dedicated lay church leaders who would hold their groups together in hard times as well as good. Her uncompromising integrity, sincerity and honesty struck home to us all and those who survived the course really felt that we had been through some spiritual commando training. Miss Goodenough well illustrated the point that I had learnt many years earlier. There are no stereotypes of action or of personality that automatically make for effective ministry. It all depends on the quality of the person and Miss Goodenough was of very high quality. The fact that house groups got going at all was largely due to her, and to the follow-up work done by the staff.

But they were never very successful and never grew in the way I hoped. Perhaps the main reason for this was that most of the congregation were quite unaccustomed to leadership roles in their work. Nor is it any criticism of them that they were not accustomed to abstract discussions.

In our attempts to widen the congregation's horizon we had a series of talks and discussions on current social problems. We thought that if we could get nationally known speakers to these meetings, as we usually did, they would attract non-churchgoing parishioners, which they usually did not. I got used to meeting our distinguished speakers at Woolwich Arsenal Station, which must be in the top ten of the most depressing stations in Britain. Before they had time to open their mouths I would say, 'Of course in Woolwich one can never tell how many people will turn up. I know you won't mind if the audience is small.' This was less than the truth. One usually did know how many people would turn up in Woolwich—a mere handful. But even if the speakers were disappointed it was valuable for the congregation to learn about abortion law reform, homosexuality, drug addiction and capital punishment. It was new ground for many of the older members. They had been brought up on a diet of church-sponsored talks on work in the mission fields, or lantern slides of the Holy Land.

Prior to Lent and before the special teaching months which we used to hold, we would send out a questionnaire asking the congregation to let us know the subjects they would like for their mid-week meetings. Our 1962 programme was typical. On Mondays the subject was 'The Church in the House'; on Tuesdays, 'The Key to Happiness'. This course, said the programme, will appeal to all those who want to hear the case for Christianity and will endeavour to give the answers to some of the questions which are thrown at Christians. It should be particularly helpful to those who are going through a period of doubt, as well as for those who are wondering whether they ought to do something about the faith. On Wednesdays it was 'The Christian Family'. This course was designed to appeal especially to women. And on Saturdays the final course, 'Getting the Best out of Life'. This was meant for those who had been confirmed in recent years or those who were thinking about confirmation.

The programme was sent out with a covering letter. It said : 'The purpose of the month is to give all sections of the congregation, their friends and those who are thinking about the claims of the Christian faith, an opportunity of deepening their knowledge and strengthening their spiritual lives. Members of the congregation often said that they would like to have the opportunity of learning more to satisfy their own intellectual quest, to resolve doubts, to be able to answer the questions of friends. Obviously nobody is expected to come to all four courses, but we do ask everyone to try and come to at least one course which involves four weekday evenings in the month.'

The congregation turned up in considerable numbers for these courses but rarely brought non-churchgoers with them. We could never make out whether they came from a sense of that wonderful loyalty which church people often show to their clergy or because they were genuinely interested in the subjects being discussed.

There is no thermometer on the market which takes an individual's or a congregation's spiritual temperature. While there were no measurable results for our teaching months I think they made a small contribution to the deepening of faith.

In order to mobilize what we hoped were the latent resources of energy, enthusiasm and expertise in the congregation we had a Christian Stewardship campaign. The effect of these campaigns, in raising more money for the church by persuading people to earmark a portion of their income for the work of the Church at home and overseas, is well known. Another aspect of the whole project was to encourage people to use their time and their talents in the service of the church and of the community. We made a list of ninety different jobs which needed doing, from tape-recorder operator to providing hospitality to overseas students. For some jobs, like helping with the Samaritan organization, we offered a special training. While we did succeed in increasing the income of the church, the response to the time and talents part of the campaign was less successful than we had hoped. This was not altogether surprising. In working-class areas once the children are old enough (and very often before they are old enough) mothers go out to work. Consequently in Woolwich there was not that pool of unused middle-aged woman power on which suburban parishes can draw, and on which they so largely depend. A further difficulty was that very few of our congregation were on the telephone, which made it more complicated arranging for people to do jobs that cropped up, as they usually did, at short notice. In spite of this a number of the congregation did start visiting the housebound old people, helping with meals-on-wheels, and other acts of service to the community.

While it would be an exaggeration to claim that the handful of churchgoers were the only people involved in unsung community service, it was my experience that they did more than any other group of people. There were a few individuals in the congregation of St. Mary's whose lives were an inspiration and as a result they were greatly respected and admired by those they served. It may not sound much to spend two afternoons a week visiting old people, listening to their woes, doing their shopping for them, reading to them or writing a letter for them, but maintaining this care, as a number of our congregation did, week by week over the years is a great test of devotion.

The size and enthusiasm of the clergy team would have made it fairly easy to steamroller the congregation. To offset this danger regular congregational meetings were held. At these meetings the congregation had an opportunity of airing their criticisms and producing their ideas. We believed this participation in democracy and involvement in decision-making would strengthen their loyalty to their church and break down the barrier between the clergy and the congregation. We were most anxious to help the congregation see that they were the Church. In the Church of England there is a tendency for the layman to feel it is all laid on from above, with the Bishop, the Church Commissioners, the Archdeacon, the Rural Dean and the Vicar dictating what should be.

We also practised the principle of accountability at these meetings by getting leaders of the various organizations to report to the rest of the congregation on how their activities were going. The theory was that the Mothers' Union would become interested in what the Boy Scouts were doing, and the house prayer groups interested in the profit and loss account of the coffee house. While these meetings

inevitably attracted the professional bores and the patho-
logical grumblers I think we went a long way to getting
the congregation to feel that St. Mary's was very much
their church in which they had a vital part to play. Unquestionably the sense of family spirit was enhanced by the
social programme we arranged. We hired a steamer and
went up the river. We hired another steamer and went
down the river. We hired coaches and went to the zoo,
the seaside and stately homes. We looked at the apple
blossom in May and ate ice-cream on the pier at Ramsgate
in September. We all went to the pantomime together at
Christmas and to a Brian Rix farce in the summer. There
was beer in the back of the bus for the men, lemonade in
the front for the children and tea all over the place for
everyone. There were constant stops on the way home so
that 'everybody could make themselves comfortable'. We
had parish breakfasts after Communion on Sunday and
parish socials on Saturday evenings. We had suppers for
the sidesmen and the Sunday School teachers. I used to tell
the staff if they ever got unfrocked they could always get
jobs in Butlin's as Redcoats. Our social programme may
have been a bit corny, but everybody enjoyed themselves
and had a good giggle.

Life with the congregation was an extraordinary mixture of farce and tragedy. At one clergy staff meeting when
we were discussing how we could help two female members of the congregation who were particularly neurotic,
a parishioner came bursting into the meeting to say that
one of the ladies concerned was at that moment trying to
strangle the other. The nearby street where this grisly
scene was allegedly being enacted was apparently in an up-
roar. The strangling session was in Brian Cooper's part of
the parish and he was quickly dispatched to deal with it.
Brian had a way with hysterical ladies. He returned to the

meeting later, and reported that all was quiet with little physical damage done.

The press always thought that the Bishop of Woolwich had some special connection with Woolwich. In fact, of course, he had no more connection with Woolwich than he did with Sutton at the other end of the Southwark Diocese. Consequently, when *Honest to God* was published journalists were determined to try and get a good story about 'Woolwich churchgoers being shocked by atheistic Bishop'. Naturally sympathetic to the duties and aspirations of journalists, and well aware of the fact that there might be a day when I might require their help, I was nevertheless determined that they should get no such story. John Robinson had walked into a minefield in publishing *Honest to God*; as far as it lay within my powers I wanted to ensure that no mines exploded in Woolwich. I told enquiring pressmen, quite truthfully, that the congregation had not yet had time to read it and added that when they did they might well find themselves in almost total agreement with it. The truth was, of course, that they could have been quite bogged down in the academic language, and the quotations from German theologians. One well-known features writer of a national newspaper was particularly persistent and clearly did not believe me. By chance we had a Parochial Church Council meeting on the evening she telephoned, and I asked her down to attend, making sure that she arrived after the meeting had been going on for half an hour. Before she arrived I warned the Council members that they were going to be invited to condemn John Robinson and his book and begged them to choose their words carefully. They rose superbly to the occasion. They explained to her that they had not read the book (most of them never did), but from the summaries they had seen in the press they found themselves very sympathetic. Indeed they claimed to be glad that a bishop in the

Church of England had put into words what they had quietly been thinking to themselves for years. The journalist then started reading extracts from the most controversial passages in the book. She had chosen them with care, in the hope of striking horror and alarm into the hearts of conventional churchmen. We were ready for this ploy. At the beginning of the meeting a few copies of the book had been given to some of the more articulate members of the PCC. I called on these people to reply. They were, of course, quite ill-equipped to do this and would have been quickly tied in knots by a fast-thinking journalist. So after each extract she read out I turned to a Councillor who had a copy of the book and said, 'I know Mr. X would like to comment. Mr. X, why don't you read the bottom paragraph of page so-and-so, it shows that Robinson qualifies the extract you have just heard read.' I was able to do this because Robinson had sent me a copy of the book in typescript and I knew it fairly well. We played this silly game for an hour or so until it was clear that the PCC had won the game, set and match. I then took her off and gave her a large whisky in compensation for spoiling her story.

Americans used to visit us in large numbers and would often ask whether *Honest to God* had helped or hindered our work in Woolwich. I answered that I did not think that it had any effect at all. The only speculations that I ever heard parishioners get involved in were on the amount of money they thought Robinson must have made from it. Our intense efforts to deepen the commitment, widen the horizons and increase the *esprit de corps* of the congregation were, I think, rewarded up to a point.

But there is no easy yardstick for measuring these things. Hence the temptation to equate success or failure with what can be measured—the number of people in the pews.

The congregation doubled to about 100 but most of the extra fifty came from socially superior areas outside the parish and were lapsed churchmen. The main reason for any success we had was the large number of clergy in relation to the small numbers in the congregation. This enabled us to take enormous trouble and give intense pastoral care. However intelligently the clergy of the Church of England are deployed it would be impossible to repeat everywhere what we were able to do in Woolwich. There simply are not enough men to go around. It was quite obvious that few of our efforts looked like being self-generating and self-perpetuating. This proved to be so, as we discovered a few years later, when many of the clergy on the staff took secular jobs and were not, therefore, able to give the same amount of time to the congregation. I had hoped that if we could raise a sufficient head of steam in the boiler the ecclesiastical train would cruise ahead without much attention from us. It was not to be.

Nine

EVEN TODAY THE CHURCH OF ENGLAND IS still in a unique position. The parochial system, for all its failings and misapplication of manpower, ensures that theoretically everybody in England comes under the pastoral care of an Anglican vicar. In rural areas there is still some connection between the theory and the practice. The country parson can know everyone in the parish whether or not they are churchgoers. The church, or more truthfully the parish hall, is often the centre of local community life and the vicar, if he is conscientious, often the anchor man of the community's corporate activities.

At the time of the Industrial Revolution the Church never really followed the people by moving its resources from the country to the towns, so that even today half the clergy work in the country and nine-tenths of the people live in the towns. Nevertheless, up to the 1914–18 war, the Church in the towns had a very considerable influence on vast numbers of parishioners who never went to church. What meagre social amenities existed, were largely provided by the Church or Church-dominated bodies. So that if young people wanted to play football or dance they had no alternative but to join the Church Club, for it alone had the facilities. If their parents wanted a holiday they joined in the parish camp pitched in the fields

140

of the vicar's county friends. The curates and the district visitors acted as the Youth Employment Exchange, the Probation Service and the Welfare Department. It was the Church that ran the soup kitchens and provided the second-hand clothes and shoes.

By the early 1960s in Woolwich there was still a small Church Primary School (almost totally financed by the State) and a small Church-run Moral Welfare Department (funded by a grant from the Local Authority) whose main work was to help girls who were having illegitimate babies. Otherwise the Church had been stripped of the props which had made it a socially significant force. There were no longer any material or social benefits to be had by being associated with the Church, however loosely. 'Rice Christianity' was out. Indeed, all the social pressures were against being a church member. I welcomed the fact that the social services were now being provided on a massive scale by the statutory authorities and manned by a whole army of professional social workers. But by losing its social props the number of people with whom the Church was in effective contact had been greatly reduced. The influence of the vicar did not go much beyond the small congregation. This is much less true in suburban areas, because there are a large number of people who consider themselves churchmen and have a residual loyalty to the Church. Attendance at Easter Day and Christmas services illustrates the difference between the working-class and the suburban areas. In Woolwich our congregation would barely increase at all on these high festival days, but in the suburban area a regular Sunday congregation of, let us say, 150, would swell fourfold or more.

Clearly the Church in Woolwich would have to stand or fall on its effectiveness as a spiritual and pastoral force. In the social service field the most it could attempt would be to close a few gaps in the existing services and pioneer small pilot schemes of social concern. This did not dishearten me.

From my personal knowledge of our non-churchgoing parishioners I was convinced that at the spiritual and pastoral level we had something to offer them which unconsciously they were reaching after and were certainly needing. They wanted a faith, a dynamic and a purpose in life. It was a commonplace that the new-found affluence which had transformed their standards of living had not brought the joy and satisfaction that was predicted. There was as much bitterness, bloody-mindedness and resentment as ever. There was less hardship, but there was probably more depression and more loneliness and more mental illness. The old inhabitants of Woolwich would constantly say to me 'Give us back the good old days'. Even allowing for the inevitable nostalgia about the past it was in many cases a real *cri de cœur*. I found the veneer of adult self-confidence and youthful arrogance so often hid a deep sense of uncertainty, insecurity and emptiness.

In our daily dealings with people at moments of great crisis in their lives the clergy, perhaps more clearly than anyone, saw how pathetically inadequate the people's spiritual resources were. I believed they needed God. But I also believed that they would not be dragooned into church. I hoped that the conversion of the church building into a multi-purpose centre of worship and pastoral care, and the generation of a life-enhancing spirit with an outward-looking attitude by the congregation would help break down the barriers between the sacred and the secular, between the Church and the people. But I also knew that much more than that was needed. We must show the people we cared about them; not as potential pew fodder or customers; not as donors whom we could milk; but as people for whom we cared, for their own sake. Consequently as soon as the staff arrived we started an intense systematic house-to-house visiting campaign with the sole purpose of making friends. We wanted to show our interest in them, their jobs and their children and to learn about their problems. We wanted to win their confidence and their trust so that if they were ever in difficulty and thought we could help they would feel free to come to us. We also believed that it would be reassuring to them when they came to us for christenings, weddings and funerals if they already knew one of the clergy personally. There was no intention in these visits of getting at them or of challenging them overtly. (In practice I think our very presence was a kind of challenge and a reminder that there is an additional dimension to existence.) We did not invite them to come to church nor tell them that, if they were to keep the promises they made when they had their children christened, they should now be seeing they were prepared for confirmation. If they raised the question of church, religion or faith, we would pursue the discussion with them. But if, as often happened, the whole visit was taken up by the man of the house talking about his job, we did not feel the visit was wasted. Above all we remembered we were guests in their homes. They had not invited us. We had invited ourselves.

Our visiting campaign must have been one of the most intense that has been carried out in any town parish since the war. Brian Cooper and Richard Garrard did at least six hours house-to-house visiting a day, five days a week. The rest of us did almost as much. We never had a door shut in our faces. Most were pleased to see us, although in some houses the television was kept on which made conversation a little difficult. If the man answered the door he would usually say, 'I'll fetch the wife.' Clearly he thought the parson and the Church were for the women. For the first minute or two they were apprehensive lest we were the harbingers of bad news. Once we had reassured them on this, they expected us to preach at them or unload tracts on them, as is the practice of the Jehovah's Witnesses. They really found it hard to believe that we had no ulterior motive for calling; not surprising because strangers who call almost always do want something. But once we had broken through this barrier of fear and suspicion it was not difficult to establish a relaxed and easy relationship. I used to get the backwash of my colleagues' visits on my occasional calls to one of the local public houses. I used to be told how 'one of the vicars called' (anybody in a parson's collar is a vicar), 'what a friendly lad he was' and 'how the wife was tickled pink that he thought her curtain material was pretty'.

At a superficial level our visits were unquestionably a success. From time to time we would unearth a pastoral problem, in which case we could help either by putting the family in touch with the appropriate statutory social service or by keeping an eye on them ourselves.

In fact it was the discovery of pastoral problems which was one of the reasons that eventually forced us to discontinue our house-to-house visiting. Each of us built up such a caseload of families who needed constant revisiting that we had no time to break new ground. We must have visited nearly seventy per cent of the homes before we had to call it off. Certainly I had 'spiritual hopes' for our visiting campaign, but we purposely approached it in an open-ended and open-minded way. We were determined to be sensitive to follow any leads that appeared. None of us expected people to flock to church as a result of it, although as one said goodnight on the doorstep, parishioners often used to say, 'I must come and visit your place one of these fine days.' What I did hope was that a few people, once they realized the clergy were on their wavelength, could speak their language, understood their doubts and really cared for them, as I believe we did, they would give the Church a try to see if it would meet their needs. Barely half a dozen families came to church as a consequence of our house-to-house visiting. So much for the old adage, 'A house-going parson makes a churchgoing people.' And I doubt whether our house-to-house visiting campaign would have been more successful if we had presented 'the Lord Jesus as Saviour' and challenged them to admit their sinfulness. Unquestionably it would have offended many and convinced them that we were not the kind of people to whom they could have taken their personal problems. I have no regrets that we did not make this kind of approach.

We were all conscious that most of the people we visited had had no connection with the church in their lives except sporadic attendance at Sunday School from the age of five to eight. We realized that the jump into immediate church membership would be too much for them, indeed might put them off because everything would seem so strange. I was hoping that as a result of our visits we would build up a halfway house church in people's homes. Had we found a few people who were reaching after God and a faith for their lives but were critical, doubtful or nervous of the organized Church, we would have suggested the formation of discussion groups in their own homes where together we could have wrestled with the problems of faith. After an incredible amount of care and coaxing Richard Garrard did get two groups going for a short time but only one lasted. Another of my hopes was that we would find people who were concerned about the community. We wanted to encourage them to form little groups of like-minded people in the area who would help care for the old and the house-bound and over-burdened young mothers. We were able to get such groups going from time to time for a short period to deal with a specific problem but no self-sustaining on-going group emerged.

House-to-house visiting was only one of a number of ways in which we tried to show our concern for parishioners. Theoretically, at least, the Church of England still has a special opportunity for pastoral care: it christens, marries and buries the majority of the population. We were determined to make the maximum use of all these opportunities. We believed that when a young couple bring new life into the world they feel a deep sense of awe and responsibility. It is a moment in their lives when they ask deeper questions and have hopeful thoughts. We tried to make the christening a tremendous occasion—something they would remember all their lives. Instead of having christenings every Sunday at 4.00 pm, when two or three families whose babies were being 'done' would gather rather lethargically round the font in a back corner of the church, we had mass christenings once a quarter. They were done with as much splendour, dignity and panache as the service for the consecration of a bishop. The christening itself was preceded by the most careful preparations. When parents came to the church asking if they could have their child 'done' they were given a little pamphlet explaining christenings at St. Mary's. This was followed by a visit from the clergyman in whose area they lived. The sole purpose of this visit was to make friends and establish confidence. At the end of the visit we would fix a time for our next call and leave a handsomely illustrated magazine which described what christening was all about. At the second meeting we would explain in the simplest way to what they were committing themselves by deciding to have their baby christened. We never refused to christen a child as we felt that ultimately the decision must be that of the parents. We never encouraged anybody to have their children christened if we thought that they were only going ahead with it to please 'Nan'. We would ask them whether perhaps it was not rather hypocritical if they themselves thought Christianity was 'a load of old rubbish'. We explained how, when one joined a trade union, in return for the privileges there were certain obligations and how the same was true about joining the Christian Church.

The next step was to invite the parents and godparents to a rehearsal. We even offered to provide a baby-sitting service so that they could be free to come. The rehearsal evening started with refreshments in the coffee house, at which we introduced all the families to each other in an attempt to get everybody relaxed. We then went across to the lounge where we showed a film strip on the meaning of christening. Finally, we descended to the church and had a rehearsal of the service using a doll as a baby. We even used to practise the hymns so that the evening ended with a sing-song prior to a home-going cup of coffee. The staff used to take it in turns to do the talk in the lounge at the rehearsal and we used to compete with each other on who could get them all laughing first. We all had our own rather corny jokes about babies weeing on us or two-year-olds punching us in the faces when they were being christened. These never failed. We always held the rehearsals on the Thursday before the Sunday christening so that nobody would have time to forget.

The christening itself was a moving experience. We had completely rewritten the service. Unlike the one in the Prayer Book our christening service was simple and understandable. Each service had all the excitement and expectation of a great occasion. The church was packed and each family had its own pew specially reserved for it. The regular members of our congregation and the choir were present. We had a portable font which we put at the chancel steps. For the first part of the service the mothers and the babies sat in the lounge where the service was relayed to them. Then, about a third of the way through, came the first moment of high drama. The mothers came down from the lounge and, proudly holding their babies in their arms, proceeded down the main aisle led by a robed cross bearer, servers and a priest. They stopped opposite the pews where their families were sitting and, still standing in the aisles, they were asked by the priest conducting the service, 'What do you in the name of these children ask of the Church of God?', to which the parents replied, 'We ask for Baptism.' The priest then asked, 'Why do you ask for Baptism?', and they replied 'That our children may be made Christians.' After each baby was christened we walked up the entire length of the main aisle holding the baby in our arms as we said the words 'Receive the sign of the Cross of Christ in token that thou shalt not be ashamed to confess thy faith in Christ crucified and manfully to fight under His banner against sin, the world and the devil and to continue His faithful soldier and servant until thy life's end.' At the same time we made the Sign of the Cross on their foreheads. In this way we showed off the new member of the Church to the whole congregation and everybody was able to whisper about each baby in turn, 'Isn't it lovely?' Finally, we got the whole of the congregation to say together, 'We receive these children into the congregation of Christ's flock, and we ask for the Grace of God, that by love, by prayer and example we may show them true Christian fellowship as long as they live among us.' After the service the member of staff who had conducted the christening was ready to pose for photographs holding the baby over the font. We knew that these family snaps would be put in a prominent place in the family album and hoped they would remind the parents of the promises they had made.

About three weeks after the christening we would make yet another call to hand over a large shiny christening card for the parents and a smaller and less shiny card for the godparents. On this visit we used to tell the parents that we had done what we could to explain the Christian faith to them and it was now up to them. We told them that we hoped they would become active members of the Christian family and that we would be ready to prepare them for confirmation or introduce them to a church house group. Even if they decided to do none of these things they could always count on us to help them in any way we could. Before leaving I always used to give them my visiting card with my telephone numbers on it and explain to them that I had a telephone by my bed so that in times of crisis people could ring me at any time of the night. We provided the leaders of the various organizations attached to the church with the names and addresses of all the people whose babies had been christened so they could invite them to their meetings. Then for the seven years following the child's christening a member of the congregation would call each year on the anniversary with a pretty little card.

It was difficult to see what more we could do to try and make christenings more relevant. I can only think of one family from all the hundreds of babies we christened who joined the Church. Nevertheless, I think the parents who had their children christened at St. Mary's felt something important and solemn had happened to their babies. The wives of the clergy staff were going through a fertile period when we started our new christening routine and for the first four mass christenings there was always a clergy baby. As a matter of fact our own last child was born in time to be amongst those in the first of the new-look christenings. Everybody was delighted that the Rector's baby was 'done' like everybody else's.

Practically everybody we married set up home outside the parish. They had to, as the Local Authority, in order to prevent over-crowding, did not allow their tenants to sub-let to their married children. This meant that no after-wedding follow-up was possible. Nevertheless, after every wedding we did write to the vicar of the parish in which the couple were going to live in the hope that he would call. We tried to take the same trouble over weddings as we did over christenings. In middle-class parishes the more conscientious clergy were reporting that marriage preparations with three or four couples together went better than if they were prepared by the priest on their own. Really lively discussions were developed on the best ways of handling the mother-in-law relationship or the various methods of birth control. In our parish where the young couples were very much less articulate we found that they were more ready to talk when they were on their own than when in a group. In a group they were afraid of making fools of themselves. So unless we were marrying 'college types' whom we would group together, we prepared couples individually.

I enjoyed marriage preparation. It was fascinating to see the change of attitude in the couple as my three sessions with them progressed. They often arrived hoping that they were going to have a ten-minute run-through of the service, learn where they stood and who did what and when with the ring. One could see their faces fall when I told them I wanted to talk to them about marriage first. As one of them said to me at the end of the preparation, 'When I first arrived I thought you were going to be a dreary old man who knew nothing about life and was going to give me a lot of codswallop advice.' Such was the image of the clergy in the Church! When they discovered that perhaps one knew quite a lot about life, could talk freely about sex, bringing up children, knew which local furniture firms were the most reliable they became more enthusiastic. On the spiritual side the most I ever tried to do was to discuss the merits of their praying together. I think we were often successful in persuading the man to have his bachelor thrash two nights before the wedding and I also used to beg them not to stay at the wedding reception until the end, as was the local custom. I had seen so many marriages get off to a bad start by the new husband in his cups washing up the glasses at the end of the reception with his young bride weeping quietly in a corner. I used to tell young couples that I would never conduct a marriage service if I thought the bridegroom was drunk. At one wedding I had to stop in the middle when a drunken brawl broke out between the respective families.

There were so many of us clergy on the staff that no single one of us had to conduct six marriages one after another on a Saturday afternoon. I have done this in my time and it is a gruelling experience. By the time one has heard 'Lead us Heavenly Father, lead us' badly sung for the sixth time one is ready to scream and it is extremely difficult to say the service as though one cared.

The same is even more true of funerals. We had constantly to remind ourselves that to the congregation it was a very important occasion which they would remember all their lives. I often heard from the undertakers and families in the parish how beautifully my colleagues conducted the service. It is not easy for a parson to know how he is doing and I always made a point of passing such information back to the member of staff concerned. Clergymen need encouragement too. The conduct of funeral services can be demanding. Sometimes the whole congregation will get hysterics and one needs to be fierce to get them to pull themselves together. There were other occasions when one was doing the committal standing round the grave when mourners tried to throw themselves into the open grave and one found oneself holding one's Prayer Book with one hand and grabbing somebody by the scruff of the neck with the other. Once a mourner had a fit by the grave and had I not reacted instinctively I think she would have fallen in.

As soon as we heard from the undertakers—if we did not know already—that somebody in the parish had died we immediately visited the relations. Funeral visits present difficult problems to a priest. The bereaved yearn for reassurance and it is tempting to talk glowingly of Heaven and the next life and overlook the Judgement which is an integral part of the Gospel. To censure either the deceased or those who mourn when they are knocked by a bereavement is, in my opinion, unforgivable.

As in every other part of our pastoral work the clergy staff argued out together how we could remain true to the Gospel as we understood it, and attempt to to bring the comfort the bereaved were wanting. We learnt that it was not so much what the parson says that matters as his general attitude of sympathy and concern. We found that the best way was to say very little ourselves and let the bereaved talk. They liked to describe in the minutest detail the last moments of life. 'He woke me up and asked for a glass of water. He looked deadly pale. I got him to the lavatory. He was gasping and very heavy. His tongue was hanging out of his mouth and he was shaking. I left him in the toilet for a minute on his own and rushed for the help of a neighbour. By the time we got back he was lying on the floor all crumpled up. We dragged him back to the bedroom but he had gone. He was a lovely man.' When I was a curate in Portsmouth, I discovered that the family liked one to see the corpse and say a prayer over it. So this we always did, although the practice of having a loved one lying in state in the front room was fast dying, and in many cases the body had already been taken to the undertaker's Chapel of Rest by the time we arrived at the house.

We would make a further visit to the family a week or so after the funeral. I doubt whether more than two or three widows joined the church after their husbands' deaths.

Again and again one got the sense that our Woolwich parishioners felt the Church simply was not for them. And so we were always thinking of ways in which to bridge this apparent chasm between the Church and the people.

As the reopening of the reconstructed St. Mary's had taken place in a blaze of publicity we thought that a large number of parishioners might be interested in seeing what we had actually done in an attempt to make the building better serve their needs. So we invited every family living in the parish for a coffee evening and a conducted tour of the church. We did not ask the whole of one street at a time but groups of families from half a dozen different streets. In that way our guests would know some of the other people who came, which would prevent them feeling shy, but would also have a chance of meeting people from other streets. In the letter of invitation we made it clear that the sole purpose of the evening was to show them the facilities of their church. There would be no hymn singing, no prayers nor appeals for money, and the coffee would be free. I thought that about twenty-five per cent of those invited would come and we organized it so that we would have about 100 people at a time. We all agreed that the conducted tour should be small. Consequently, we had a three-line whip on all staff each of whom would show a party of about twelve around.

I thought that many people might be curious and interested in the inner workings of a parish church so we decided to show them all sorts of details. The women would be shown the ovens and coffee-making machines and where the food was stored. Everyone would see the menus. We would take them to the parish office where they could see the typewriters, telephones and dictating machines which we hoped gave an impression that the whole show was efficiently organized. It would be explained to them that the wall between my office and the parish office had been built with special soundproof material so that people could talk to me in complete confidence knowing that nothing they said could be heard outside. We would show them the safes where the church silver was kept and the vestments too. We would take them to the Samaritan office in the crypt and explain what happened when a suicide call came through. We would point out the church notice-board in the porch, over which we took so much trouble with displays of photographs of the work of the Church at home and overseas. They would see the range of books and pamphlets on the bookstall. Those who were interested could inspect the organ console with its multitude of stops. And then at the end of the evening we would give them a little pamphlet which listed the names and addresses of all the staff and gave details of all the church organizations from the Cubs to the Old People's Club in which they might be interested.

I was inordinately proud of the church. I loved showing people around and was greatly looking forward to the first of these evenings. The ladies of the congregation were mobilized to provide the coffee and the staff, as usual, were all smiles ready to receive the expected flood of guests. About fifteen people turned up. But those who came enjoyed themselves greatly and were obviously enormously impressed. We assured ourselves that the turnout for the next party, which had been arranged for three days later, would be better. It was worse, and the staff actually outnumbered the guests. We carried on undaunted but thereafter had only one member of staff on duty. Perhaps altogether five per cent bothered to turn up—not from hostility but from an extraordinary lack of curiosity which is a feature of this area.

I had never been greatly enamoured of the traditional parish magazine and the Rector's letter starting, 'My dear people'. I agreed with the alleged reaction of the late Dick Sheppard of St. Martin-in-the-Fields, that whenever he saw a parish magazine he tore it up to stop it doing any more harm. As a pioneer of the tabloid parish newspaper I was keen that we should distribute in the parish the syndicated *National Christian News*, which we called the *Woolwich Beacon*. We hoped that it would have two benefits. First, the monthly issues would help to show that the Christian faith and the Church had something relevant to say about the every-day issues with which people were confronted. Secondly, it would mean that members of the congregation who delivered the paper each month to nearly seventy-five per cent of the homes in the parish would be able to make friends and answer the questions of our non-church-going parishioners. We instructed the distributors to report to the clergy if they discovered cases of sickness and sadness so that we could make a follow-up pastoral call. I think it was successful in both respects, but it was never quite self-financing and unfortunately we eventually had to discontinue it when we could no longer afford to subsidize it from our meagre church funds.

Our house-to-house visiting campaign coincided with the tombola craze of the early 1960s. At every home we went to we made a point of asking if there was anything we could do for them in particular or for parishioners generally. From all corners of the parish requests for a tombola club, and, even more significant, offers of help to run it, came pouring in. There was a delightful irony about it. Here in Woolwich we had a group of clergy all of whom had spent some five years in training for the sacred ministry of the one Holy, Catholic and Apostolic Church. We had collected between us some five first-class honours degrees in various subjects. We had worked hard to try and raise enthusiasm amongst our parishioners with conspicuous lack of any measurable success. And it was not until we started bingo in our church Primary School Hall that we struck a chord in the area. Frankly I do not think we should have ever have started it if we had not thought we would make a good deal of money out of it. I, who carried the burden of our constant financial worries, was the most enthusiastic. The staff were more reluctant and the PCC positively unhappy. I told them they need neither help nor play, and I asked them to choose which of the two members of staff should be fired if we could not pay their stipends. The latter point went home and won the day. All those who had volunteered to help run it were sent round to other tombola clubs in South-East London to learn the snags. To ease our tender consciences we kept the entrance fee and the buying of the card, down to 2s. 6d. which we felt old-age pensioners could afford. We did not allow anybody to buy extra cards halfway through the evening to chase their losses. We also distributed lots of little prizes. The top prize was about £12. We did, however, have a raffle in the interval when soft drinks and crisps were sold. The profits from these were about the same as the cash collections in church on a Sunday. In a typical squeamish and Anglican way I felt mildly guilty and ashamed of the whole venture, and suggested that we should keep publicity to the minimum. All I would allow was a leaflet for every door in the parish. It was enough. It was more than enough. People started queueing half an hour before the doors opened. Latecomers had to hang on the wall bars in the hall and mark their cards at the same time—a considerable feat. Flushed by success we opened another bingo centre at the Mission Hall in another part of the parish.

The committee which ran this church hall were only linked with the church through a member of our staff, Richard Garrard. They distrusted St. Mary's so deeply that the formality of passing their takings through the Church Council accounts provoked a full-scale revolt. The money they made from bingo went to provide coal and Christmas parcels for those living in the vicinity. They were so enthusiastic and efficient about this that they scrapped the official list of elderly people in the area, did their own survey and came up with a list which was accepted by the Local Authorities as definitive. These sterling committee members who would have blacked the eye of anyone who called them do-gooders, took to sneaking around to visit and redecorate the homes of old people whom they had met during their parcel distribution and survey.

Bingo is an inane and fatuous game. I could not endure the tedium of sitting through a whole session with the entire audience giving the predictable wolf whistle when 'Legs Eleven' was called. But I used to pop in at the end; this gave me an opportunity of meeting lots of people I would not otherwise see. This was valuable as someone would always come up and ask me to visit a relation in hospital, or make some similar request. I do not think there was anything we did in Woolwich which was more effective in drawing the community together and developing a sense of *esprit de corps*. Old people living alone who rarely went out pottered round to the hall for their weekly game of bingo and gossip with their neighbours. If any of the regulars were sick there would be a whip round so that flowers could be bought for them. The men of the parish who ran it for us gave up two or three evenings a week without any charge and one of them, who had a drink problem, stopped going to the pubs. When I was lecturing at theological colleges students would ask me which of all our activities in Woolwich contributed most to the building of the Kingdom of God. They thought I was being flippant when I replied, 'Running bingo clubs.' This impression was confirmed when the principals discussed the students' syllabus of studies with me and I ventured that from my experience in a working-class area it seemed more important for the young clergyman to know how to run bingo in such a way that it did not contradict the Gaming Laws than it was to understand New Testament Greek.

The success of bingo taught us an important and somewhat discouraging lesson. If we provided what people actually wanted instead of what we hoped they wanted or thought that they ought to want, the activity flared into life with the minimum of effort, fuss or publicity. But if they were not wanting what we were providing there was virtually no response, however imaginatively and energetically it was promoted and run. The agony of so much of our pastoral work in Woolwich was that the things people did want from us—the name of a safe, cheap abortionist; the loan of £20; a roof over their heads, or a new husband—we were unwilling or unable to provide. But the things that we were able to give they did not appear to greatly want.

Ten

THE MISSION OF THE CHURCH HAS TWO aspects. On the one hand there is its work to promote personal conversion, private prayer and public worship. Older theologians, referring to this work, defined the Church as a 'school for sinners', and as a training ground for sanctity.

On the other hand there is the Church's role as an influence on the structures of our society. Believing that all men's activities should be brought under the sovereignty of God, the Christian recognizes that some problems can only be solved by political action. Education, social, economic and housing policies of central and local government provide the background against which individuals are helped or hindered in their full spiritual, mental and physical development. Enlightened and compassionate legislation does not necessarily make enlightened or compassionate people—but it helps.

There are few clergy I meet who are able to hold these two aspects together in a creative tension. Those who are keen on 'personal conversion' and 'bringing men to Christ' often seem unconcerned about the power structures of our society. And vice versa. In Woolwich we attempted to do justice to both aspects of the Gospel.

The title Rector of Woolwich and, therefore, leader of the mother church of the 150,000-strong Borough of Woolwich, sounds impressive. Many years ago the holder of this office would have had automatic *entrée* to the civic, political, educational and commercial structures of the community. Indeed, he would himself have been one of the civic and educational powers. In 1960 this was no longer true. In the community at large the Rector of Woolwich counted for very little. My hard-pressed predecessor had not put a very high priority in his ministry on being a public person. His departure was given two lines in the local paper and on an inside page at that. I was virtually starting from scratch. It is easy enough to use grandiose phrases about the Church influencing and permeating everything that was going on in the community. I had used such phrases many times in speeches and sermons. But in practice how is this actually done? St. Mary's was pathetically weak in numbers and resources. Its image as a holy huddle was not a helpful one. The clergy staff were already desperately busy. It was no fault of the congregation that it was beyond their capacity to get close to the sources of local power. About the nearest any of them got was that one of the ladies in the congregation had a brother who was chauffeur to the Town Clerk. None of the leaders of the community lived in the parish or worshipped regularly at St. Mary's. How I envied those clergy who, in some other countries in the world, are alleged to have several Cabinet ministers sitting at their feet at the Sunday morning service! Whatever one might say or even secretly think about 'having the key to human happiness' or 'the hope of everlasting life' in one's hands, in tangible terms being the Rector of Woolwich often felt like being a General without an army. Nevertheless, there were, I thought, two things that could be done. First, we (and in practice this meant the clergy) could attempt to be associated with every significant group in the Borough and encourage them in the good work that many of them were trying to do. And whenever they required the support and help of the Church in ways that we were actually capable of giving it, we would do so.

Each year a civic military service to commemorate the granting of the freedom of the Borough to the Royal Artillery was held at St. Mary's church. These services with their bands, their flags, their parades, their jingoism and their summer bonnets are open to criticism on many grounds. I sometimes felt that any connection between what went on at such a service and God was purely coincidental. But it did mean that once a year many of the leaders of the Borough gathered together in a church building. The Labour Councillors (who were the large majority of the Council) would turn up in force together with the handful of Tory Councillors. So would the MPs and the chief officers of the Council, the Presidents of the Rotary Club and Chamber of Commerce and leaders of various voluntary bodies. As luck would have it, this annual service took place soon after my arrival which gave me a chance of preaching about what I saw as the role of the Church in the civic life of the Borough. I told the congregation, as I firmly believed, that in the last forty years the Labour Party in Woolwich had done more to build the Kingdom of God than the official Church had done. I did not mention the Conservative Party not because of any political prejudice of my own but because they had not held power. I told the Councillors that whether they knew it or not, or liked it or not, they had been and were being fellow workers with Christ. I said, 'Christ is concerned about homes as well as hymns, about parks as well as prayers, and about sewers as well as sins.' I pointed out to them that their progressive and far-sighted housing policies and social welfare work had transformed people's lives and protected the weak and the infirm. I endeavoured to explain to them that Christian work was not necessarily that which was done under the umbrella of the Church or by clergymen. I said, 'It is a sad thing that the idea has emerged that doing Church work means sitting on Parochial Church Councils and teaching in Sunday schools. Nobody would deny the importance of these activities but sitting on the Borough Council and Employers' Federation or Union Committee is Christian work of equal importance.' I illustrated this by saying, 'The most Christian meeting that I have been to since I have been in Woolwich was a meeting of the Woolwich Trade Council, at which the members talked constructively, charitably and acted generously on four of the greatest social questions of the day. At no point did they discuss any matter which concerned their own self-interest.'

I knew that Councillors and leaders of voluntary organizations often used to get depressed and discouraged. They wonder whether the hours of unpaid and unsung work they put in is worthwhile. I wanted to lift their hopes, their courage and their horizons, to help them see they were truly doing God's work and playing an important part in building His Kingdom. I pledged the official and organized Church to be their servants. Finally I told them, 'Inward-looking Christians are as useless as a power station that shoots power round a closed circuit. We at St. Mary's are not concerned with becoming an organization but a power house where all can come to have their spiritual batteries topped up. The busier one is in public service the more necessary it is to have one's batteries recharged.'

In the last few years I have learnt somewhat painfully that telling the truth as one sees it does not always further one's own interests or increase one's popularity. This occasion was an exception to this general rule. The leaders of a local community get few perks and precious little thanks. I learnt later that they were grateful for what I had said and had been helped by it. Apparently they had not been accustomed to being talked to in this way and had not always seen their work in this light. I think the occasion helped us to get off to a good start with the local leaders. From time to time we would invite one of the key figures in the Borough to our regular staff dinners and get him to talk to us about his work and its problems. When Christopher Mayhew was our guest we quizzed him on what he thought made his constituents tick. We were both encouraged and surprised when he told us we ought to know better than him.

Looking back now after an interval of years I think the happy partnership that developed between the leaders of the Borough and myself was one of the most fruitful aspects of our work in Woolwich. To have written or spoken about it at the time, as we did about other things we were doing, might have had the effect of undermining the mutual respect and confidence on which it all depended. It was a privilege for me to become the friend and confidant of the men and women carrying the heaviest responsibilities in the life of the Borough. I am sure I leaned on them more than they leaned on me. Their friendship was unquestionably a source of personal and private strength to me. There were many times when I thought that of all the jobs in Woolwich mine was the most difficult and the least rewarding. But when I heard of the problems with which my friends were wrestling I used to count my blessings. If I played a part contributing to the good relationships which existed in the Borough and had some influence on the power structures of the community it may have been the most worthwhile thing that I did. Of course, I would have tried to work closely with anybody who was the Member of Parliament and leader of the Borough Council or Town Clerk. But the fact that one admired and trusted them as people and knew that they were dedicated to the Borough made one all the more determined to help them.

We had a very close relationship with the MP for Woolwich East, Mr. Christopher Mayhew. We used to invite him and his Conservative opponent to be questioned by the congregation during election campaigns. Once we did this within the context of a church service. In defending this action I told the local press 'We have prepared six questions we think that thoughtful Christian people should be asking their candidates. I am very anxious that the Church in Woolwich should play its part in trying to see that we have a responsible election campaign, and that the voters should wrestle in their minds with the fundamental questions that confront our society. I think it right that the candidates should answer the questions in a church building. All men, including politicians, come under the judgement of God. Moreover, what the politicians say in Westminster should be influenced by what goes on in church. And what Christians do in church should influence their attitude to politics. It is a happy coincidence that the beginning of the election campaign should coincide with our Harvest Festival. At Harvest Festival Christians thank God for the fruits of the earth and man's skill—in other words, we thank God for wealth. One of the main subjects of the election is about the creation of wealth—more wealth—and the way it should be used and distributed.' I was asked whether I thought that a political meeting in a religious service would cause controversy and I replied, 'At St. Mary's we are concerned to try and do what is right and responsible. If this causes controversy, let us have controversy. In fact I believe the old lie that politics and religion do not mix is now dead and buried. I am sure that the congregation of St. Mary's realizes that an essential consequence of being Christian is to take politics seriously . . . Political parties in a large measure decide the sort of society we shall have. If this isn't the concern of Christians, what is? I believe that there are a great number of people in Woolwich who will want to attend the service and the meeting. They will all be very welcome.'

From time to time Christopher Mayhew and I would join forces over some issue. One such occasion was when a neo-fascist body called the Anti-Violence League threatened to run a campaign in Woolwich, during which it was rumoured that Sir Oswald Mosley might speak. In backing an appeal from Mr. Mayhew, I said, 'I give warning that my colleagues and I on the staff of St. Mary's Church, Woolwich, will mobilize all progressive and caring people from all religious and political beliefs to counter the proposed campaign of the Anti-Violence League. Our appeal will not aim to stimulate hysteria, fear, hate or revenge, but rather we shall endeavour to present the facts about crimes of violence, their causes and their possible cures— calmly and soberly.' Christopher Mayhew knew that if there was ever anyone who came to his 'surgeries'— when he saw constituents about their problems—whom we could help he could pass them on to us.

But it was with the Borough Council that we had most dealings. Their writ ran everywhere. Nothing could happen in the Borough without their support. For most of my time in Woolwich the Town Clerk was Mr. Roderick Doble, who must have been one of the most imaginative town clerks in Britain. He was always bursting with exciting ideas which would enhance the community spirit. I thought some of his ideas were unrealistic (as he did of some of mine) and I would tell him so privately. But once his scheme was endorsed by the Borough Council I did everything to see that the Church played its part in supporting it. I never became the local Labour Party's yes-man, but only once, and then after I had been in Woolwich seven years, did I attack the Borough Council in public. This was not, I hope, from any lack of moral courage but because I believed I could achieve more by making my criticisms privately behind the scenes. Sometimes I would publicly defend the Council. There was a frightful row over the automatic multi-storey car park which Princess Margaret opened; it had never worked, stood empty for several years, and then had to be pulled down. I attended a public meeting called to censure the Council. One of the local papers reported, 'Shouting above jeers and catcalls at a rowdy meeting called to look into the auto-stacker fiasco the Reverend Nick Stacey, Rector of Woolwich, told angry ratepayers, "If you think you can be better Councillors—get elected and run the Borough." Shouting loudly, Reverend Stacey said, "You can question the Council on many grounds but not on their integrity. They had had very bad luck. The only Councils who do not have bad luck are those who do nothing." ' The report in the local paper continued rather sinisterly, 'While he was speaking two policemen arrived and stood in the gallery.' It did not make clear whether their task was to protect the audience from me, or me from the audience.

In another, but private, row between the Borough Council and the diocese, I backed the Borough. After the war when few people had realized the potential value of land in the cities, sites owned by the Church were unquestionably sold too cheaply. In order to get the best value for Church property in future, Mervyn Stockwood recruited some property advisers, who were not, some of us had warned him, men of the calibre to be advising a diocesan bishop; advice which sadly turned out to be right but was not accepted by Dr. Stockwood at the time. On the recommendation of these men, the diocese was trying to pull a fast one on the Borough over a site which it was selling to them. I told Dr. Stockwood bluntly that if the diocese went on pressing its unreasonable point he could not expect me to maintain good relations with the civil authorities.

As I was trying to forge links with the Borough, other

members of the staff were doing the same in other fields. Bob Hughes, as Industrial Chaplain, was visiting factories, running courses for apprentices and occasionally organizing an industrial service at St. Mary's, at which products of local industry were displayed all over the church.

Local industry often seemed surprised at being considered a part of God's concern. We wrote to ask all large firms in the area for products to be lent for exhibition at an Industrial Service. The brewery replied that they 'had no products suitable for exhibition'. We replied with a quotation from a recent remark by the Archbishop of Wales, that beer is a gift from God and regretted that they did not think their beer good enough in quality to be worth exhibiting. The reply was two cases of beer and a message that they did not want it back as they were sure that we could put it to good use after the service. It went to an old people's home for Christmas and became a regular feature of future industrial services.

Bob Hughes also kept in touch with the Woolwich Trades Council. Brian Cooper became Chaplain of the Woolwich Polytechnic, and Richard Garrard developed a particularly valuable partnership with the District Nurses who, like us, were in constant touch with the local people. We worked particularly closely with the Woolwich Council of Social Service and all of us were attached to various voluntary bodies. We had close links with the police, the Probation Service, the Employment Exchange, the Youth Employment Officers and the various welfare departments of the Borough. The London probation service used to send us a group of its trainees for a day as part of their course. All social workers in the Borough meet monthly for a sandwich lunch and discussion in the lounge of the church.

After we had been in Woolwich for a year or two we took on the Chaplaincy of a large local hospital. We divided it up so that each of us had four or five wards to visit each week as well as doing emergency calls. Our involvement spread everywhere. There was no pie in which we did not have our fingers. Occasionally we burnt them. I preached what I thought was an innocent Remembrance Day service at St. Mary's. I told a congregation of Old Contemptibles and British Legion stalwarts that Remembrance Day was fast losing its appeal and no longer capturing the imagination of the nation. I commented that some people were suggesting that it should be discontinued before it became a bore and degenerated into becoming an empty formality. If that was to happen I recommended that we had a Peace Sunday to take its place. The national press took up the idea, and the British Legion took up their arms against me. 'British Legion men slam Rector of Woolwich—but he gets round of applause' ran the headlines in the paper after a special meeting called to denounce me.

One important advantage of working with a team of clergy was that if any one of us had personality difficulties with one of the leaders of a particular voluntary organization with which we were working we would arrange for another member of the team whose personality we thought would be more acceptable to take his place. As well as trying to work with all the different voluntary bodies we used to look for opportunities for running some short 'one-off' campaigns on special issues.

We ran a 'Let's Be Proud of Woolwich' campaign. I felt the Borough had an inferiority complex and was concerned that most people's first ambition was to get out of Woolwich as fast as they could and join what I called 'the scramble over Shooter's Hill into the suburbs'. This attitude was breeding discontent and unhappiness and I was determined to fight it. In those days I did not mince my words. Whatever else I was criticized for nobody could accuse me of not making myself clear. When launching the campaign I said, 'I would much rather live in Woolwich than in some sprawling, soulless, dreary, keep-your-self-to-yourself, chromium-plated suburb with half the population falling flat on their faces in the rat race to keep up with the Joneses.' Reporting the campaign the local paper said, 'The Rector hopes to get the support of every-one in the Borough for his campaign and said they need not be churchgoers to join, as this would cut out about ninety-eight per cent of the parish straight away. The rules laid down by the Rector for his campaign are simple. They are that "members" will be debarred from saying that Wool-wich is a dump and will be expected to defend its reputa-tion at all times.'

Another of our many ventures was our 'Bread and Cheese' week and 'Miss-a-Meal' campaign to assist World Refugee Year. We managed to secure the services of the English Cheese Maiden. I thought we must exploit her to the full and in order to launch the campaign I borrowed a costermonger's barrow and pulled her through the shop-ping centre of Woolwich. It nearly killed me. The caption to the front page picture with which my efforts were re-warded ran, 'Barrow boy priest. Miss a meal, but don't miss this unusual sight. Looks of amazement followed the Rector of Woolwich, the Reverend Nick Stacey, when he made his unorthodox appearance in Beresford Market Square on Monday. Mr. Stacey doesn't believe in half measures—as the people of Woolwich are finding out. Unflagging he hauled his cargo Cheese Maiden, Miss Mari-lyn Hardy, and a large Cheshire cheese round the town centre. Every sixpence his scheme raises will provide a meal for three refugee children.'

It was one thing to help, to encourage and to stimulate existing statutory and voluntary organizations and to have short, sharp campaigns into which we would throw all our resources for a few days. It was quite another to set up a new organization of our own which would close a gap in the existing social services. We were already running the traditional parochial organizations from Cubs to a Women's Fellowship. We were determined anything new we undertook should be really well run.

It was Bob Hughes who was particularly keen that we should start a branch of the suicide Samaritans. The Samaritan organization had been started some years earlier by the Reverend Chad Varah from his London City church. Like most brilliant ideas it was simple. A telephone with an easily remembered number would be manned day and night so that those in despair could ring for help and advice. Many of those who rang were contemplating suicide and some, as we were to discover for ourselves later, had actually taken an overdose before ringing, had had second thoughts and were wanting help urgently. Chad Varah's scheme had proved such a success and was obviously meeting such a real need that he was encouraging the formation of branches all over the country. Understandably perhaps, the Samaritan service had come under some criticism from professional psychiatrists who complained that amateurs were meddling in areas which were properly the domain of experts. We saw the validity of this criticism, but did not believe that it carried the day. The professionals, as the humbler ones among them admitted, were not themselves all that successful with suicide cases. They were also overburdened by work and were unable to give their patients the time that they needed. All my pastoral experience had convinced me that genuine care and a bit of commonsense could complement or even replace drugs. Another criticism was that many of the people helping Chad Varah with counselling and befriending were themselves either people who had contemplated suicide or at best neurotics. It was, the critics said, 'the nuts leading the nuts'. This was partly true as a comment, but invalid as a criticism. I believed some of the best counsellors and befrienders are those who had themselves personally experienced the agony a client was suffering. In any case, Chad Varah made an important distinction between counsellors, who had some professional training, and befrienders, who never pretended they were other than amateurs. To counter any possible criticism we determined from the outset to work closely with the professionals to whom we would refer clients, provided we first got their agreement. With a characteristic energy and enthusiasm, Hughes poured himself into getting the Woolwich branch going. It was a big task.

First he had to recruit and train some sixty helpers to man the telephone, to act as befrienders and as counsellors. Almost all our voluntary helpers came from outside Woolwich. Once this was done we had to give the maximum publicity to the telephone number of our Samaritan office which was in the crypt of the church. Although the telephone in the Samaritan office was manned until 10.00 pm we did not attempt to keep people on duty in the church throughout the night but arranged for calls to be transferred to whomever was doing night duty. Hughes himself took more than his fair share and the strain on him was immense. I became worried about his health. He was already working about eighteen hours a day and frequently dealing with Samaritan calls at night as well.

The greatest difficulty of the work was that one could never tell which calls were genuine and which were hoaxes. A person would ring up in the middle of the night from a call box and say that unless someone came at once he would do himself in. Sometimes he would refuse to say exactly where he was and one would climb out of bed to do a tour of call boxes in the area where he claimed to be. One was almost sure that it was a hoax or an hysteric drawing attention to himself but one could never be sure and was unwilling to take the risk. If we could elicit from a caller, or trace from where he was ringing, our tactics were to keep him talking while someone else would get to another telephone and arrange for a third person to go to the caller. At night it was usually wisest to make such visits in pairs.

One night, for instance, Hughes was called out in this way by the Samaritans' Head Office. They were talking to a man in a call box at Woolwich Ferry, who boasted that he would be dead before they could reach him. Hughes and the rugby-playing son of one of the church members reached the box, in record time, to find there a giant, one-eyed merchant seaman, who fiercely resisted all attempts to get him to go to hospital. Eventually the tablets he had taken began to take effect and he agreed to go to Hughes' house for coffee. There he became delirious and imagined that he was back in the Red Sea, clobbering and stealing pearls from Arab fisherman. Narrowly escaping the Arabs' fate, they got him into the car and drove to hospital. Before losing consciousness, he made spectacular efforts to take charge of the car, shouting, 'The Maoris are after us'. Swerving wildly through deserted streets, they got him to hospital and there, because the Casualty Department was short-handed, they stayed on to help wash out his stomach and get him to bed. He was later sent to a mental hospital for fuller treatment.

I have never been able to make up my mind about the right attitude to suicides. Part of me feels that if someone wants to put an end to his life it is not for me or anyone else to interfere. Yet in practice I have always prevented suicide whenever I was able to do so. I had one case which did not come through the Samaritan service, and to this day I wonder whether I did the right thing. The lover of a woman rang to say he had left her for good and was fearful that she would commit suicide, and would I go round at once to her flat, which he had just left. It was the middle of the night. I knew the woman well. She had been in and out of mental homes for years. As a result her children were in and out of children's homes and foster homes. It was a tragically mixed up and unhappy family. Wearily I put on a cassock over my pyjamas and called at the woman's flat. We talked inconclusively for an hour before she left the living room and locked herself in the bathroom. After a minute or two she shouted at me, 'I've done it this time.' I knew she had an eighteen-year-old daughter sleeping somewhere in the flat, and I thought I had better wake her and explain the position. It occurred to me that it might come as a slight surprise to her to be awakened by a clergyman with only a cassock covering his pyjamas. I visualized what a good headline it would make in the *News of the World*. After a considerable amount of shaking I woke her and told her 'Your mum is locked in the bathroom, and says she has taken an overdose.' The daughter replied, 'Mum's always doing that', and turned over and went to sleep again. I left the woman locked in the bathroom and wandered back to the rectory through the deserted Woolwich streets at dawn wondering whether or not to call the Police and the Ambulance service. In the end I did, but only just in time and her life was saved—for more unhappiness.

We ran the Samaritan service from Woolwich for several years with Richard Garrard taking over the directorship when Bob Hughes left. Eventually we decided to move it to Bexley as most of our helpers, and indeed the clients too, came from the suburbs. It was never possible to assess accurately how many of the people who called were genuine suicide risks. I would guess that it was in the neighbourhood of ten per cent. One breakdown of cases which we attempted put twenty-five per cent down to matrimonial problems, sixteen per cent financial, fourteen per cent accommodation, eleven per cent loneliness, six per cent emotional relationship problems and five per cent alcohol, the remainder being miscellaneous, although of course many of the cases could have come into more than one category. We had about 200 to 300 new cases a year. We referred those we could to other bodies qualified to deal with their problems. But it often happened that by the time people came to the Samaritans they had already been through many of the statutory and voluntary social services, in which they claimed to have no confidence. We were a long stop—the last resort. For Bob Hughes, Richard Garrard and the gallant band of people who worked with them it was noble and demanding work.

Throughout my ministry in Woolwich I was convinced that it was the general image of the Church in the eyes of our parishioners which was an important factor in their lack of interest in the Church. I was hopeful that the conversion of the church building, the pastoral care we were attempting to give, and the outward-looking vision we were trying to inject into the congregation would slowly alter people's attitudes towards the Church. Through all our various activities we were in touch with more people than most other downtown churches, but I was constantly concerned in trying to get across the new image to as many of the people as possible. I wanted everyone to know what was going on at St. Mary's, Woolwich. And if the people of Woolwich would not come to church to hear the Gospel preached, other ways of reaching them must be found.

The three local weekly papers were an obvious medium for our purposes. A very high percentage of homes in the parish took one or other of them and I discovered they were read more thoroughly than the national newspapers. I think the links we developed with the local press were mutually beneficial. The church got enormous publicity for its activities and views and the papers got some good copy. On the smaller stories I used to try and give each paper an exclusive in turn. On the big stories, in which, of course, we involved them all, I always tried to time press releases and conferences so that the local papers could carry the story on the same day as the nationals, or even before. In the local paper which was most widely read in our part of Woolwich I had a column. It was given such prominence that it was more than a column, it was a splash. The paper got articles from me for a fee in shillings which the nationals would have paid an equal number of pounds. I got a very valuable platform. My column was widely read and commented on. I usually dealt with serious subjects but on one occasion I told readers that my doctor advised me to take up swimming. I went on to extol the virtues of the local public baths, and invited other middle-aged men to improve their health and reduce their waistlines by joining me at the baths for a swim, a practice, I am afraid, which I did not keep up for very long. For weeks afterwards I was greeted in the streets with 'How is the swimming going?' Others just did the breast-stroke movements with their arms whenever they saw me.

Apart from writing about what the church was doing and attempting to give Christian insights to local and national questions, I was able to write about anything that was going on in the Borough. If the Borough Council or a voluntary agency were trying to launch some new scheme I would endeavour to help by writing about it in my column. As a result of our close connections with the papers, everything we did was highly but responsibly publicized. The benefits were great. The Church became a talking point. I think people began to feel we were trying to do a good job and we went some way to creating a new image. But as parishioners constantly pointed out, St. Mary's was not like the rest of the churches. What we may have achieved was, I suspect, largely nullified by the total image of the Church throughout the country. Once or twice I thought that the Church was in danger of being over-exposed and I would reduce the flow of stories, for a time.

It is ironical that while the publicity we got was enormously beneficial to the church in Woolwich it was, I believe, one of the main causes for the suspicion, not to say, distrust, in which I am personally held in the Church of England. Of course the dilemma for anybody who uses the press is that people make better news than ideas. Therefore it was inevitable that many of the stories revolved round the clergy staff in general, and myself in particular. Consequently, those who did not understand, or did not want to understand, what we were trying to do criticized me as seeking personal publicity. I felt the remarks of my critics were often more of a comment on themselves than on me. I sought, and I valued, publicity because I thought it would help me in my work. And so it did. It was partly responsible for the fact that when I spoke people listened. When I espoused a cause people sat up and took notice. When I rang up strangers to seek help for parishioners they knew of me and were often more ready to co-operate. Sadly churchmen are not immune from the tedious sin of envy. But as I used to say to fellow vicars in South-East London they too could develop the same close links with the press as we did. We were publicized because we took the press seriously, and only gave them newsworthy stories. I told the staff that before sending in a story they should put themselves in the position of the news editor and then ask themselves whether they would think it was worth printing. Sometimes we wanted publicity for something which I did not think was of much general interest. We would always try and find a newsworthy angle to it before releasing it to the press. And if we failed we never sent it in. As a result I do not recall an occasion when the papers did not use our stories. If I was being interviewed by a young and inexperienced reporter, I would try to help him by suggesting how he should write the first paragraph of the story and would then give him two or three quotes to strengthen it.

All this led to the criticism, some of which came from high places in the diocese, that all we were interested in was gimmicks. It was inevitable that the more unusual things should have received the greatest publicity. This did not mean that we were failing to do the more traditional things as well. In retrospect I think it was naïve of me not to realize that I would come under fire from others and I should have taken as much trouble in getting them to see what we were trying to do as we took with the press. All my life I have had a simple faith that in the long run integrity and truth will prevail. I believed deeply in the rightness of what we were trying to do, and the way we were attempting to do it. I knew that the motives of my colleagues and myself were above reproach. I knew as well that they would be on me like a ton of bricks if they ever thought I was doing anything that was superficial, slick or second-rate. We were never sensational for the sake of being sensational. But from time to time we did things in a sensational way because we wanted to get the point across. I wanted the Church to be involved and to be seen to be involved in everything that was going on in the life of the Borough. I hoped eventually that those who had been so quick to criticize and sneer would realize that they had judged us wrongly. But we never imagined that our effectiveness in building the Kingdom of God could be measured by the column inches about us in the newspapers. Nor did we think it could be assessed by the number of peripheral committees a clergyman can waste his time sitting on. Unquestionably the impact we made was great. But impact by itself is of no consequence. The task of the Church is to change lives and transform society. Those were the yardsticks by which I would judge the success or failure of our mission.

Eleven

THERE WERE AN AWFUL LOT OF CHURCHES near the centre of Woolwich. In fact, there were too many. There were three Baptist churches, one of which was an enormous barn-like Tabernacle with temperance texts painted over its dark brown walls. There was a Congregational Church, in whose vestry the famous Woolwich Equitable Building Society had been born. There was a Presbyterian Church, a Methodist Church, and a Salvation Army Citadel. There was also, of course, a Roman Catholic Church, with an octogenarian priest and friendly young Irish curates: this was the only one that flourished. The rest were like the Anglican churches—ill-attended and impoverished, with the faithful struggling to keep them going. The congregations of all the Free Churches in the town would easily have fitted into one church and still left room for all the Anglicans too. But they were no less keen than the Anglicans to hold on to their buildings.

I had not been there long before I was pleading privately and publicly with Free Church leaders to rationalize their church resources by having one well-attended, well-equipped, well-staffed and multi-purpose Free Church centre, such as the Anglicans were trying to achieve. I spoke at a lunch given in honour of the Moderator of the General Assembly of the Presbyterian Church of England when

179

he visited Woolwich. I advocated that the Free Churches should get together rather than squander their resources separately and before apathy picked them off one by one. I stressed that if there was a Free Church revival in Woolwich it would help the Anglicans too. I was convinced that denominational differences were irrelevant to the modern situation. Within three months of my arrival we got representatives of all the non-Roman Catholic Churches together to discuss the formation of a Woolwich Council of Churches. I expressed my ambitions for it to the local paper. 'I hope this is going to be the start of a new and exciting chapter in the history of the Church in Woolwich. In a missionary situation such as we find ourselves it is absurd and unrealistic for individual churches to go it alone.'

The local Council of Churches was formed and I was elected its first Chairman. In my speech at the inaugural meeting, I tried to inject a sense of urgency. I wanted the Council to be an action group and not just a talking shop and an excuse for setting up yet more committees. I told the clergy and lay representatives, 'I am convinced that the evangelistic work and pastoral care which each individual church is doing should be planned and carried out in co-operation with the other churches in the neighbourhood.' I pointed out that there were seven different places of worship in the small area of Woolwich that St. Mary's was meant to be serving, and went on, 'So much of our effort is wasted by overlapping. The Council must be an action group mobilized to build the Kingdom of God in Woolwich.' It got off to a good start with an open-air service which we held in the shell of the Royal Artillery Garrison Church, which had been bombed in the war but never rebuilt. The Reverend David Sheppard, now Bishop of Woolwich, who at the time was working across the river in the Mayflower Family Centre, came over to preach at it. The Council of Churches did useful work. The churches started working together in such ventures as Christian Aid Week. Joint services were held on Good Friday, and occasionally a church would cancel its Sunday evening service and the congregation would go off *en bloc* to worship at one of the neighbouring churches of a different denomination. I think some of the local ministers and their congregations were suspicious of St. Mary's in general, and of me in particular. They thought we wanted to gobble them up. But one Methodist minister, the Reverend Ray Billington, and the Presbyterian minister, the Reverend Derek Baker, and his congregation trusted us and shared our vision. What happened as a result was remarkable and unique.

Ray Billington had become minister of the Herbert Road Methodist Church in Woolwich shortly after I went to St. Mary's. He was one of the ablest of the young ministers in the Methodist Church. He was exceptionally articulate and a fluent speaker on a wide range of subjects. He was a good teacher, journalist and broadcaster. Above all, he was great fun—an enormously life-enhancing person. He was as realistic about the churches as we were, and if anything more impatient and more critical. This had not made him universally popular in Methodist circles. He had had a fairly stormy career in the Methodist ministry, and consequently had never been offered jobs commensurate with his talents. We worked closely with him from the moment he arrived in Woolwich, but unfortunately the particular Methodist church he was serving was not the one that was in the parish. Nevertheless, we got the Anglicans at St. Mary's and the Methodists at Herbert Road together whenever we could. After the first of the many reports on Anglican/Methodist unity was published we arranged for representatives from the two congregations to have a series of meetings to discuss the official proposals. After they had met about twice, they reported back that there was no point in continuing the meetings as they agreed about everything and could not see what all the fuss was about. 'Let's stop talking and get united,' they said. I could not have agreed with them more, but alas I had no power to pre-empt Anglican/Methodist unity, which at the time of writing is still being held up by an unholy alliance of the very high and the very low in the Church of England.

After Ray Billington had completed his three-year contract as minister of the Herbert Road congregation we all thought that it might forward the cause of Church Unity if he were to join the team of Anglicans at Woolwich Parish Church and at the same time remain a Methodist minister. This would mean giving up his charge at Herbert Road, but he would be able to earn his living partly by teaching and partly by taking over Bob Hughes' job as Industrial Chaplain. The Parochial Church Council of St. Mary's were enthusiastic and unanimously resolved that Dr. Stockwood be petitioned to agree to Billington preaching, taking services at St. Mary's, other than Holy Communion; administering the Chalice at Communion and he and his wife (an ex-Roman Catholic) receiving Communion themselves. The bishop was co-operative and gave all the permissions asked for except the administration of the Chalice at Holy Communion. In his letter he showed the extent to which a Bishop has to guard his flanks. He said, 'I should prefer you not to press me to give permission for the administration of the Chalice. I shall be prepared to reconsider this request at a later date when the position is more stabilized. As you will appreciate, the experiment will be closely watched and the critics will be anxious to pounce on anything which is illegal. If Mr. Billington were to administer the Chalice in the early days of the scheme it might become a case for a wretched ecclesiastical controversy which would get into the press. And if I were attacked I should be compelled to admit that I had not the authority to give permission.' Although we were disappointed we saw his point and did not press him. He kept his word and later agreed to him administering the Chalice. At the same time Billington was getting the necessary approvals from the Methodist Conference. In the press release announcing this unique appointment, I said, 'The walls of denominational differences are beginning to crumble. In Woolwich we are hoping that with a few more powerful blows on the trumpet they may, like the walls of Jericho, collapse altogether.'

The move was widely welcomed except by the *Church Times* and some of its readers. One wrote:

'I was a Methodist at midnight, an Anglican at noon.
And I hope to be a pious Presbyterian very soon.
And an anti-paedo-Baptist at the rising of the moon.
Blessed be the Bishop who has taught you to combine
The Luther and Calvinistic views of the divine
And to cultivate the Quakers without needing to
   resign
O sweet and happy compromise when Christians shall
   agree
To adopt a new religion every Sunday after tea
Till we all get mixed together in a glorious kedgeree.

'At your ordination you promised before God to "give your faithful diligence always to banish and drive away all erroneous and strange doctrine . . ." and, no doubt, you join the litany and pray to be delivered "from all false doctrine, heresy and schism . . ." How do you justify this with your doings as reported in the *Church Times* of yesterday?'

While I was at Woolwich I found increasingly that it was not the apathy and indifference of the parishioners that wore me down, but the constant attacks of those who were meant to be on the same side.

Billington became enormously popular with the congregation of St. Mary's, but continued to maintain close links with local Methodist churches at which he preached regularly. He was a very stimulating person to work with, always bursting with ideas and rarely out of controversy.

Billington left Woolwich shortly after I did to go into academic work. It is a sad comment on the Methodist Church that it never really tried to hold or to use a man of such great ability.

While we were negotiating for Billington to join the staff of St. Mary's we were involved in a much more ambitious and difficult scheme which had never been tried before in England. It was for the minister and congregation of St. Andrew's Presbyterian Church in Woolwich to give up their own church building and share Woolwich Parish Church as equal partners on a permanent basis. From time to time the church of one denomination has acted as host to another while their church is being rebuilt, and occasionally in new housing areas small district churches are used on a shared basis, but never before had an attempt been made to share a Church of England parish church with another major denomination on a permanent basis. Our experience illustrated the appalling difficulties of getting anything done in the Church of England.

When I first met the Presbyterian minister in Woolwich, the Reverend Derek Baker, I realized that he was a man of integrity and courage. He combined realism with vision and was psychologically tough enough to face honestly the facts of the church's situation in the town. He was clearly a man with whom we would be able to work closely. His own job was not an easy one. The Presbyterian Church in Woolwich had been founded in 1662 by the then Rector of Woolwich, who was ejected from the parish church after the passing of the Act of Uniformity. The present St. Andrew's Church had been built in 1842 and seated 1000 people. Its congregation 120 years later was rarely more than fifty and drawn from many miles around. Nevertheless, by Woolwich standards, it was strong and solvent.

The congregations of St. Mary's and St. Andrew's tried to do nothing separately that they could do together. It was not much, but it meant that slowly and quietly the two congregations came to know, like and trust each other. In 1962 John Robinson preached the sermon at the Tercentenary Service of the Presbyterian Church in Woolwich. He suggested a good way of celebrating was to return to the ancient parish church from which they had been ejected 300 years earlier.

A year later when we were having one of our occasional joint meetings, one of the laity took up his idea and suggested that the obvious next step should be for both congregations to share the same building. There was enormous enthusiasm for the idea. Nobody thought it would transform the church situation in Woolwich, but everybody believed that it would make good, pastoral, economic and administrative sense. It would be a step forward towards Church unity and release the energy of the congregations from raising money and maintaining church buildings for pastoral and evangelical work in the area. The Anglicans could have exclusive use of the building for their services at certain hours on a Sunday, and the Presbyterians the same at different hours. Hopefully, we could have a joint evening service. The amenities and expenses of St. Mary's Church would be shared. The more we talked about it that evening, the more excited we became. I put the scheme to Mervyn Stockwood. In my letter to him I said, 'The Presbyterians will rightly be anxious to maintain their separate identity and traditions, and any scheme we put up would have to be, and be seen to be, one of genuine sharing between equal partners rather than a takeover bid by us . . . Clearly any scheme of sharing would inevitably commit my successor. We cannot expect the Presbyterians to give up their place of worship without reasonable security of tenure here, nor would I ask them to consider doing this.' Dr. Stockwood was keen, but his legal adviser, Mr. David Faull, said that as laws stood I could not tie the hands of my successor.

The Southwark Diocese was extraordinarily fortunate in having David as its legal adviser. He was a great personal friend and an unfailing ally who worked unceasingly for us, for virtually no remuneration, trying to find ways round the outmoded ecclesiastical laws. It was a tremendous encouragement knowing one had a really helpful ecclesiastical lawyer on one's side. But even David could not find a way round and was doubtful about the legality of the scheme.

So I told the Presbyterians that once their congregation was installed at St. Mary's even without legal safeguards they were safe. Public opinion would not tolerate them being thrown out at the whim of any of my successors as Rector. The Presbyterians took the point and we made the scheme public. In the press release announcing it, Baker said, 'I believe it could be a pilot scheme of national importance and significance to the Anglican and Presbyterian Communions in England.' I added, 'By being prepared to give up their church building the Presbyterians have shown that the claims of the Church of God have priority over the emotional attachment many Christians have to their buildings. If similar arrangements could be made by congregations of different denominations throughout England, not only would it greatly increase the witness of the Church but it would release vast resources for new housing areas and the Church overseas . . .'

The ink was barely dry on the press release when we came up against a new problem. The Registrar General at Somerset House decreed that as the laws of the land stood it was illegal for Presbyterian marriages to be solemnized in a Church of England building. It was a bitter blow. The only way this could be circumvented was for me to promote a private Act of Parliament which would be both expensive and slow. My blood boiled and I decided that if it was the last thing I did in this life I was going to get the Presbyterians into Woolwich Parish Church. I would promote my own private Act of Parliament, but not before I had brought the Archbishop of Canterbury into the act. I wrote to him with much more restraint than I felt and explained the whole grotesque situation. I suggested he might care to promote the Act of Parliament. In the best Anglican tradition he set up a committee of top ecclesiastical lawyers who reported that apart from the problem of marriages the Act of Uniformity in 1662 prohibits preaching and the administration of the sacraments by non-Anglican ministers. Our whole scheme was illegal from beginning to end.

I met Mervyn Stockwood at the Athenaeum to discuss the situation. I was very cross. In language that is not normally used by members of the Athenaeum and their guests I told him what I thought of the Church of England. I further asked him to give my compliments to the Archbishop of Canterbury and kindly suggest to him where he could conveniently place the Act of Uniformity of 1662. I ventured that it was ridiculous for bishops and other Church leaders to urge the Churches of different denominations to pray together, to get together and to work together, only to find that when they obeyed their leaders' instructions they were thwarted by 300-year-old laws. Mervyn listened to all that I had to say and agreed with most of it himself, but asked me not to swear at him in front of the Club servants.

It was Election Day 1964. As I motored from the Athenaeum back to Woolwich I wondered why I had decided to become a parson. I knew that politics was risky and frustrating, but I asked myself where I would now be if I had gone into politics instead of into the Church. I thought however disappointed I might have been in politics, it could not be as bad as working in the Church.

Christopher and Cicely Mayhew were dining with us at the Rectory that night prior to us all going down to the count at Woolwich Town Hall. Labour won the election, but Mayhew, alas, did not get a job in the Cabinet.

I started trying to pick up the bits of our church-sharing scheme over which I had worked unceasingly for a year. I told Dr. Stockwood in a letter, 'I find the whole Anglican attitude to the law exasperating. When Harold Wilson comes up against a law which is against the public interest, he instructs his legal men to prepare legislation to get it altered. He does not meekly acquiesce to an intolerable legal situation . . . If it only concerned Woolwich I would not be making such a fuss, but as you have probably heard, the Woolwich experiment was mentioned again and again in the Nottingham meeting of the British Council of Churches as a pattern which must be followed throughout the country as soon as possible if there is any hope of unity by 1980. My own view is that if we can get the congregations from different denominations sharing buildings the psychological and social barriers between them would disappear.'

The Archbishop of Canterbury did pledge himself to get the laws changed. I was inclined to think he might have thought of doing so before. But the Presbyterians who had

shown remarkable patience and understanding throughout decided that the plans for sharing would have to be
postponed. However, the door was kept open and they
said that once it looked as though legislation amending
the existing laws was going to be enacted they would reconsider the position. Both congregations in Woolwich
were deeply disappointed and utterly baffled. They were
good people who just wanted to do something which they
were convinced would help the building of the Kingdom
of God in Woolwich and further the cause of Church
unity. They thought that this was what the Church leaders
were keen on too. What they found was a tangle of Archbishops, Bishops, Registrar Generals, Registrars, Chancel-
lors, lawyers, Acts of Uniformity, Consistory Courts,
faculties, licences and God knows what else. One of the
most devoted members of St. Mary's congregation asked
me what all this had to do with Jesus of Nazareth and His
way of love. It was impossible to explain.

The Archbishop of Canterbury raised the whole question of sharing the churches in the following January at
the meetings of Convocation, where he was asked to
appoint a Commission. This was enough for the ever-
understanding and splendid members of the Presbytery of
London South, who gave the go-ahead to our Woolwich
scheme knowing that eventually the arrangement could be
put on a proper legal footing. The service inaugurating the
scheme took place in the spring of 1965. The whole
arrangement became one of the most successful ventures
we ever undertook. It raised the morale of both congregations and freed the Presbyterians of financial worries.
While each congregation had its own separate services on
Sunday mornings a joint evening service that was held
from the inception of the scheme has helped the congregations to grow together. I do not recall a single disagreement, either between the congregations or between the

Presbyterian minister and the Anglican clergy. While the scheme at Woolwich went smoothly enough, the same cannot be said about getting the laws changed.

The Archbishop set up a Commission under the Chairmanship of the Bishop of Leicester, which included four Bishops and four Archdeacons. Some eighteen months later it produced its report, called *Sharing of Churches*. The headline of the editorial in the *New Christian* commenting on it ran, 'Mouldy Morsel'. 'The report is undoubtedly one of the most lamentable documents ever to be laid before an assembly of responsible churchmen. It presents without sign of shame some of the most unattractive features of Anglicanism and includes a number of statements that even a most dyed-in-the-wool supporter of the established Church would regard as repulsive . . . It is incredible that the year 1966 should find a Commission consisting of Bishops, Archdeacons and other notable figures speaking of "how far it is our duty to preserve in as undiluted form as possible the special ethos of our Church", and of plans for the sharing of churches undermining "traditional attitudes to the mission of the Church of England". How is this to be squared with the Archbishop of Canterbury's challenging statement that "the Church that lives for itself will die by itself"?'

As I was largely responsible for the Commission being set up in the first place it was something of a surprise to me that neither Dr. Stockwood's legal adviser nor I were asked to give evidence. I was doubly surprised when I read at the beginning of this official report that the sharing of Woolwich Parish Church with the Presbyterians was 'a special case' which must be 'dealt with as wisely as possible under the existing law'. The whole point of setting up the Commission was that it is impossible to regularize the present position under the existing law. In an article I wrote on the report in the *New Christian*, I said, 'The only redeeming feature of this unimaginative and unin-spiring document is that it suggests a Church Assembly measure to deal with some of the legal obstacles to prevent the sharing of buildings. But if the spirit of this report accurately represents the Church of England's attitude to the Free Churches I do not think the Church Assembly need spend their precious time passing such legislation be-cause I cannot believe that any Free Church congregation would ever want to share anything with us. The report admits that some Free Church leaders whom the Com-mission met at the last of its five meetings wished the re-port had gone further. In fact I take a more hopeful view of the mind of the Church of England and I have no doubt whatever that the Convocations of Canterbury and York will throw this report out as unworthy and inadequate.' It says on the inside cover, 'The report has only the authority of the group by which it was prepared'. May it ever remain so.

I was deeply concerned about the effect the report might have on the Presbyterians in Woolwich. They had every reason to think that they had been conned into sharing a spiritual home with Dracula. But by a stroke of good fortune a group of us were able to go a long way to re-deeming the situation. Through pressure of business the Convocations had to postpone discussion of the official report for several months. This gave some of us time to produce an alternative unofficial report which we circu-lated to all members of Convocation prior to the debate. In the Convocations of the Church of England it is almost unprecedented for an official report of an Archbishop's Commission not to be 'received' however awful it is. It is 'received' and, if disliked, then amended out of all recogni-tion. This is what happened in the case of the Bishop of Leicester's report. A new committee was set up on which John Robinson was asked to sit because of his connections with Woolwich. It was very sympathetic, and the Bill that went before Parliament amending the existing laws largely incorporated the recommendations of our unofficial report, which was warmly welcomed and approved in the debate.

It took seven years from that exciting evening when the idea of the Presbyterians joining us at the Parish Church was first mooted until the amending legislation went through the Houses of Parliament. Had we acquiesced to the ecclesiastical Establishment's entreaties to be quiet, to show patience and to await God's good time, I very much doubt whether the laws of the land would now be changed. As a result of our efforts, what we did illegally in Woolwich can now be done legally by every church in Britain. It was Derek Baker, the Presbyterian congregation of St. Andrew's, and the Presbytery of London South who showed the patience, took the risks and had the faith. The credit for the victory is theirs.

With the Presbyterians and their ministers happily installed at St. Mary's, with a Methodist minister on the staff, the Parish Church was beginning to have an ecumenical ring about it. I was keen to extend it. The Presbyterian and Congregational churches were having official top level talks about merging, and Derek Baker and I hoped that we might be able to persuade the minute congregation of the Congregational church in Woolwich to join us at St. Mary's. Their own church which was next door to the Rectory was so large and draughty and the congregation was so poor that in the winter they worshipped in a squalid little hall at the back of the church huddled round a leaking gas fire. I felt they would be happier in the warm gay atmosphere of St. Mary's with their Free Church Presbyterian friends. They felt otherwise. Their part-time lay preacher was convinced that a churchgoing religious revival was just about due and we should need every church and pew available to accommodate the multitudes. I thought he was possibly being a little over-optimistic.

In logic, the case for the equally small Methodist congregation joining us was as strong. But in church affairs, as in most of life, sentiment is much stronger than logic. Billington could easily have looked after the handful of practising Methodists in his spare time. This would have relieved the burden of their elderly and delightful minister, the Reverend Maynard Wilson, who was also the minister of a very thriving suburban church several miles away in Welling. It was there he lived and the Welling church took most of his time. Sadly two or three Methodist families wanted to hold on to their own enormous and un-suitable building, and as they were able to let their halls at a handsome rent to a school for its midday meals, the church was financially solvent. Understandably Maynard Wilson felt that his days for fighting battles were over. A complicating factor may have been that some of the Methodists were a little suspicious of Billington's radical-ism and possibly frightened of me. I believed that both the Congregational and Methodist congregations missed a great opportunity. In a few years if a presence by these two churches is to be maintained in Woolwich at all, economic pressures will force them to share buildings with other denominations. It is a constant source of disappoint-ment to me that so often when the Churches do the sensible thing they do it too late and for the wrong reasons.

We were never close enough to the local Baptist churches to consider joining forces although paradoxically our next step in the ecumenical direction was to appoint a Baptist minister to the staff of St. Mary's.

The Quadrant Housing Association, which I shall des-cribe in detail in a later chapter, was expanding fast and

we required a Housing Manager to look after the homeless families we were housing. A number of them had
pressing pastoral and personal problems and we felt that
a minister might be as effective in helping as a professional
Housing Manager. Consequently, we appointed a young
Baptist minister, the Reverend Brian Challis, who was in
charge of a church in Wolverhampton. In the Baptist
Church no minister may undertake work outside the Baptist ministry without the permission of the Baptist Union.
The Union turned down Challis's request to join the staff
of Woolwich Parish Church and help homeless families.
For Challis to have defied the Union as he was wanting to
do would have meant that he would have ceased being a
Baptist minister and it might have been difficult for him
to return to the Baptist ministry at a later date. With typical courage Challis argued that his loyalty to Christ was
more important than of that to his Church. He further felt
that the job we were offering would give him better opportunities for Christian ministry than the traditional Church
pastorate. Nevertheless, I was unhappy about such a dedicated young man with the responsibilities of a wife and
two small children cutting himself off from his Church.
I took up the cudgels on his behalf. I wrote to one of the
great and liberal figures in the Baptist Church, Dr. Ernest
Payne, who fortunately was at that time General Secretary
of the Baptist Union. I explained to Dr. Payne that members of the ecumenical team at Woolwich Parish Church
were never required to do anything that was contrary to
the discipline of their own denomination. I stressed the
demands that the team would make upon Challis for Sunday duty at St. Mary's were inevitably limited because
there were already so many priests and ministers attached
to the church. This would mean that he would be free to
preach and take services at local Baptist churches on a
Sunday. I told Dr. Payne that as the Baptist ministers in

our part of London and North Kent were on the whole aligned with the fundamentalist groups in the Baptist Church I was hoping that by Challis having a foot in the liberal and radical ethos of St. Mary's and another in the conservative ethos of the North Kent Baptist churches he would be able to help break down some barriers. Dr. Payne came to the rescue and shortly afterwards Challis was told that he could be retained on the Baptist Ministerial List. Another hurdle in the ecumenical race had been safely negotiated! Challis proved an excellent choice as a Housing Manager and stayed with Quadrant for several years before returning to the traditional Baptist pastorate.

Our final step in the direction of ecumenicity took place only a few months before I was to leave Woolwich. This was to have a Roman Catholic priest on the staff. He was the Reverend Father Henri du Halgouet, a fifty-two-year-old Frenchman. Du Halgouet was a member of the Congregation of Missionaries Oblates of Mary Immaculate, a missionary Order. Before coming to England he had been the Superior Provincial of his Order in Southern France with fifteen Communities and 175 Religious under his control. Du Halgouet, who was working in a Catholic parish in North London, had come to Britain to explore and hopefully to further the ecumenical movement among Catholics which had been given so much impetus by Pope John. On his day off he came down to Woolwich with no other intention than to see the various uses we were making of the church. By chance I happened to meet him and was able to tell him what we were trying to do. He showed enthusiasm and understanding. Above all he struck me as a man of much sanctity, wisdom and experience, gained, as I was to discover later, from his work in Canada, Central Africa and Corsica. I was determined that the rest of the team should meet him. At the end of the team's second meeting with him he asked if he could join us provided we could all get the necessary permissions. John Grigg, who at that time had a column in the *Guardian*, wrote, 'What he [du Halgouet] saw and heard from the team in Woolwich impressed him very deeply—especially the candour with which they discussed their problems and the practical orientation of their work. Eager himself to promote goodwill between Churches and aware of the inadequacy of the traditional parish organization, he was inspired by the spectacle of a Presbyterian, a Methodist and a Baptist joining with the Anglicans in a common social ministry without prejudice to their distinctive rights and tenets. He resolved to throw in his lot with them.'

It was one thing to resolve, it was quite another thing to get the agreements required. The team at Woolwich were, of course, thrilled and honoured that he should want to come. The Anglican and Presbyterian congregations were delighted. A local girls' comprehensive school was only too ready to give him a job teaching French. Mervyn Stockwood was keen but cautious lest we should do anything that would spoil his own good relationships with the Roman Catholic Archbishop of Southwark. The Catholics were what one could only describe charitably as hesitant. The tale of the negotiations with them is too tedious, tortuous and in many ways too tragic to tell. Suffice to say that it involved the Vatican, the Apostolic Delegate in Britain, the Roman Catholic Archbishop, the Superior of du Halgouet's Order in France, among others. Although we did not get all we asked for, many considered it a triumph that we were able to announce publicly that the arrangement was made with the knowledge and 'qualified permission' of the Roman Catholic Archbishop of Southwark. It had to be stressed that Father du Halgouet's association with the team would be on an informal basis as no sacramental involvement was possible. But he would be able to join us in prayer, fellowship and social work. And he did. With du Halgouet's appointment we only lacked a Congregational minister to be able to include all the major English Churches. No other parish in Britain had ever had such a team.

Twelve

THROUGHOUT MY TIME IN WOOLWICH WE constantly tried to assess our work. After about three years it was becoming very doubtful whether we were going to achieve our churchgoing targets, modest as these were. After four and a half years I was convinced that, whatever we did, we would not get a churchgoing breakthrough; I even became increasingly doubtful whether we were going to hold what we had got. Throughout South London congregations, confirmation candidates, Sunday School attendances, christenings and weddings were declining at an unprecedented rate, some as much as thirty-three per cent. Although our congregation in Woolwich was still growing very slowly, the numbers in our Sunday School and youngsters coming forward for confirmation were following the same pattern as the rest of the diocese, despite all our efforts. It was a disappointing and a discouraging situation. For years we had poured big resources of men and money, love and prayers, thought and energy, in what I believe was a well-conceived, carefully planned and thoroughly executed mission. We had maintained for nearly five years a tempo almost similar to that of a three-week General Election campaign.

Of course we could point to the many good things that had been achieved: The church was well known. The

198

clergy were popular and respected. By our very presence around the streets and in the homes we were symbols and reminders of another dimension to life. I have little doubt that thousands had been comforted, reassured and encouraged by our love, our smiles and our words. Perhaps people were also helped by our prayers. We were doing much pastoral counselling. We were meeting some social needs. I hope those we were marrying felt they were being well launched and the relations of those we buried felt their loved ones had been laid to rest with reverence, dignity and hope. I had no way of telling, but perhaps thanks to Woolwich Parish Church the town was a happier, better and more contented place. I am sure we gave the congregation a lot of gaiety. Certainly each of us clergy could think of the handful of people who claimed to have found a deep, abiding and life-transforming faith as a result of our ministry. But the number of young people whom we prepared for confirmation with such meticulous care, but who had left the Church within a year, was very much greater. I am prepared to grant that in all these immeasurable ways, the value of which God alone can judge, we may have been ten times more effective than I imagined even in my most optimistic moments.

Nevertheless by the terms with which the Church has traditionally measured success or failure—our mission was a failure. The fact that in similar areas in London the Church was failing too did not alter the point, although it might soften the blow. It merely meant that at other parish churches the failure was even greater. Ours was probably one of the most 'successful' Anglican churches in working-class riverside London. But our achievement was that in four and a half years the regular members of the congregation had increased from about fifty to 100 mostly drawn from socially superior areas outside our parish. Yet if each priest from our staff had persuaded ten new people each year to join the worshipping community we should have had a regular congregation of 400.

As I realize now, we failed because we never had any chance of succeeding. It was naïve of me to imagine that we could have succeeded—a naïveté, let it be said, that was shared by many others in the leadership of the Church of England. At the time there were many moments when I thought it must have been my fault. But I consoled myself that however bad I was, my colleagues were superb, and I was never so bad as to have prevented them doing their jobs. If I had been they would have been quick to tell me so. The truth was that, as in politics, it is very difficult to go against a trend. Whatever the local candidate does or does not do he has only the most marginal effect on the way people vote. In the 1960s among all classes throughout Britain the trend was away from the Church. Like so many others I believed that if only the Church was more caring, imaginative and energetic, as we had tried so hard to be, it would come alive. In practice, the sociological factors were massively stronger and more influential than we were.

In Woolwich non-churchgoing habits had deep roots going back many generations. They were not to be lightly cast aside. New modern pressures and aspirations were confirming people in their old habits and pulling them further away from the Church. The Church was an institution that looked back. The working men very understandably wanted to forget their past of poverty, squalor and struggle, and the free handouts of a bountiful but patronizing mother Church. They wanted to look forward to the new age that beckoned. An age free from want and bursting with material prosperity. Day after day the television commercials were telling them that lasting happiness lay in the washing machines, the wall-to-wall carpets and the package holidays to the sun in the Costa Brava. The Church of God was no match for this with its message of sin, sacrifice and salvation. And presented so much less professionally as well. As if this was not enough, there was the breakdown in authority which provided release to some and increased uncertainty in others. The days when what the 'vicar says', 'the Church teaches' and 'the Bible reveals' carried weight were fast disappearing. The age of paternalism was over, the age of fraternalism had not yet arrived. We were in the limbo land of the age of adolescence; the age when authority is rejected but when most people lack the maturity to work things out for themselves. My own attitude to these things was contradictory and ambiguous. I welcomed many of those changes in society which may well have been the main causes for our own failure. I could see the standards of living of the people of Woolwich rise before my eyes. It was exciting to see them enjoying things which to their parents twenty or thirty years ago would have seemed inconceivable. There was the pride they were able to take in their well-furnished homes. There was the drudgery from which they had been emancipated by their washing machines. There were the pretty dresses they were able to buy from Marks & Spencer. There was the well-stocked cocktail cabinet in the front room and the sophisticated cheeses from Woolworth's. And as for the pram and layette for the first baby—no Royal babies rode in grander carriages or had softer nappies. When I first went to Woolwich the church cleaner went to Ramsgate for her holidays. By the time I left she was going to the Canary Islands. She had graduated from Torquay, Jersey and Majorca. But more important than this were the bright new purpose-built comprehensive schools and the exciting new ways of education. There were the educational trips the children took to the Continent and the universities and polytechnics for further study. It was the Inner London Education Authority not the Church which was raising hopes, widening opportunities and increasing vision. If a full church was dependent upon having a society of impoverished, struggling peasants keen to keep in with the Rector for the crumbs that might drop from his table, I would rather that the churches be empty. If the only way to get a large congregation was to have it consist of servile, forelock-touching, ill-educated people too fearful to question the wisdom of the 'men of the cloth' proclaiming away above contradiction then I would rather have empty churches.

Of course, I was disappointed about our failure. I had longed so much and had worked so hard to try and take the old traditional ways of the Church, polish them up and give them a face-lift so that God might better use them for the building of His Kingdom. I had staked so much on my belief that it could be done. I was ambitious to see the enormous resources of the Church of England being better used, as I believed the present parochial system was inefficient and wasteful. I believed we had a plan and a policy which could give new life to the Church of England. I went to Woolwich to prove I was right. We wanted to develop a pattern and strategy of parochial ministry, mission and organization which might show the way to the rest of the Church. I hoped that if we could get results the Church at large would follow our lead. Of course, I still believe that our way of doing things and our policy of basing a large staff on a multi-purpose building was more effective than the normal pattern of having a church building on every street corner serviced by a single-handed vicar. But I could not demonstrate it in terms that would be understood and accepted. I knew that our minimal, measurable and definable achievements would be insufficient to convince the Church at large that a drastic face-lift would give it new life.

Nearly twenty years earlier I had lain in my hammock

in HMS *Anson*, sailing the Pacific, and wrestled with the idea of resigning from the Navy in order to become a priest. I knew virtually nothing about the Church of England: but I was aware that it was big and sleepy. I had a feeling that it could be vastly more effective than it was in helping men find faith and so making the world a better place. Everything I saw in the intervening years demonstrated to me the rightness of my hunch and served to increase my determination to play a part in the Church's reformation. But the inescapable lesson of our experiences in Woolwich was that the Church's problems were great, deep, complex and puzzling. A much more radical reappraisal was necessary. The reforms for which I had been pleading and working remained desirable but if implemented would only expose the real problems more clearly. At the theological level radical reappraisals were being made by those more qualified than I. I started trying to work out what it would mean at the parochial level.

I distilled the fruits of my new thinking in a paper which I circulated privately to a few friends. I called it *Stop the Machine, I Want to Get Off*. In it I explained my disillusionment with the traditional role of the parish priest; an amateur all-rounder, called upon only to be nice to everyone he meets. I said, 'There is a sense in which it is true, and not just cynicism, that an automated priest with a perpetual grin on his face, everlastingly wandering around the parish and automatically "mouthing" what would be only quite a small repertoire of platitudes, would meet the vast majority of needs.' I suggested that if the clergy should take up secular employment there would not be any dearth of openings for the parochial clergy in the secular structures. Many of the statutory social services to which clergy may feel drawn are desperately undermanned. In fact, many of the things the clergy do in an amateur way, at the moment, they could be paid for doing—after a 'conversion' course—by the State. Conscientious parish priests spend hours with people who are marginally mentally ill and inadequate, so do psychiatric social workers, who, apart from their greater professional know-how, have the whole resources of the mental health service behind them. And so the list could be extended: Citizens Advice Bureau workers, Youth Employment Officers, Welfare Officers and personal service workers. I concluded, 'Many years ago I stumped the public schools of Britain recruiting men for the parish ministry. I could not do it again. It is not that I regret being a priest. It is that I deeply regret having no other trade or skill. At thirty-six it may now not be too easy for me to break out of the ecclesiastical structures in which I am entombed, but I very much hope that the hundreds of dissatisfied and disillusioned curates will consider doing so—not as a retreat from which they feel guilty, but as an advance which will give them a greater opportunity of serving their God and their Church.'

By chance at this moment, Mr. Graham Watson, the head of Curtis Brown, the literary agents, invited me to lunch. He had heard about what we were doing in Woolwich and was trying to persuade me to write a book on how the Church of England could be resurrected into new life. I told him that was asking too much as I was not sure how it could be done. I went on to tell him about our experiences in Woolwich. He thought they would make a good feature for one of the Sunday colour supplements. The idea appealed to me. I felt we had a good story to tell and deductions to draw from it which were vitally important to the Church. The fee was attractive. It would pay the salary for a member of staff for a year. As the tombola craze was on the wane and the income from it correspondingly down, I was desperately pressed to meet the monthly salary cheque for the staff. The fee for a major article would take me off the hook for a month or two.

I have little doubt that the *Observer*, to whom Graham Watson first offered the idea of the article, would have taken it and paid the same princely fee if I had written, as I easily could have done, a fundamentally dishonest article: the exciting story of a Georgian ecclesiastical white elephant on the banks of the Thames being transformed into a multi-purpose centre used by 1500 people a week. The life-saving Samaritan service had produced a host of moving human stories which could have been turned into several columns of readable copy. The very idea of young men with knapsacks full of first-class Honours degrees turning their backs on the world's rewards, to slog round the hard pavements of working-class Woolwich might sound very like the *Boys' Own Paper*, but it could also have been dressed up in a way to appeal to the radical, intelligent middle-class readers of the *Observer*. And the Church of England would have been very pleased with it and with me! The Church was looking for straws to clutch at. The fact of 'grand chaps' doing a 'grand job' in a 'grim place' would have reassured its leaders. It would have been worth a couple of minutes' comment at a bishops' meeting or over dinner at the Athenaeum.

I could not write such an article because it has always seemed to me that the first task of the Church is building up the worshipping community. Failure at this point is not compensated for by successful suicide squads, housing associations, coffee bars and tombola games. There are plenty of other organizations doing these things. The uniqueness of the Church is that it claims to be the Body of Christ in the world with the message of salvation. When I was inducted as Rector of Woolwich my duties were set out for me in the service by the Archdeacon. He said, 'Hear the words of Our Lord. Go ye therefore and make disciples of all nations.' To this I replied, 'I will do so the Lord being my helper.' I had sealed my brief down a bit and substituted the people of Woolwich for all nations. And it was in this, my very first task of making disciples, that we had so clearly failed.

It is no credit to me that it never occurred to me to write an article that would be acclaimed in the Church. It would have been out of character for me to do so. And so the article I wrote was a summary of the tale I have tried to tell in the last few chapters of this book. It aimed to be a truthful account of what had happened at Woolwich during my first four and a half years as its Rector. I started, 'We have had a remarkable opportunity of making a breakthrough in getting people to come to church. We have played every card in the pack. We have done everything we set out to do. But we have achieved virtually not one of the modest things we hoped for . . . We have no excuses. These have been the most dramatic and exhausting years of my life. We have laughed and occasionally wept. We have tried to pray and to love. We have been as brazen as a Dean Street publicity agent and we have tried to be humble and sensitive. We have raised a fortune and spent it. We have quite obviously failed.' I then listed the things we had done. I went on to say, 'Living among the trees it is not easy to see the wood and if I try to discover the lessons of the last five gruelling years I am faced at once with the absurd contradiction—God is desperately needed and yet I have reached the point where I can see little chance of our capturing people's imaginations by the traditional methods however lovingly, vigorously and imaginatively performed over however long a period. Indeed I believe it may get harder still as the residue of formal Christianity disappears and the secularization of society is completed.' I continued by describing our future plans about the clergy taking secular jobs and finished, 'No doubt some would interpret this as a council of despair—a retreat for those who have lost their nerve and whose faith has got wobbly. To us it seems an advance. For hundreds of years the ecclesiastical structures have served society fairly well. Today they are becoming increasingly irrelevant. It is the secular ones that determine the shape and tone of the world. If the Christian has anything to say he must say it from within them. It will be disastrous for us to generalize for the Church at large from our particular experience at Woolwich. But I suspect that we, and perhaps the Church too, have more to learn from our failure than we would have done had we in fact been successful.'

The piece was written in one night between midnight and dawn because I was pressed for time. (I remember thinking that it was the first time in my life that I had earned so much money for a night's work.) Despite the speed I took a lot of trouble over it. Before sending it to the *Observer*, my brother Tom, who at that time was Chief Foreign Correspondent for the *Sunday Times* and a highly respected journalist, worked over it. After the article came out, the *Sunday Times* rang me to say that they were disappointed that they had not been offered it in the first place. It was offered to the *Observer* because I thought its readers would better understand and be more sympathetic to what I was trying to say. In fact I had a slight *contretemps* with the Deputy Editor of the *Observer Colour Supplement*. We agreed that the article should be called 'A Mission's Failure'. But I thought it ought to have a question mark after it. I was told that it would weaken it and did not press the point. Perhaps I ought to have done.

Some of my friends told me that the piece I wrote was a compulsive article. By that they meant that I was so disappointed that I had failed to achieve the unrealistic targets I had set myself at Woolwich that I had to get my failure off my chest, before the largest possible audience.

It was, they said, a kind of public self-flagellation, or was it like the murderer who creeps back to the scene of the crime almost hoping that the television cameras will be there to film him re-enacting the event? How else, they asked, can one explain that someone like me, who, to some extent, needed and thrived on success, could proclaim failure to the world. I know how easy it is to rationalize one's actions after an event: nevertheless, I believe I was quite clear about my reasons for writing it the way I did. Above all I wanted it to be an article of integrity.

Incidentally the same kind of integrity was shown by Ian Berry, who took the photographs which illustrated it. Berry, who first made his name with his photographs of Sharpeville, arranged to come and see me at 11.00 one morning. We were well accustomed to photographers visiting us and had a stock routine. We would chat them up for half an hour while we were giving them a cup of coffee and then take them to three or four points from which they could get a good photograph and pack them off back to Fleet Street by lunchtime. I was planning the usual routine for Berry, but I found him such an intensely interesting and fascinating person that we talked for an hour and a half. By 12.30 I suggested that he ought to take his photographs and that he would just have time to do so before lunch. He gave me what I can only describe as a peculiar look and explained that if he were to get under the skin of Woolwich and get the feel of our work there he would want to be by our sides day and night for at least ten days. And so he was. The only thing he did not do was to photograph us in bed. The same integrity and concern were shown a few months later when Mr. Guy Brenton did a documentary on our work for BBC television.

But I wanted the article to be more than just truthful. I wanted it to alert the Church. After all, in Woolwich we had been able, through no merit on our part, to put into operation many of the policies, reforms and ideas which were being widely canvassed as the answer to the Church's ills. In most parishes in England, the cry was, 'If only . . . we should be able to make a breakthrough in winning the hearts of men and women to a living faith. If only we had more staff, more cooperative church-wardens, more progressive congregations, more friendly parishioners, more money, etc . . .' We had in Woolwich almost everything the rest of the Church was asking for. And yet we had failed. Another reason for writing was in the hope that it would be an encouragement to large numbers of dedicated clergy and church people who, I knew, felt that the lack of response they had experienced in their parishes sprang from some personal failure on their part. I remembered so well the extreme depression felt by many of the clergy working in the intractable areas in Birmingham; how they felt, how they cried, how some of them had breakdowns—all this was written on my heart. I hoped that when they read my piece they would feel less of failures themselves. Finally, I wanted to show that while in the respect of churchgoing we had been prepared to admit failure we were not defeated and were searching for more relevant ways of ministry.

Anyway, the article caused a stir. It touched a sensitive nerve in the Church of England. Letters poured in in their hundreds and just as I thought we were about to break surface from the flood that overwhelmed us, the article would be reproduced in another part of the world and the flood would start all over again. It was like bathing in a rough sea. No sooner had one picked oneself up after being bowled over by one mighty wave than one was hit by another. I had everything thrown at me from the inevitable used lavatory paper to a bishop saying I was killing the Church of England. Reactions were interesting.

w.c.—o

There were a few who were grateful that I had exposed the real position and faced the facts of the Church's situation. Such people believed that this was a necessary first step in the radical renewal of the Church. In percentage terms these letters were a minority. In the terms of the people who wrote them the quality made up for a lack of quantity. At a time when I was being almost battered into sensibility, it was an encouragement that those whose judgement I valued most welcomed and understood the article. Underlying the vast majority of the letters I sensed a deep reluctance to contemplate the failure and possible collapse of the present ecclesiastical system. I was told that one could not measure anything by numbers in church, that five years was too short a time to assess results, or results are unimportant anyway. It is being faithful that matters. Of course, I had not said that the number of worshippers is the only yardstick for measuring the effectiveness of a church. Nevertheless, I had always understood that the traditional teaching of the Churches throughout the ages had been that regular worship with one's fellow Christians round the Lord's table on the Lord's day is an essential but not the only expression of the committed Christian life.

There was much doublethink in letters which took me up on this point. Because the Church was not being successful in persuading people to worship many were shifting their ground and saying it was Christian kindness, the giving of solace or helping people in their personal relationships which was the real test. I thought the Church must make up her mind what she was aiming to do. At the moment the whole massive and time-absorbing and enormously expensive ecclesiastical organization, with its 22,000 Anglican places of worship in England and Wales alone, was being kept going because the fundamental *raison d'être* of the Church is worship. If in the Church's strategy it has ceased to be a top priority or if it is incapable of fulfilment it seemed to me grotesque to go on appointing priests to be vicars of churches with a seating capacity of 1000 and a congregation of twenty. To those who wrote to me in this vein I replied if kindness is all, would not the Church be better working within the social services and should not we stop trying to maintain a vast and expensive structure geared to encourage worship? I was not persuaded by those who told me that five years was too short a time to learn in which direction the pendulum was swinging. The correspondents who stressed this point gave me the impression that they were really only whistling to keep up their own spirits. My belief is that society is changing so fast that five years today is like fifty years a generation ago. Although it was contrary to conventional wisdom, my experience in the ministry has always been that one either gets results soon or not at all. Much as I would liked to have thought otherwise I can find very little evidence that I have reaped where others have sown, or vice versa. The inescapable fact was the ever-increasing alienation of modern man from the Church. To those who stressed the need for faithfulness I tried to point out that having said that they had not said all: it was important to be faithful about the right things and in the right way. Faithfully maintaining the parochial structures and ministry or even Cranmer's services might not necessarily mean that one was being faithful to the Kingdom of God.

Hundreds more wrote in to tell me what I should have done to have made the whole thing a success. Brian Cooper who had a beard should have cut it off. We should or should not have worn cassocks. God could not have possibly blessed our venture because we organized bingo. There was one comment widely made in condemnation of my article. It was that the team at Woolwich was unsuitable for the task. Its members were too bright, too impatient, too articulate and too fast-moving. Surely, said these armchair critics, who had never been near Woolwich, far less seen the team at work, slower, plodding men would have done better and the parishioners would not have been overwhelmed by such a star-studded cast. I know these criticisms to be totally untrue. I have learned, the more gifted the priest the better he was at the job. When I peeped over the parochial fence into other parishes in South London and saw how little was being done in many of them by those men, who, it was being claimed, were more suitable for the parochial round, I used to get very cross.

The loudest protests of all came from the bishops of the Church of England. The Archbishop of Canterbury devoted the whole of his monthly letter in his diocesan leaflet to the subject. He finished it by saying, 'As soon as this sort of success or failure discussion starts, by its very nature it secularizes the issue and carries it far from the joy of the angels over one sinner who repents.' The Archbishop of York accused me of 'rocking the boat'. The Bishop of London said that, 'Defeatism must be completely and utterly rejected,' to which one correspondent to *The Times* commented, 'Too often the word "defeatist" is used for those who draw attention to the unpalatable facts of a situation and who call for that situation to be dealt with as urgently and courageously as the facts warrant. There is no greater problem before the Church today than that of its mission to the masses of the people in the great cities. But there is little evidence that the general body of the Church either realizes the extent of the problem or the radical action required to remedy it.' He put it well, and indeed one of my reasons for writing in the first place was to try and shake the Church out of its lethargy and complacency. One bishop, who had better be nameless, said there was no need to believe what Stacey said as he only did it for the money. I must say it was somewhat daunting being described as a kind of male whore by a bishop of the Church while one was trying to serve as a priest.

As Mervyn Stockwood never discussed the article with me, I do not know what he thought about it. But writing in his Southwark diocesan news sheet three months after the article was published, he sat on the fence, an unusual position for him. He said, 'There are still reverberations from the article written by one of our clergy, Mr. Stacey . . . without subscribing to all that Mr. Stacey wrote I hope a sensible discussion will continue.' He then suggested five good points for consideration by the diocese which made me think that he had a lively understanding of the situation. Amongst the bishops Robinson alone openly supported me. My first reaction to their onslaught was to feel hurt. I thought it was a pity that a number of the bishops should have doubted my motives and questioned my integrity. I believed it was I who was caring about the Church, showing moral courage and attempting to point the way to the future: it was they who were dodging the issues. Instead, all I got was abuse and they accused me 'of washing the Church's dirty linen in public', 'of being a traitor' and of being a 'self-seeking publicist'.

Hurt turned into anger; anger that the leaders of the Church were either so blind or so complacent or so insensitive or so fearful that they could not see that I was saying something true and important, however unpalatable it might be. I realized that some of them thought my article would discourage the parochial clergy and they wanted to protect them. I think they gravely misjudged the effect it had. My massive postbag suggested that it had helped the clergy. As a result of it I think that many parochial clergymen became more relaxed, less anxious and introspective about what they wrongly considered to be their personal failure to fill the churches. In a paradoxical way it gave them encouragement and hope. They began to feel that if we could not do it in Woolwich with all our advantages they would not be able to do it either and it was now no good worrying about it. It seems to me a denial of episcopal leadership to try to persuade the clergy that all was well with the Church of England. The effect on the clergy was merely to convince them that the bishops were out of touch. No one is impressed by the captain who sings lullabies, mouths platitudes and issues bromides when every member of the crew and the passengers can see the ship is sinking. Surely it is the captain's job to get the crew to trim the sails, and plug the holes.

In retrospect, perhaps I was too harsh in my judgement of the Church leaders. I understand now what I did not altogether understand then. Their inability to face facts springs from a psychological defence mechanism. For many of them I believe it is only by continuing to live in a fantasy world that they are able to carry on and continue to operate the largely irrelevant ecclesiastical machine. If they acknowledged the true situation to themselves I am sure that many of them would collapse. That an increasing number of ordinary clergymen have at least understood the situation accounts, surely, for the high breakdown rate amongst the clergy in recent years.

When one is the centre of a controversy, which in this case went on for many months, one is not always the best person to assess the effects. It has been said that what John Robinson's book, *Honest to God* was to theology, my article, *A Mission's Failure*, was to parochial life. This may be an exaggeration but I sense that since my article nobody any longer expects a working-class parish to come alive in the traditional way. Certainly many of the predictions that I made in this and other articles have come to pass. There is a certain irony in the fact that many of the things for which I was roundly condemned seven years ago have now become part of conventional wisdom and are today incorporated in the sermons and speeches of some of those who were loudest in their accusations of me.

But there was one certain effect of the article. The ecclesiastical establishment has not forgiven me for it. Over two years later, Dr. Stockwood was dining quietly at my home. He was the only guest. We had dined well and, in a relaxed mood in the early hours of the morning, I mentioned to him that after six years in Woolwich I felt I had given what I could to the place and ought to move. He told me that apart from the Bishop of Birmingham, whose chaplain I had been, in his opinion no other bishop in the Church of England would offer me a job for many years to come. He went on to describe his own experiences and how he was in Bristol as a vicar for fourteen years before he was offered another job in the Church. I kept the thought to myself that he had made more enemies than I ever had. And so I only half believed him. I promised myself that I would wait a further two years—until my fortieth birthday—to see if the Church came up with an offer. If nothing had happened by then, I would consider seeking full-time employment outside the Church.

Thirteen

THE AFTERMATH OF 'A MISSION'S FAILURE' was a flood of invitations to do lecture tours, broadcasts and more articles, especially for the American press. I declined most of them, as I was still involved in a punishing fourteen-hours-a-day programme at Woolwich, but I did agree to appear on a couple of television programmes.

One was *Not So Much A Programme* which at that time was at the height of its popularity. Apparently in the programme the week prior to my appearance a considerable amount of time had been devoted to making fun of church-going. In an attempt to redress the balance it was thought that they ought to have a clergyman on to have his say. Presumably I was invited because I was in the news at the time. Actually I was the first clergyman ever to appear on the programme. In talking to David Frost I made it quite clear that I would only appear on the condition that he interview me on the *Observer* article and its implications for the Church; that mixing it with a panel made up of the highly intelligent, articulate, amusing and somewhat cynical literary figures who appeared regularly, was well out of my league. David Frost knew that as I had been buried in Woolwich for the previous five years I was out of practice at witty pseudo-Oxbridge high-table television talk. He was given a list of clergymen whom I thought would be more suitable. He insisted that I appear and agreed to the stipulated conditions.

It was to be a Sunday evening programme. I was preaching at the Evening Service at St. Mary's and therefore arrived after the three other distinguished literary guests who were on the panel that week. They had already started on the drinks that preceded the luxurious dinner we were to have before broadcasting. (In the BBC the more prestigious the programme, the more lavish the hospitality. *Not So Much A Programme* was very prestigious.) The talk before dinner was mainly about the bizarre activities of various well-known theatre personalities: I was not able to contribute to this. All the current television lions were at the dinner party—Donald Baverstock and Alistair Milne and the BBC's two whizz kids, Ned Sherrin and David Frost, the panel and myself. I felt like the country cousin visiting London for the day and was able to take little part in the dinner-table conversation with its 'in' jokes about the entertainment world.

But halfway through the dinner the female member of the panel, who the television correspondent of the *Church Times* described as 'violent with her vituperation', turned to me at the other end of the table and asked what I was doing there. The remark was made in a tone of voice which implied that she thought the butler should have swept me out with the crumbs of the previous course. I told her that Mr. Frost was going to interview me on a recent article of mine. She responded by saying that she thought this was an extraordinarily boring idea. The other members of the panel quickly agreed with her and the woman suggested that it would be much more amusing to have a general discussion in which the panel could take part on some theory that had apparently recently been propounded about Christ being mentally deranged. I told them that I had not heard of this particular theory and was totally ill-equipped to discuss it and had in any case only agreed to appear on the programme at all on the condition that I was interviewed by Mr. Frost on his own. David Frost supported me, but I began to feel more and more unsporting, feeble and dim. By then there was about an hour before we were due on the air and I suggested that if this new subject was the one they wanted to talk about there was just still time to get a suitable clergyman. I mentioned possible names. After a few minutes of further discussion it was decided that it was too late to get anybody else and the general opinion was that they were landed with me who I am sure they felt to be a boring and inadequate little man. Trying not to be too pompous, but feeling very insecure, I stuck my toes in and suggested that much the fairest thing to do was either to carry the item in the way that had been arranged or cut it out altogether. The producers did not want it cut out because they had promised the powers-that-be that a clergyman would appear in that week's programme. I sensed they were rapidly losing confidence in me. Equally they did not want to upset the panel who were determined to air their views about this new theory on Christ. By this time there were only a few minutes before we were due on the air for what was a live show.

Literally, as we were being called to the studio for voice-level tests, Ned Sherrin suggested a compromise: David Frost would interview me first for a few minutes and then throw the discussion open to the panel. I was reluctant to agree but was in a terrible dilemma. Had I walked out it was likely that it would have caused a row in the newspapers because everything that happened or did not happen on the programme was news. I had little stomach for being the centre of yet another controversy. Further, my general contention about the Church was that it should mix with the world and not always want to have the last word. To have run out would have been to do the very thing that I was often accusing the Church of doing. But by going on I thought there was a real risk that I would be massacred by this formidable trio and do harm to the Christian faith. I would also be put to another disadvantage, which may seem small but can be significant as I had learnt from my experience in previous television programmes. Anyone who joins a programme in the middle (as it was planned that I should do) to argue with a panel which has been on the set and participating throughout, finds them relaxed, warmed up and confident, while the newcomer is still trying to get the feel. I decided that the lesser of the two evils was to appear.

My item was last on the programme and I think some ten to fifteen minutes had been allocated to it. The earlier sketches and discussions had over-run and by the time I came on there were only about five minutes left. I was relieved at this as I thought that with a bit of luck I could spin it out with David Frost and so keep the vultures out of the act altogether. But David Frost, too, had obviously been keeping his eye on the clock, and instead of spending a few minutes interviewing me he spent what seemed to be only a few seconds before turning to the panel for their say. Two of them were like a pair of hungry hounds poised to tear apart an exhausted and cornered hare. It was their very viciousness that saved me. No sooner had one finished a spiel of ill-thought-out criticisms of Christianity than the other would come in and take up the cudgels. Every time I tried to open my mouth to answer some of the points they were making I was subjected to another barrage. The more they snorted, the more I smiled. Baverstock, the Head of BBC Television, who was in the Control Room, and had the authority to extend the length of the programme, thought all this was splendid television and allowed it to run overtime. While I was able to get in the odd interjection here and there it was not until the end that I was given a chance of answering back. The *Church Times*, which rarely misses an opportunity of attacking me, was gracious enough to comment, 'And then for a few seconds Mr. Stacey—or Nick, as he was called—was given an opportunity to reply. He did it very well but he had to talk at breathtaking speed to comply with the timing.'

Going back to Woolwich in the taxi that night I was very gloomy. I did not think I had done very well and I thought I might have let the Church down. The outcome was interesting. While I gathered that official complaints were made to the Archbishop of Canterbury and to the BBC about the unfairness of the programme—complaints which I did not join in—I had never before received so many letters from viewers congratulating me on my performance in a television programme. It was not what I said, the way I said it or that I smiled. It was, I am sure, because the British are instinctively on the side of the underdog. And that night I was clearly the underdog numerically as well as intellectually. I suspect there is an important lesson for the Church to learn from my unnerving experience. When it seems to be beaten in debate it often wins in reality. The more the Church is persecuted, the more it comes alive.

I recall the other television programme for different reasons. It was a 'religious slot' BBC television programme (therefore very low prestige—coffee and sandwiches instead of the wine, brandy and butlers laid on for *Not So Much A Programme*). The subject was *A Mission's Failure*. The format was a short film on Woolwich with street interviews on what local people thought of the work of the Church, followed by a statement from me summarizing my article. The programme was to finish with a studio discussion between Mervyn Stockwood, the Reverend Eric

James, James Mitchell—a young publisher—and myself. Mr. Robert Mackenzie was in the chair. The BBC were delighted that they had got Dr. Stockwood to appear. I was apprehensive. I did not want to have a row with him on television because he was, after all, my employer. On the other hand, if he decided to attack the article, as I had been tipped off was likely, or mouth episcopal platitudes, I was determined not to let him get away with it. We sat in the studio watching the film on Woolwich which I had not seen before. My heart sank when the splendid man who was doing such an outstanding job running bingo in our miserable little mission hall and whom we had seconded on to the PCC said, 'You don't have to go to church to be a Christian. And I rarely go myself.' I winced at the thought of the letters that would appear in the *Church Times* and was glad that I would be safely out of the country in Nigeria when the programme went on the air a couple of days later. I feared that this innocent and harmless remark would be used as a stick to beat us with, and give church people an excuse for dismissing what we did at Woolwich as gimmicks.

My predictions were accurate and the following letter actually appeared in the *Church Times*. 'Sir, if the bingo operator at Mr. Stacey's church, Woolwich, who we saw on Sunday's *Meeting Point* is typical of the Parochial Church Council of the parish church it is hardly surprising that the church's minion there has been regarded as a failure. As a non-churchgoer this person has no right to hold an opinion, let alone be on the PCC. His attitudes towards the Christian faith is doing irreparable harm to the Gospel of Christ and obviously he hasn't the faintest notion as to what Christianity is about.' It was typical of the hundreds I received.

The film ground on and the discussion started with Mac-kenzie asking Mervyn Stockwood whether in his judgement our work at Woolwich had been a failure. Dr. Stockwood did as I feared: he never attempted to answer the question and replied with irrelevant platitudes. I told him he was ducking the issue but otherwise held my fire. And I was glad I did, because by the end of the programme, he had done a complete *volte face*, and in the view of one commentator on the programme, took up a position almost indistinguishable from mine. I thought the most significant feature of an otherwise uninteresting programme was the way that it showed up Dr. Stockwood. He is able to maintain the Establishment position for a short time, but in the end, and with his friends, in a state of exasperation he comes down on the side of truth and humanity.

Another drama took place behind the scenes. We were all in the hospitality room chattering nervously, and nibbling nuts prior to the programme, when we were introduced to a blind Indian journalist. It is not unusual for journalists, PROs and personal assistants to hang around hospitality rooms at television studios before and after programmes, and as my mind was focused on the extent to which it would be wise to clobber Mervyn Stockwood, I did not take much notice of him. I gathered he was writing a series of articles on the new theologians and recall telling him that I could not be much help to him as not even my greatest fan would ever describe me as a theologian new or old. When the programme was over Eric James and I were about to share a taxi home when we saw the blind journalist standing by the outside doors of the studio looking lost. (I later discovered that he was Mr. Ved Mehta, who was a distinguished writer for the *New Yorker*.) We offered him a lift. Eric James, who was a very old friend of mine, and I were in a relaxed mood after the strain of the programme and were gossiping and joking away in the back of the taxi. We dropped Mr. Mehta at a tube station and Eric James actually saw him on to a train. I flew to Africa the next day and thought no more about it. Some months later a sub-editor on the *New Yorker* rang me from New York to check two facts in Mehta's article. He wanted to know how many clergy there were in the Diocese of Southwark and whether Mehta was accurate in reporting that I had been paid a certain figure for my *Observer* article. I told him that it was none of the *New Yorker*'s business how much I got paid and any reference to a sum must be taken out of the article, which he agreed to do—a promise that was not kept. A week or two later Mehta sent me a copy of the *New Yorker* from America, asking for my comments. He had devoted pages to an almost verbatim account of the television programme, spiced with extracts of the conversations he had had in the hospitality room plus even spicier bits of what he claimed to be part of my conversation with Eric in the back of the taxi. The imaginative details he used were damaging and embarrassing to Mervyn Stockwood and Eric James, and libellous to me. There was nothing I could do about the *New Yorker* in America as the issue had already been distributed. My solicitors told me the article was defamatory and libellous and that I could take out an injunction in the High Court preventing that issue of the *New Yorker* being distributed in Britain.

I decided there was no point in joining battle with the *New Yorker*, but would try and get Harper & Row, the highly respected American publishers, to make the necessary changes in the book of Mehta's articles, which they were bringing out. By chance I happened to be in New York for a few days in order to do a series of broadcasts. It was at the time other people (who included most of the leading British theologians) were writing to Harper & Row to complain that Mehta had misunderstood, misrepresented or misquoted them. The publishers soon realized that it was not just me making an unnecessary fuss, and promised to make the changes for which I was asking. The book did eventually come out but certainly aroused little interest in Britain. Nevertheless, this transatlantic *contretemps* was a diversion I would rather have done without.

I also went on a five-week whirlwind tour of Africa. After five years in Woolwich and a couple of months' hammering as a result of the *Observer* piece, I felt I needed a break to get my second wind.

In my very first weekend in Africa I took part in a service in the back streets of Lagos which had everything we had failed to achieve in Woolwich. I had told the African Bishop of Lagos that I wanted to go to a typical downtown Anglican African parish church. It was lucky that I arrived twenty minutes before the service was due to start else I would not have got a seat. I was the only white person in the congregation, the service was Cranmer's Matins which has never greatly excited me and the whole thing was in Yoruba so I did not understand a word. It was indescribably thrilling. It was what I had always felt, but so rarely experienced, the worship of God to be all about. It was warm, sincere, uninhibited, uplifting and enormously vital. Everyone was taking part, enjoying it, believing it, and getting something out of it. I was profoundly moved to know that they could do in Lagos what we could not do in Woolwich. I have not had the answer. I thought how fabulous and enormously worthwhile all the sweat, tears and toil of Woolwich would have been if we had been able to recreate just something of what the Africans had created.

There was a similar experience in Accra only a couple of days later. The revered and saintly Anglican Bishop of Accra, Richard Roseveare, was my host. The Bishop, who was a monk, was so respected and loved that he was the only man President Nkrumah had deported whom he had to allow back to the country.

My visit coincided with a Church festival and the Bishop asked me if I would like to go to Communion. Naturally I fell in with this plan and he told me that I would be roused at 4.00 am. I suggested that this was really rather overdoing it and as I assumed that only he and I and perhaps some of the servants would be at the service we might consider holding it at a rather more civilized hour. He explained that we were going to a local parish church near the Accra market, which was well patronized by the famous market mamas, who would be making their Communion before opening their stalls. The service would therefore start at 4.30 am. To me it was almost unbelievable to see the next morning 900 people at a mid-week Holy Communion service starting at that hour. The Anglican Church arrived in Ghana fairly late in the day. The first Bishop was only appointed in 1909, and yet after this comparatively short time they had congregations which no Church of England cathedral or parish church in Britain could get within a mile of mustering.

On the way to the service the Bishop told me that the market mamas were one of the most powerful groups in Ghana and once they had decided that they had had enough of Nkrumah his days would be numbered. I sat in the gallery of the church so that I could better absorb the totally memorable scene. The view I got was a sea of gay multicoloured skirts covering huge upturned bottoms as they knelt in humble reverence and awe to receive the Communion of the Body and Blood of Our Lord. As the market mamas held out their rough pink hands to take the consecrated bread one realized that these were the hands that were not only holding the power of God in the Sacrament, but a considerable part of the political power of the land as well. My mind switched back to Woolwich where there might have been three or four people, without any influence or power, at a similar service.

W.C.—P

In the evening of the same day I joined an enormous procession of the faithful on a march through the streets of Accra. We all carried lanterns and sang hymns as we went. The inhabitants came out on to the pavements and sang the hymns with us as we passed. Hundreds of children ran along with us clapping and chanting, grinning and smiling.

I recalled how the world leader of the Salvation Army had come to visit the Salvation Army Citadel at Woolwich: I wanted to try and make it a very special occasion and invited him to preach at Woolwich Parish Church and arranged for the Salvation Army band to sit all round the altar in the sanctuary of the church during the service. In return it was arranged that I should join the Salvation Army chief and give a talk with him in Beresford Market Square, the normal Salvation Army Sunday meeting place, prior to us all marching from the Square to the parish church. As we moved down the streets of Woolwich the inhabitants closed their windows to shut out the noise of the band and our half-hearted singing. Those who we passed by on the pavement gave us that 'Why can't you belt up?' look. It was all very different from Accra. Yet it is, I fear, no more than a romantic dream that the African Christians will come as missionaries to Britain to convert us. The relentless forces of secularism, for good or ill and much of it is for good, that have swept the advanced nations of the world are already beginning to sweep Africa.

The Bishop of Accra's household was remarkable. There seemed to be hundreds of hangers-on living in the very modest and somewhat scruffy episcopal compound. Impoverished as he was himself, he provided a kind of haven for some of the unemployed and unemployable. On the last evening of my three-day visit I asked him to tell me who I should tip and how much, as I was anxious not to do the wrong thing. His eyes twinkled at this, and he drew

up a list which seemed to cover several sheets of foolscap.
Even though the services I had received from most of the
people on the list had been no more than marginal. I told
him I thought I was paying the wages for his entire household for a month and that it would have been cheaper, but
not so much fun, to have stayed at the Hilton. With another twinkle he told me that I had assessed the situation
very accurately. I was very happy to do as the Bishop advised me. After the largesse that had been so delightfully
winkled out of me, it came as no great surprise that large
numbers of enchanting youngsters of the household came
to say goodbye to me on the following morning, and indeed fought as to who should carry my case to the car.
They not only wanted my autograph but were equally
keen to have my address in Britain. I wondered why they
were so particularly anxious to know the day by which I
would be at home. Innocently I gave them all the information they asked for. By some extraordinary coincidence the
mothers and fathers of the children of the episcopal household all seemed to go sick together at a time which coincided with my return to Britain, which, as the letters to
me from their children pointed out, meant that they would
not be able to pay their school fees. It was just as well that
I had begun to earn my living in secular employment otherwise I should not have been able to educate the children as
well as pay their parents' wages. As I told the Bishop later
it was one of the most enjoyable and expensive three days
of my life.

   After visiting the Congo, Zambia and Rhodesia, I went
to South Africa. I told the people of Woolwich of my im-
pressions in an article which I wrote for the local paper.
I said, 'The fundamental difference between South Africa
and the independent African nations, is that the former
is going absolutely in the wrong direction and the latter,
in spite of all their difficulties, are staggering forward in

the right one. Time, I believe, will solve many of the problems of the new African states. Time must make the situation in South Africa worse.'

A number of my liberal friends in South Africa begged me to contact and try and look after those young members of the African Resistance Movement who had been tortured by the South African Police after their arrest, turned State evidence against their friends, were released in return and had fled to Britain feeling ashamed and dispirited. I felt deeply for them. I could well have imagined myself being a member of the African Resistance Movement had I been living in South Africa and more easily still, imagined myself cracking under torture and continuous cross-examination by the highly professional South African Police. I was able to find one of them when I returned to Britain and he made our home a base. The Movement, which was involved in sabotage, was being much criticized at the time as being childish, amateur and ineffective. I was glad to be able to write a long article on its activities in the Weekend Review of the *Observer*. I finished the piece by saying, 'I believe that when the tragic history of the past few years in South Africa comes to be written what is now dismissed as a futile gesture will be seen to have been a brave effort of a group of whites to bring their fellows to their senses.'

Fourteen

THE CLOSING MONTHS OF 1964 WERE dark days for me. I had become a priest in the Church of England because as a Christian I thought that of all the institutions I knew, the Church of God was the one that should be the most concerned and effective in changing lives and transforming society. I spurned the possibilities of a career in politics, Fleet Street or the City, all of which had styles of life which I would have found much more congenial. From the day that I visited Hiroshima my concern was to use my life to help play a part however small in making the world a better place. It may have been immature and idealistic of me but it was genuine. The priesthood as a mere job—as a way of earning a living—had never greatly appealed to me. The places where one was expected to live were not ones that I would have chosen for my wife and family. If one was conscientious the hours were long and because one lived above the shop one was never off duty. One rarely had a weekend off and the pay was ridiculous. I used to earn in two hours writing articles for newspapers what I earned in two weeks as Rector of Woolwich. I had no taste for theological hair splitting. Ecclesiastical jokes, gossip and tittle-tattle bored me. But all this and more was a price I would have gladly paid and to some degree was paying in Woolwich, if it was actually doing any good. But if it was to prop up an institution which was slowly dying and having little influence on men or affairs, then it was a heavy price to pay.

I was becoming increasingly doubtful whether the Church of England had the energy or the will to reform itself. All my hopes that this mighty organization could be mobilized and galvanized into becoming a great power for good were ebbing away. A group of us had raised enough money to enable the Reverend Eric James to leave his South London parish in Camberwell and stump the country. He was attempting to raise the banner of radical reform and persuade the clergy to welcome the Beeching-type report on the Church produced by Mr. Leslie Paul in 1964. For, if his recommendations in this report were adopted, it would at least have ensured that the Church's resources of men and money were deployed where the people are living today instead of the present system which deploys them where the people lived in the Middle Ages. James reported that there was little enthusiasm for drastic change. I did not doubt his word. All the evidence pointed the same way. My deep fear was that, if the Church continued along its present path, it would, instead of dying graciously and willingly in its present form, use its last gasps to complain bitterly about the hardness of men's hearts and the faithlessness of our generation. I knew that many Church leaders were pinning their faith on the Church being able to reform its structures, as Leslie Paul recommended. But, as was shown in the debates at Convocation over reunion with the Methodists, when the crunch comes it drags its feet, loses its nerve and compromises fatally. I had been clamouring as loudly as anyone for reforms, but I was beginning to realize that in the very unlikely event of them being pushed through they would merely save the Church as a religious club. This upset me greatly. For some time I had had a love-hate relationship with the Church of England but I had never lost confidence in its potential. Now I was beginning to be overwhelmed by the tragedy and futility of its situation. On the one hand, one knew that people were hungry for something which would give meaning to their lives which they certainly were not finding outside the Church. On the other hand, there was this massive ecclesiastical organization—by far and away the largest voluntary organization in Britain with its 15,000 clergymen in full-time employment and its annual income from the living and the dead of £42½ million—floundering around like a great dinosaur. It would have to die before it could live again.

So I began to see that the resurrected Church would no longer express its life in mighty buildings, massive organizations, and in its own schools and colleges, all of which symbolize a Church concerned with worldly power and status. The new Church some of us were wanting to see would not be a great estate of the realm rivalling the Institute of Directors and the Trades Union Congress. It would bear no resemblance to a religious club. Its work would be done without fuss or publicity through small groups of people meeting in their own homes and places of work—for communion—working out together what it meant to be a Christian in the world, for friendship at a deep level and for planning how they could best serve the community through the secular, statutory and voluntary organizations. As I saw it, the new-look Church would require the maximum of trained, articulate laity and the minimum of paid clergy, organizations and buildings. Indeed, I began to wonder whether there was any reason why Christians should not hire the local school for an hour on Sunday for their act of corporate worship. This was all very different from the hopes I had of the Church when I was ordained. It was wildly different from what

I thought the Church would ever voluntarily accept for itself. I was very doubtful whether it would be prepared to lose its life in order to find it. I reckoned that time and economic pressures would gradually bring this about. But the enormous inherited wealth of the Church administered by the Church Commissioners would enable it to keep going for many years even if there was little life or relevance left in it. The parochial clergy would increasingly become part geriatric nurse, part undertaker. This was not a role that I had envisaged for myself when I decided to become a priest.

Perhaps I expected too much and worried too much. Perhaps I cared too much.

Anyway, for me it was a poignant situation. If my theological insights were right and the growth points in our society did lie mainly in the secular structures then the most worthwhile places to be were in those very professions on which I had reluctantly turned my back fifteen years earlier. Thus, at the very time some of my friends were becoming Ministers in the Government, editors of papers and partners in merchant banks I was doubtful whether the organization I had joined was doing much good. It seemed to me that I had two alternatives. I could either try and go into politics or stay at Woolwich and attempt to develop the new pattern of ministry I had outlined in my article, *Stop the Machine*.

For weeks I wrestled with the desire to cut my losses and seek adoption as a candidate for Parliament in the Socialist interest. Christopher Mayhew was, as ever, enormously helpful and wrote to Mr. Harold Wilson. I had one or two somewhat painful interviews with Mervyn Stockwood. At one of them, very properly, he pointed out my faults to me. I told him that I thought he was a particularly appropriate person to do so, as all our mutual friends told me how alike we were. But I held back from politics. It would have meant surrendering my Orders as a priest, because clergymen of the Church of England cannot sit in Parliament. I did not want to do this because I valued my priesthood and I had a nagging hope that if God had meant me to be a priest He would not want me to give this up. He must surely have had something in His mind when He put the idea into my head in the first place. I was also reluctant for other reasons. For eleven years I had been 'canvassing' for God. I had more affection for the Church than for either political party. I had spent so long nursing a marginal parish, hopefully in the interests of God. I thought that an ex-priest aged thirty-six nursing a marginal Parliamentary constituency in his own interests would be unseemly.

Another factor that held me back was the team at Woolwich. I did not want to let them down. Bibby had gone to a parish in Manchester, Hughes to Birmingham University and Cooper to a theological college in Canada, others of equal ability and dedication had come to take their places.

Billington had only just arrived. Baker and the Presbyterians were just about to come. Jeremy Hurst and his delightful Canadian wife, Elizabeth, had come to us via Winchester from where he won an Exhibition to Trinity College, Cambridge, and Lincoln Theological College. Before his ordination he had taught English and French at the University in Newfoundland and had given Religious Instruction at a borstal. He was just the right man for us at a time when we were all doing much soul-searching. He had a first-class mind and was mature, relaxed and detached. More than any of us he was able to laugh about the somewhat depressing situation we thought we were in. His wife was tremendously gay coping with the three children she had given birth to within 375 days. (A singleton followed by twins one year and ten days later.)

Then there was Miss Barbara Wollaston. She was one of the most courageous and hard-working girls I have ever come across. Miss Wollaston had started her professional career as a trained parish woman worker. Sadly the Church of England does not normally take its women workers seriously and they often get landed with the jobs the vicar or the curates do not like doing. After some years in traditional parish work Miss Wollaston very understandably did not reckon she was getting anywhere very fast. So she left the parish she was in to go to the London School of Economics and take a degree in sociology. It was after this that she joined us—as a sociologist. Her first brief with us was to do a sociological survey of the congregation prior to doing wider surveys of the parish generally.

Another young man was planning to join us from Wells Theological College when he was ordained in a few months' time. He was Paul Jobson. I was excited about the prospect of him coming as I felt intuitively that he was going to have an enormous amount to contribute. I first met him when I went to preach at a special service for the East Manchester group of parishes. After the service I met a group of local young people from this Coronation Street area for a discussion on the state of the Church. Among them was Jobson, who had been born and brought up in East Manchester. He was small in stature and looked somewhat like a beatnik. But he obviously had a quick and sensitive mind, considerable charm and a delightful sense of humour. But what impressed me most about him was the fact that he was an ordinand of the era after *Honest to God* and *A Mission's Failure*. He took it for granted that in the future we would have to think of God in different ways. He accepted graciously that parishes in East Manchester and East London could not be brought alive in traditional ways, using traditional methods. He was not looking back over his shoulder nostalgically to the past. He was looking forward to the future with confidence, because, like me, he was convinced that as the Church is of God, new ways of service and ministry could be found. By the end of the evening I had decided I was very keen to have him on the staff at Woolwich Parish Church and hoped that the other members of the team would agree. A young parson's first job after his theological college is important to him. It can set the pattern for the rest of his ministry and principals of colleges advise their students that the kind of vicar or rector they serve is more important than the parish. By the standards of 1965 Paul Jobson was 'way out' and I suspected that not many middle-aged clergyman would have understood him. He had committed himself to join the team at Woolwich. I felt a strong moral obligation to him which weighed heavily with me.

Paul Jobson was to replace Jeffrey Rowthorn, who had been with us for nearly three years. He too was an exceptionally talented young priest. He had two Firsts at Cambridge and had won scholarships to universities in Teheran and New York. He was leaving us to become a country vicar in Oxfordshire and is now working in America. I shared my analysis of the situation with the new team of Baker, Garrard, Hurst, Rowthorn, Billington and Miss Wollaston. We kept Paul Jobson in touch with developments in our thinking. Garrard and Rowthorn, while agreeing with many of my views, were on the whole more conservative than I. Billington was more radical. Baker, Hurst and Miss Wollaston were somewhere in the middle. Theoretically it seemed to us that there were three possible policies which the Church generally could adopt in the intractable non-churchgoing areas like Woolwich. (I say theoretically because even on the rare occasions that the Church does come to a common mind it is often impossible to implement an agreed policy because of the laws.)

The first alternative was to continue its present policy of trying to keep going lots of church buildings, each with a vicar and some with a curate as well, for congregations that sometimes did not even reach double figures and were rarely more than thirty or forty strong. Lay members of Church Assembly and Diocesan Boards do not usually come from downtown working-class parishes. The vicars of such parishes want to present the brightest picture to the bishop—in the understandable hope that he will be pleased with them and offer them a more responsive parish in the suburbs. As a consequence, very few people actually know how utterly dismal and unproductive for the Kingdom of God these parishes are.

In the parish immediately next door to us at Woolwich the congregation rarely reached double figures. There was no Sunday School, indeed no parochial organization of any kind. The church next door to that one had a congregation of twenty to thirty and a good troop of Boy Scouts. The next parish down river had a congregation of fifteen or twenty. Some clergymen came to these parishes for a couple of years, worked hard, found they achieved little and left. Others got into a rut and stayed long after they should have gone. It was an almost totally pathetic situation, in which, in my opinion, no blame should be attached to the clergy. They were being broken by the system. The team at Woolwich all thought that the Church's present policies gave it the worst of all possible worlds. None of us saw any merit in splitting up so that we could each take on a downtown church.

A second policy would have been to accept that there were far too many church buildings and that it was unlikely in the foreseeable future that the present rapid decline in churchgoing would be halted. Therefore, all that was needed was one church building for every 100,000 of the population, which could be adequately served by a vicar and a couple of curates. (In the Woolwich area which had a population of 90,000 there were sixteen Anglican churches with an insured value of £1¾ million, used once a week by a total of 800 people at the most.) In a highly populated area no parishioner would have been more than two or three miles away from one centrally placed church serving as many as 100,000 people. Buses could have been hired to bring the car-less and the elderly faithful to church. Just in case there might be a church-going revival in the unforeseeable future, the sites of redundant churches could be leased rather than sold so that they could be reclaimed by our descendants if they ever wanted to build new churches. None of us liked this policy because it showed the Church in retreat. Nevertheless we saw that by adopting the first policy the Church could be slowly but inevitably driven to the second one. Indeed it was beginning to happen. When a vicar left his parish and it was discovered that the building needed £10,000 spent on it to make it safe it was closed and pulled down and the parish amalgamated with the one next door. The Church was being relentlessly nibbled away.

The third alternative was to keep three or four church buildings for a population of 100,000 but make them multi-purpose and multi-denominational, such as we were doing at St. Mary's. In this way they would be widely used for serving the community in many different ways throughout the week as well as on Sundays. And instead of having five or six full-time clergy as members of staff whom the congregation could not possibly afford to pay, there would be ten or twelve clergy attached to the church, most of whom could earn their living in secular occupations. This would have the negative advantage that the

clergy would no longer be a financial drain on the church,
but more important, it would have the positive advantage
that the clergy would be able to exercise a more effective
ministry in the secular structures than they were being
able to do in the parochial ones. Such a plan was a practical expression of my own thinking in *Stop The Machine,
I Want To Get Off*. It was creative and outward-looking.
In different ways, and for different reasons, this was the
plan that made the greatest sense to us. We agreed that
we should stick together, work out what secular jobs we
might take and attempt to develop a new-look church
life in Woolwich.

Garrard, like all of us, saw very clearly that at the heart
of a parish priest's job was a paradox. He is needed, but he
is not wanted. One saw this most vividly in hospital visiting. As part-time hospital chaplains we each spent four
hours a week on bed-to-bed visiting. For the most part
the conversation with patients was cheerful and superficial. And this is how they wanted it. Only very rarely did
we appear to meet a spiritual need. Then, out of the blue,
discharged patients for whom letter-writing was a great
effort, would write to say that without our weekly visit
they would never have got through. We used to recall
vividly that with that particular patient we had never got
further or deeper than talking about the flowers and the
picture of the children on the bedside table. But on balance, Garrard decided that he himself wanted to continue
in the traditional parochial ministry, anyway for the time
being. This could not have suited our plans better, as we
all agreed that we should need at least one priest in the
team fully engaged in parochial duties. We decided to call
Garrard the Sub-Rector. He would be responsible for the
worship of the church and the pastoral and spiritual care
of the congregation. He would look after the choir and
servers and co-ordinate the part-time parochial work of

the honorary clergy. Garrard was a first-rate priest and nobody could have been better equipped for these duties.

Billington was becoming increasingly doubtful about the value of his work with the South London Industrial Mission. He felt that gossiping to youngsters at their lathes in local factories about the football team was not a very productive activity, especially when he could have been teaching them Liberal Studies at a local college of further education, to which they were compulsorily released for one day each week. The purpose of Liberal Studies was to widen the students' understanding and knowledge of the world. The lecturers were given a free hand and within certain limits could teach much as they liked. Billington had noticed that a number of Liberal Studies lecturers were Communists. They had realized that it was a position which gave them considerable influence over the young apprentices. Why should the Communists, who are often so clever at finding and infiltrating the points of real power, have it all their own way? We enthusiastically supported Billington's plan to get a job teaching Liberal Studies which we thought would give him an unrivalled opportunity of bringing Christian insights to secular events, to young people with whom the Church had no effective regular contact.

Hurst had spent the previous year pounding the pavements and knocking at the doors in the Woolwich Common area of the parish. He was the first to admit that he had personally learnt a lot about people from this experience, but, as for the good that he had been able to do, he could not see any point in continuing it. He pointed out his opportunities for giving Christian teaching in parish life were confined to a handful of small children who spasmodically attended Sunday School and an even smaller number of confirmation candidates. Yet, by giving religious instruction or teaching Social Studies at a comprehensive school he would be in touch with hundreds of young people whom he never saw, let alone ever taught, in his parochial work. The logic of his case was indisputable.

Miss Wollaston was already using her expertise as a sociologist in the surveys she was undertaking. Therefore, for her, no changes were necessary. Since Baker was about to bring his congregation to St. Mary's, he thought he should concentrate on getting them happily settled in and therefore would not take another job.

I insisted that when Paul Jobson came he must spend a few months learning the basic skills of a parochial parson's job, such as conducting funerals properly, after which he could decide how he could best spend his time. Jobson assures me that on the day of his ordination at Southwark Cathedral, I told him, 'I am not sure that I know what the parson's job is, but stick around and see what happens.' In practice, things started to happen to him fast. I was worried about the way the coffee house was being run by the professional manager we had at that time. I did not feel that its full potential as a pastoral centre as well as an eating place was being fully exploited. Paul Jobson was keen to take it over. While most vicars would have been horrified at the idea of a young clergyman running a restaurant within weeks of being ordained to administer the Word and Sacraments, I thought it would give Paul Jobson a good opportunity of getting to know the local people and generally getting the feel of the area. I also thought he would bring style, panache and his particular brand of imaginative and sensitive caring to the whole operation. And he did. He ran it superbly; under him it became what I always dreamed it ought to be but had never fully achieved. A few months later, as I shall describe in a subsequent chapter, Paul Jobson became virtually fully employed as a youth leader paid for by the local education authorities.

My position was a bit more complicated. The team insisted that I continued as its Chairman and Co-ordinator. They also thought it important that I carried on the work I was doing with the local secular leaders. In their opinion the range of my responsibilities was such that whatever secular job I took I would have to do from my office in St. Mary's Church. In practice, this led me to increasing my output of freelance journalism, and starting and running a Housing Association for homeless families. We also decided to appoint a layman as Parish Bursar, to deal with the endless administrative chores. In the end we never did this, because the calibre of the people who were prepared to do the job at the salary we were able to pay was depressingly low. My own secretary, Mrs. Crawford, was so much better than they would have been and so we decided to appoint an additional secretary, Mrs. Bowles, to help her, and between them they looked after the administration with charm, efficiency and understanding.

We spent a lot of time trying to work out the relationship between the worker priests and the congregation. We thought that as they would not be in such close touch with the congregation as they were when fully engaged in parochial work, it would be wrong for them to have too big a say in its direction. Consequently, we decided that everything should be done through the Sub-Rector, who would distribute to the various worker clergy the jobs he wished them to do in their spare time. But it was agreed that there were some things that the worker clergy should definitely do. They would all take it in turns to conduct Sunday services and preach. They would also do baptisms and marriages and the interviews that preceded them. Funerals were more of a problem. I believed strongly that the priest who has visited the bereaved should also conduct the service. As funerals take place during working hours the worker clergy could not always get away in order to take them. This meant that the burden of funerals fell on the Sub-Rector and myself. The worker clergy also looked after church house groups, took Communion to the sick in their homes and visited individuals as required by the Sub-Rector. But as I said in my summary of the decisions we made, 'The amount of time honorary priests will have available will vary, and I would like to see them having a great deal of freedom enabling them to use their spare time in the way they believe it would be most effective.' I added, 'It must not be thought that the honorary Rector and clergy are making a good thing out of the new arrangements. They will probably not be working any harder for the Church in the evening than many members of the congregation who do not get rent, rates and free accommodation in return.' Finally I said, 'It will be most important for the honorary clergy not to neglect their wives and families or fall down on their secular jobs by being over-tired or doing insufficient preparation. On the assumption that the clergy are working a five-day week, I would suggest that no one is under any obligation to do more than two evenings a week, say two hours of services on a Sunday and four hours over the rest of the weekend.'

When a priest has spent years being trained for a particular type of ministry, and in my case actually exercising it for ten years, it is not easy to make the mental and psychological adjustments required for moving into a new pattern of life with a new set of aspirations and goals. I was, therefore, tremendously pleased and excited about the way the team came to a common mind on our new policy and how readily we were able to agree on its detailed application. It was typical of the largeness and elasticity of their minds and the honesty of their thinking. It was an expression of their faith and moral courage. It was an enormous encouragement to me. For a couple of months or so I had lain back on the ropes being punched from all directions above and below the belt. All my old enthusiasm returned. The adrenalin started shooting round my body again. I was back in the centre of the ring and full of fight. Our first plan for the church in Woolwich had not been the answer. Now we had another.

Our next problem was to get the agreement of the Parochial Church Council. Understandably they were confused. For years it had been drilled into them how important was the parish priest's job, how necessary it was that they should pray for more vocations to the ordained ministry and how, as a congregation, they should be encouraging the best young men in it to consider offering themselves for ordination. Now in effect we were saying the job was something of a waste of time—although we did not put it as crudely as this. I told the PCC that they had a choice between accepting the new plan or reverting to the traditional set-up. This, I explained, would not be a Rector and five assistants such as they had had for the previous five years, but a Rector with possibly one curate. They knew that I had personally raised much of the money for the clergy's wages over the last few years in the confident but, as things turned out, misplaced expectation that with a large staff we would greatly increase the congregation. Thus, I expected the clergy would generate their own wages from the enlarged congregation. With all the goodwill in the world I could not go on raising and earning money to pay for a large full-time staff of clergy, even if I had thought it desirable to do so. We told the congregation that on our part there would be no hard feelings if they decided for the traditional set-up. We would all leave so that Dr. Stockwood could appoint an appropriate man as Rector. The PCC voted overwhelmingly in favour of the new plan. And so we stayed.

I wanted the congregation to understand that our new strategy was not just the lesser of two evils, but hopefully a positive and creative way forward for the Church of God in the future. Accordingly we arranged a series of meetings and discussions. Before one of them I circulated a paper which spelled out our new aims. In the introduction I said, 'One of the strengths of the last five years is that the staff and congregation have known what we have been trying to do together . . . Now that we are moving into a new gear, it becomes as important, if not more so, that we know our aims, because to a large extent we shall be breaking new ground. It is most important that the congregation should accept that there are a number of things which we have been able to do in the past which we shall not be able to do in the future. Apart from any good we may do in Woolwich, I believe the most significant thing we have to do in the next few years is to develop a pattern of ministry and Church life which can be copied in similar areas.' Then in a section under 'Our Aims', I said, 'In the previous five years our fundamental aim has been to breathe new life into traditional patterns. Much as I personally would have liked to see the old pattern brought alive again I am now convinced that in riverside South London it cannot be done by the Anglicans. I think it may still be possible for the Catholics in the short term, but in the long run I believe they are going to be faced with the same problems as we are now. I propose that our aims for the next stage should be more modest and so, perhaps, more likely of attainment. They should be:

1. The successful working of a mixed manned interdenominational team from one church centre. (By a mixed manned team I meant some clergy and ministers in full-time secular work, some in full-time parochial work and

some, like myself, partly involved in secular and partly involved in parochial work.)

2. Pressing ahead towards Christian Unity with the development of St. Mary's as an ecumenical centre.

3. Concentrating on the training of the laity using the house group method, i.e. in small groups of people with common interests such as Miss Wollaston's sociological survey had thrown up.

4. Attempting to build up St. Mary's as a centre of dialogue and meeting for the Borough.

Finally I warned the congregation, 'We must be prepared to see a reduction in the congregation, confirmation candidates, marriages and baptisms. We have got to face that we cannot even attempt to care pastorally for the whole parish although we can by good use of the local press keep the work of the Church and the challenge of the Gospel before the parish. Church organizations, i.e. Mothers' Union, Women's Fellowship, uniformed organizations (Scouts and Guides, etc.) may have to die unless there are lay people to run them.'

That anyway was the theory. How did it work out in practice? I was not altogether surprised that the congregation did not go down during the last four years of my eight years in Woolwich when we were in this new gear, in spite of the fact that everywhere else congregations were fast declining. The sociological fact seems to be that if people want to go to church they will do so almost regardless of the clergy: if they do not want to there is nothing much the clergy can do about it. I remember Cooper saying to me in the early years, 'You cannot help but admire the people of Woolwich, they are resolutely resisting every pressure we are putting on them!' In my experience every local church which is to be effective needs at least twenty intelligent and dedicated Christians to give its worship, witness and life a hot centre. But in working-class conurbations where those who have got on get out to suburbia, the number of theologically trained and articulate laity is bound to be small. However, with the clergy staff of ten, which we were soon to have, together with the ten leading laity of the congregation, I think we were able to maintain a really vital Christian community in a way that simply would not have been possible if there had only been two full-time clergy and the laity. Anybody who wanted to worship God in the Anglican way would have found at St. Mary's a Christian family worth joining. Another enormous advantage of a large staff is that every member of the congregation could find one member of it to whom they could take their troubles and from whom they would feel they would get good advice. In a parish with just one priest it is inevitable, however good he is, that some members of the congregation will not feel on the same wavelength as he.

We were able to maintain the same careful preparation for confirmations, christenings and marriages as we did under our old methods of working. We were also always able to see every parishioner who actually came to us for help and advice. We were not able to seek out the non-churchgoing masses as we had done before. House-to-house visiting for friendly chats also became impossible.

Of course, the congregation would have been happier if they had had five or six full-time staff looking after them. But I am sure they would have been the first to agree that they were better off spiritually and pastorally by having a large number of worker priests giving them a little of their time than one or two parish priests giving them all their time. On the financial side the church became nearly self-supporting because it was no longer having to find the stipends of the clergy. But I have little doubt that the greatest gain was to the clergy themselves. They felt more fulfilled. They reckoned they were exercising a much more effective ministry in their secular jobs than they had done when they were full-time parish priests. As I write some years later, even Garrard, who was the strongest believer in the traditional parochial ministry, has now left it, for a job at a college of education.

We discovered what we thought in theory was in fact true in practice. It was an advance and not a retreat for the clergy to earn their living within secular institutions. We found that we could make a more effective contribution from within them than from the parochial periphery. There was no dearth of openings for us and we actually lived among the people who went to the institutions we were working in. This was unique in our area, as none of the other school teachers and social workers lived in the same areas as the people they were serving. Consequently, we became more truly involved and identified. It was not an impossible strain for the worker clergy to fulfil their church functions in their spare time in spite of the fact that most of them had young families. Had their children been grown up they would have been able to give even more time to 'church work'. But I am convinced that the fundamental secret of its success was the strength and unity of the team. We drew up a simple code of rules:

1. Decisions affecting the life of the team are taken by all and binding upon all. But none may be asked to contravene the explicit policy of his denomination.

2. Attendance at the weekly evening act of worship which is private is obligatory upon all. Each ordained member of the team will conduct the service in rota.

3. Attendance at the fortnightly team supper and meeting is obligatory upon all members.

4. The team shall have two one-day conferences a year.

5. All Anglican members of the team are expected to attend the parish Communion on Sunday morning unless otherwise engaged.

The rules were only the outward and visible signs. The inner power was a mutual confidence, loyalty, respect and affection which team members had for each other. It was underpinned by the conviction that what we were trying to do together was a creative way of serving Christ as well as being a way ahead for the Church of God beset as it was by problems and perplexities. Often the best test of whether something is worthwhile is whether other people want to join. We never set out to recruit other clergy who wanted to leave the parochial structures, but we had many requests from all over Britain from priests who wanted to join us. We thought it wise to expand very slowly and not to grow to about twelve in number. In fact, when I left Woolwich there were five Anglican priests, three Free Church ministers, one Roman Catholic priest and two Anglican lay women in the team. I remain convinced that we did develop a pattern of ministry for the Church that would be applicable throughout the industrial conurbations. Indeed I think it may be the future pattern for the whole Church.

In the last year or two there has been a sixty per cent drop in the number of men accepted by the Church as suitable for training for the priesthood. Unless the Church lowers its standards so that it attracts men of such poor calibre that they will find the financial and social rewards of the priesthood an advance on anything they would achieve in the secular world, I cannot see many able men ever again offering themselves for work in the full-time traditional parochial ministry. Nor would I encourage them to do so. I can see, and would enthusiastically support, men big in heart and mind willing to combine the priesthood with secular employment. I long to see the theological training given to ordinands reorganized so that they could train for a secular profession as well. As a start I would do away with most of our existing theological colleges and attach them to the Church's colleges of education. It saddens me, but no longer surprises me that, as far as I know, what we pioneered together in Woolwich has not been repeated anywhere else.

Fifteen

AFRICA REFRESHED ME AND I RETURNED ready for another stint at Woolwich. Shortly after I got back I was elected by my sixty fellow clergy to be the first Dean of the new London Borough of Greenwich. The Church of England is organized in Rural Deaneries, which normally consist of ten or fifteen parishes. A Rural Dean's responsibilities are somewhat nebulous and, as in so many things in the Church of England, the job depends on what the man makes of it. The Rural Dean is responsible for the pastoral care of the clergy in the Deanery, with whom he has regular meetings to discuss common problems. He acts as spokesman for the Church in the area and is very often the go-between for the clergy and the Bishop. In most dioceses it is the Bishop who appoints the Rural Dean, but Mervyn Stockwood introduced a system whereby the clergy of the Deanery elected their own man. My election happened at the time when London was being reorganized by the Greater London Act into larger Boroughs of some 250,000 people. This involved the merging of the old Metropolitan Boroughs of Woolwich and Greenwich into a new Borough which, much to the disappointment of the Woolwich Councillors, was to be called Greenwich. Straddling the area of this new Borough were the three Church Rural Deaneries of Woolwich, Greenwich and Eltham. Dr. Stockwood was as keen as I was that the Church should organize itself along civic boundaries, and the amalgamation of the three Rural Deaneries into one new large Deanery was agreed by the clergy.

I was pleased and heartened by my election, which I gathered caused embarrassment to the Diocesan hierarchy. The election took place at the height of *A Mission's Failure* controversy, when many of my critics were telling me that I had undermined the confidence of the parochial clergy. 'Stabbing them in the back' was how one Church leader described it. For five years Woolwich Parish Church had made the running in the area and we had a far larger staff than any other parish. This always tends to make other vicars somewhat envious, so there were many reasons why the clergy should not have put their confidence in me. The ecclesiastical establishment might disown me, but at least my peers were ready to give me the only job, albeit part-time and honorary, in the Church of England for which democratic elections are held.

The new Borough Deanery over which I presided consisted of thirty-two parishes, about forty churches, some sixty clergy in full-time parochial employment and perhaps a further ten priests in secular work. I was instituted as Dean at the civic service to celebrate the inauguration of a new Borough. At the first meeting of the clergy and laity of the new Deanery, I was determined to show that I had some constructive policies for the Church to counter any suggestions that my criticisms in the past had been negative. I reminded the Deanery conference, 'If there are times when we are disappointed at the numbers attending church services, we have only to reflect how low also are attendances at such things as ward meetings of political parties. We are not the only organization affected by apathy. The times call for courage, vigour and action, not depression, defeatism or destructive criticism.' I went on to spell out a four-point programme for the Church in the Borough. First, I wanted to try and mobilize the resources of the Church in Greenwich to serve the community at every level. I thought that one way of doing this would be to appoint a priest and layman to act as the Church's liaison officers with the various groups in the Borough. I would liaise with the Borough Council myself, while others whom I appointed would liaise with industry and the unions, the Council of Social Service, old people's organizations, the Probation Service, the Police and the press. Secondly, I asked the Churches to concentrate on the training of the church laity. I told the Conference, 'The concept of the clerical shepherd protecting the theologically illiterate lay sheep is out of date. In the Church of tomorrow we must all be shepherds, able to advise, instruct, reason with and understand the doubts of the thousands outside the Church whose theological understanding is very limited.' Thirdly, I wanted to see an expansion of house churches throughout the Borough, where small groups could meet for prayer, study, discussion and fellowship. I suggested, 'The strength of the house group lies in its flexibility. They can be sub-divided, they can move house or be disbanded. They require no money and little organization.' Fourthly, I called upon the Church to try to recruit people for community service without any ecclesiastical strings attached. 'I know from personal experience that there are many people who will respond to the parson's call for service, although they would neglect his calls to services.'

I was gratified by the comments made about the meeting in the local papers. One paper ran a banner headline 'After that Church "failure" . . . Triumph.' The opening paragraph of the report said, 'Anyone who imagined after all that discussion last year about the "failure" of a mission in Woolwich that the Church of England, or the Rector of Woolwich, were about to pull out of the town would have been given the lie triumphantly at the first conference last week of the new Greenwich Deanery. It was held symbolically perhaps in the Town Hall and not in a church. The Rector (the Reverend Nick Stacey) is, of course, the new Rural Dean and this first conference was a test of his capacities to offer constructive answers to his own past criticisms and to point a possible road ahead through the swirling mists of secular indifference. His suggestions were crisp, forthright, practical and burning with enthusiasm.'

I never imagined that as Dean of the Borough I could do much to change the Church. Rural Deans have virtually no legal powers. Moreover, I had long felt that, because the parson's job is so personal, effective supervision of the clergy is very difficult. If a priest is good at his job he does not need much supervision, and if he is a weak performer then there is very little that supervision can do to help him. Nevertheless, we made modest progress along the lines of my four priorities. The secular authorities really began to feel that the Church wanted to serve, as was shown by the parishes using their church halls for old people's clubs and pre-school play groups. The Woolwich part of the Deanery had far too many churches. Consequently I took every opportunity of trying to persuade the parishes to close churches, and was successful in three cases.

But it was at the personal level that I felt that I was able to be of most use. Like every conscientious Rural Dean, I tried to encourage the clergy when they were depressed and stand by them when they were in trouble. I well understood the frustrations felt by the junior clergy and helped them think through whether they should take secular jobs. There were times when I was deeply concerned about the strain on the clergy in the Deanery, and the need, as I saw it, for a total reorganization of the Church. In early 1966 I wrote to Dr. Stockwood, 'I become more and more concerned about the morale and general state of the clergy. In the few months that I have been trying to keep an eye on things in this Borough, priest A has died in circumstances which look remarkably like suicide, B has died prematurely, C has had a nervous breakdown, D is having one, E probably about to have one, F has chucked his hand in, G has had to resign his living for reasons which I suspect are basically psychological. And these are just the most glaring cases. It seems to me the whole show is creaking and groaning to a standstill. The diocese is hopelessly overstretched. You and the rest of the hierarchy are under appalling strain trying to hold things together, but are clearly fighting a losing battle. All the signs are that things are going to get even worse. I should suspect that you would broadly agree with my diagnosis. But what can be done about it? If a few bishops agree with you, couldn't you demand that crash legislation be put through Church Assembly making certain areas of some dioceses, "special areas" which would give you freedom to reorganize from scratch. And if you do not get your way, resign *en bloc*. While I am sure the resignation weapon has got to be used with great caution, I believe that there are times when the crisis is so serious that it is right to use it. In any case, those like myself, who are deeply concerned about your health, wonder how much longer you can stand the present strain. I think you may well kill yourself if you go on as you are and your death will have been of little avail. If you can mobilize just a few of the bishops to act courageously and decisively with you, you might pull something off and if you had to resign it would give the Church the shock it so desperately needs. I think you realize that most of the best young clergy still in parochial work are nearly at the end of their tether, and many will, I would guess, be pulling out to secular work in the next few years. Oxford and Cambridge are full of ex-ordinands who have seen the red light and have withdrawn in time.'

Dr. Stockwood, while agreeing that the diocese was overstretched, was less pessimistic. I fear that the intervening years have proved me more right than he was. For today, some six years later, the chickens are really coming home to roost in the Southwark diocese. It is about to face an unparalleled financial crisis.

Canon Eric James who is in charge of urban mission in the inner city's areas of Southwark reports that if the diocese cannot find an additional £200,000 per annum it has the choice of cutting its work by this amount or reducing the number of clergy. As there is little chance of raising this additional money and as the laws governing the freehold make vicars virtually untouchable, the first clergy who will have to be got rid of are the assistant curates and those engaged in specialist ministries—very often the men doing the most important 'frontier' work.

It gives me no pleasure to say that I warned that this would happen in reports, speeches, letters and articles. It was exasperating and frustrating to be told at the time that one was being alarmist, defeatist and lacking in faith. Had the Church acted five years ago when it still had some room for manoeuvre it might have been spared from making the arbitrary and ruthless cuts in men and work which are now virtually inevitable.

My work as Dean highlighted for me the incredible way the Church deploys its resources. I was responsible to the Bishop for the work of the Church in an area serving 225,000 people. For this task the diocese gave me £25 a year expenses. Had I not been earning my living as a freelance journalist, which also enabled me to pay a personal assistant and secretaries, I do not see how I could have even pretended to do the job. The Diocese of Hereford, on the other hand, had a population that was smaller than the Deanery of Greenwich but which had two bishops, two archdeacons, a dean of the Cathedral, three full-time canons and 218 full-time clergy. As most of the money for the stipends of the clergy comes from the Church Commissioners, the financial subsidy from headquarters given to Hereford would have been about four times as great as that received by Greenwich with only sixty clergy. I find it hard to see how the Church can expect people to take it seriously or imagine that it has a job of significance to do as long as it goes on organizing itself in a way that no secular organization or business would tolerate for ten minutes. I enjoyed the Deanery work to which I devoted probably less than one-fifth of my time. I hope I established that the job of Borough Dean was a worthwhile one. In any case, after I left Woolwich it was made into a full-time post.

I had hoped that when we reorganized the activities of Woolwich Parish Church to allow for some of the clergy to take secular jobs the tempo of life would slow up a little. It was not to be. This was partly due to my becoming the Dean of the Borough, which I had not allowed for in my plans, but it was also because I came to see increasingly the enormous potential of the Housing Association which I had started. It all began some two years earlier in 1963. I had been invited to give a talk to the 1958 Dining Club which met regularly at Quaglino's restaurant in the West End. Its membership consisted mainly of young men in their late twenties, who had been to the 'better' public schools and then at Oxford and Cambridge together. They wanted to keep in touch with each other and thought it would be fun to meet from time to time over a good dinner. I spoke to them about some of the problems of riverside South London. After the dinner, the Club's Chairman,

Mr. Gospatric Home, told me that he and some of the members of the Committee had been thinking that as well as meeting for a sumptuous dinner the Club ought to do something socially worthwhile. We both agreed that it was a waste of everybody's time for privileged young men to go down to South-East London youth clubs to play ping-pong with under-privileged boys. The Club members wanted to do something which would be worthwhile and, as important, would enable them to use their various professional skills. I suggested that we started a Housing Association in Woolwich.

Homelessness was much in the news at the time, and like every parish priest, I had been involved in the problem ever since I went to Woolwich. More people had come to see me about housing problems than any other single problem; also there was a hostel for the homeless with which I was in close contact just outside the parish in Plumstead. I remember well going back to my comfortable Rectory ofter my first visit to this 'refugee camp' and asking my wife how we and our three young children could endure existence in such a place. It was a prospect too awful to contemplate. The hostel, which was run by the LCC at that time, had been converted from an old workhouse into one-roomed flats with shared kitchens and lavatories. Although it was much improved later, it had an all-pervading smell of boiled cabbage and stale urine. The residents had approached me in order to enlist my support in getting the LCC to improve the place. I had great sympathy for them, even though I knew that some of the families had brought homelessness upon themselves through fecklessness, stupidity or lack of foresight.

How often throughout my time at Woolwich a family from the north would appear on the doorstep. They usually seemed to arrive when it was dark, cold and wet. The children were always crying and hungry. How often I was told the same story of stupidity. The man had heard that wages were better in London, had chucked his job and given up his accommodation in the north, put his family's belongings in a couple of suitcases, used what savings he had to pay train fares for himself and his family to London and then came on to Woolwich because he had been stationed there as a soldier during his National Service. It usually seemed to be at the weekend when they came to me with a wife and three children but with no job, nowhere to live and no money. Whatever one might have felt it did not help the children to tell the man what a fool he had been.

Although I did help bring pressure on the LCC I was very aware of the difficult position they were in. A minority of the homeless familes was very tough indeed and were weeks behind on their rent, highly subsidized though it was. If the hostels were made too comfortable some families would have settled down in them for life, and if the local government officers were not very strict in the way they defined what constituted homelessness, hostels would have been flooded out by literally thousands of families. I felt that many Local Authority officers and caseworkers who were not in a position to speak out for themselves had been unfairly criticized by press and television for being hard-hearted, insensitive and uncaring. I was in daily contact with them, and, considering the way their patience was tested, the remarkable thing was how dedicated they remained. But no blame could be attached to the vast majority of families who were in desperate housing need. This is not surprising when it is realized that in the mid-1960s 150,000 families (half a million people) were on the housing lists of all the Greater London Boroughs. Daily I saw the broken homes, the mental illness, the alcoholism that resulted from London's housing problem. I had done much speaking, writing, broadcasting and some television interviews about the human casualties of this tragic situation, but I longed to be able to help them in an immediate and practical way by offering them a decent home at a rent they could afford.

These were the reasons why I suggested that the 1958 Dining Club might help me start a Housing Association in Woolwich. Lest there was any doubt of the need, I arranged for the Club's Committee and a few other friends who I thought might be ready to help, to visit the hostel for the homeless in Plumstead. This clinched matters. Some members of the Club were enormously enthusiastic to go ahead; I introduced them to an exceptionally able friend of mine, Hugh de Quetteville. At that time he was a director of S. H. Benson, the advertising agency. He was later to become the Managing Director and Chairman of Colman, Prentis and Varley at the very early age of thirty-seven. He brought in another very talented man, John McBride, who was Marketing Director for the *Sunday Times*. In no time we were set up and ready to go. Between us we knew quite a lot about a considerable number of different subjects but we did not actually know very much about housing. Nor did we have any money. We thought it would help to raise money if we collected some heavy-weight patrons. McBride collected his employer, Lord Thomson of Fleet, Charles Adeane, who was associated with us but tragically killed in an air crash shortly afterwards, collected his father Sir Robert Adeane, and I pulled in most of the others, who included my godfather, Mr. Esmond Durlacher, Canon John Collins and Lord Soper.

In 1963 we bought our first house and converted it into three flats. We bought two more houses in 1964 and a further four in 1965 which produced another nine flats. We bought the houses on mortgage from the Woolwich Borough Council, whose Treasurer, Mr. Frank Hewlett, was extremely helpful, and we met shortfalls out of the £3000 of charitable money we raised in the first three years. The rents paid by the tenants covered mortgage repayments, rates and a small allowance for repairs and maintenance. Progress in our first two years was painfully and pitifully slow. But it was not time wasted, because we were gaining vital practical experience. It was from this experience that I became convinced that there was one way, hitherto insufficiently exploited, of making a really significant contribution to London's housing problem.

The main official emphasis was on four fronts. First, slum clearance, though this often involved a housing loss because human density per acre in the rabbit hutches which were demolished was higher than was being allowed for in the new building. Secondly, building on unused land, the stock of which was fast running out. Thirdly, decanting Londoners into new towns. And fourthly, dissuading people from coming to London at all. I believed that conventional wisdom on housing was putting insufficient emphasis on modernizing and converting two-storey pre-1914–18 war terraced houses and thereby creating additional units of accommodation. In certain parts of London, like Notting Hill, Kensington and Paddington, where there were rows of three- and four-storey houses, conversion was going on but the real potential lay with the two-storey ones because there were so many more of them. Quadrant, as our Housing Association was now called, had discovered that these two-storey three- and four-bedroomed houses with long back additions could be bought and converted, thereby creating two excellent self-contained two-bedroomed flats for about £3500 a flat. This was little over half of what it was costing the Borough Council to build new two-bedroomed flats. There are in London tens of thousands of these larger, old, but sound two-storey houses with thirty or forty years of life in them. By present-day standards and size of family they were too big for single-family occupation—anyway for the kind of family who lives in the twilight areas where they are situated. Furthermore, by modernizing them and converting them it would prevent them from becoming slums before their time. I reckoned that housing associations were well qualified to tackle this work leaving the Local Authority Housing Departments to concentrate on slum clearance and new building. The accuracy of my assessment was confirmed several years later by the Ministry of Housing whose 1968 White Paper was called 'Old Houses into New Homes'.

But there were two problems. First, housing associations were having to meet mortgage shortfalls from charitable sources, and, even if the shortfall was only five per cent, the amount of charitable money required soon mounted up. Indeed we reckoned that if Quadrant was to expand at the modest rate of fifty flats a year we should have to raise £15,000 a year, plus management expenses. Consequently, the rate of a housing association's expansion was directly dependent upon the speed at which it could raise charitable money. Secondly, those in greatest housing need were the low wage earners; but with the ever-increasing cost of borrowing money it was becoming harder and harder for a cost-rent association to provide flats at a rent the most needy could afford. What was wanted, therefore, was a scheme which would enable Quadrant and other housing associations to buy and convert old but sound properties on a large scale using Local Authority loans; these would be let at sufficiently low rents to make them within range of the most needy tenants. There would then be no need to raise large sums of charitable money.

I wrote to the Minister of Housing outlining my scheme which would enable us to do all these things. His senior officials saw the possibilities and eventually I was put in touch with the GLC, whose officers had themselves made much the same analysis of the situation. To cut a long story short, by December 1965, Quadrant became the first housing association to work out and adopt a new partnership scheme with the GLC. It was a major breakthrough for ourselves and for the whole housing association movement. I told the Quadrant Committee that as a result of it we would expand at the rate of 200 flats a year: they thought I had taken leave of my senses. By 1970 Quadrant was expanding at the rate of 400 flats a year, and is growing faster than any other housing association in Britain.

I was surprised how slow other associations were to adopt the scheme. It is no credit to the voluntary agencies that there remains a residue of suspicion of the statutory authorities. I have never seen the Local Authorities as bureaucrats or competitors but as friends and partners. There was great goodwill on the part of the GLC, but there were also miles of red tape to disentangle before the scheme got going smoothly. Patience is not normally one of my virtues, but I was convinced that this scheme would at last enable housing associations to make the kind of contribution that every report said they ought to make but which they had never yet done. If so, it was worth all the wooing and cooing that was involved. The Greater London Council was the goose that was going to lay the golden egg. I cannot believe that its feathers had ever been stroked so lovingly, or its officials smiled at so sweetly as they were by me.

But we had one more breakthrough to make. Traditionally the conversion of old houses in twilight areas was being done by small building firms. But once Quadrant started expanding fast we soon had more work on our hands than the local builders could manage. Neil Wates, a director of the nationally known firm bearing his name, was an old friend and I urged him to set up a new department to deal with our work. He was enthusiastic about the idea, and now for the first time a major building firm, using modern methods and techniques, is involved in this vital task of conversion work. The sky is now the limit.

Quadrant, which is no longer linked with the Church, is now spending £2 million a year on housing homeless families. I imagine that many important schemes have been conceived over brandy in the restaurant of Quaglino's. I doubt if any of them have brought more happiness and saved more families than the plot that was hatched during the 1958 Club's dinner.

My unpaid work as Quadrant's Chief Executive meant that I was having fewer and fewer hours each week in which to earn my living, but few things that I did in Woolwich gave me a greater sense of fulfilment than the work I was able to do with the homeless. I had gone to Woolwich in the first place to try and serve the people. Here at last I had found something which people desperately needed, and which literally changed their lives and gave new hope. I could point to family after family who took on a new lease of life after we had come to the rescue. For years I had been saying to the officers of the local welfare, children's and probation departments that I wanted the Church to help them in their work. Now at last we could. Every day they were on the telephone asking whether we could house this or that family, who had been struck down by some tragedy. There were a number of murders while I was in Woolwich, but there was one particularly gruesome one in which the assailant had murdered a young husband and father of a small family in front of his wife: he then turned on her and injured her seriously. The young wife was not only widowed but left homeless as well. By a lucky chance we had an unexpected vacancy on the day I was rung up about this sad case and we were able to house the family within hours.

Of course, we were only able to house a fraction of those who came to us for help, but the Committee members, who gave generously of their limited time, always visited every family that applied to us. In almost every case we found that we could be of some constructive help even if we could not put them on our own top priority list. We could, for instance, ensure that they were on the Local Authority list, tell them how to set about getting a mortgage, put them in touch with the local Rent Officer or, in some cases, suggest how they could make their existing accommodation more agreeable. We found that our applicants fell into two main categories. First, there were the young married, lower paid workers with two or three children; secondly, mothers who were separated from their husbands: these we found to be exceptionally good tenants.

In all our housing operations we were faced with a dilemma. Our criterion for housing a family was that they should be in need. But unless they paid their rents we could not meet mortgage repayments, and some of the families in the worst plight had very bad rent records. We tried, therefore, to limit the number of problem families we took on, but faced with heart-rending cases we allowed our hearts to rule our heads and took many risks. That we kept our rent debts so low was largely due to members of the congregation of St. Mary's, who in the early days acted as rent collectors. We discovered that it was kind to be tough, because once a family got behind on their rent it was very difficult for them to catch up. While we were totally unpaternalistic I thought it would be a nice gesture if I took a little present to the children of all our tenants on Christmas Eve. Hugh de Quetteville came with me, and while we were doing this tour of houses we took the opportunity to look at their rent books. A great many had not paid because it was Christmas week. Hugh de Quetteville and I found ourselves giving boxes of

Smarties to children with one hand and trying to shake the rent out of their fathers with the other.

Housing the kind of people we did, it was inevitable that we should have our tragedies. We had cases of manslaughter, of incest, and of rape. But the worst of all was a fire. One Sunday afternoon de Quetteville and I were visiting prospective tenants and came across a family living in conditions the like of which I have never seen. They had two children, one of whom looked so ill with bronchitis that I thought he was going to die. The mother was in an advanced state of pregnancy and the father out of work. We were so appalled by what we saw that we put them straight into the car and took them to a flat which had unexpectedly become vacant the previous evening. This was in a house which we had just bought in memory of Charles Adeane, which we had converted into three self-contained flats with all safety regulations rigorously adhered to and passed by the Borough Council prior to them paying out the improvement grant. When we offered the family the middle flat of this house they burst into tears of gratitude. I told my personal assistant to beg, borrow or, if necessary, steal some sticks of furniture and help move the family in the next morning. The house they came from I reported to the Medical Officer of Health, who was eventually able to close it. I was worried by the general condition of this family and decided to try and look after them myself. The mother had her baby which lingered on the edge of life for several weeks before dying. I never succeeded in getting the mother to visit the sickly infant when it was in hospital. The funeral, which I took, was on a bitterly cold day: only the mother and father and myself were present. Neither parent had a proper coat and I got them to huddle under my cloak as we stood by the graveside for the committal. It was very pathetic. As the months passed, in spite of all my urging and coaxing, the family got further and further behind on their rent: but I could not bring myself to threaten eviction. I decided I would postpone action until I returned from my holiday.

At about 11.00 pm on the day we returned from our holidays, when I was feeling full of enthusiasm for the fray and ready to take anything that Woolwich could throw at us, my secretary rang to say that there was a fire in a nearby road and that she was afraid that it was one of Quadrant's houses. I rushed off there and I came down one end of the street as the fire engine came down the other. The mother of the family in the top flat, in an understandable panic, had unnecessarily thrown her children out of the window; mercifully they had all been caught by neighbours holding out blankets. Just before I arrived, the crowd that had gathered shouted to the woman to jump too, which she did. It was poor advice and the fall killed her. Had I got there seconds earlier I might have been able to prevent her from jumping because, as I discovered when I inspected the house later, there was no fire in the room she was in. The fire had started in the middle flat occupied by my problem family. One of their remaining two children died. I followed the procession of ambulances to the hospital and later that night had to tell the parents the sad news. I discovered what had happened later. My family had gone to visit the family on the ground floor flat but, in case their children should wake up, they had left the television on, to reassure them that their parents were still at home. The set was faulty and was thought to have caused the fire. But the parents also propped open the spring-loaded, fireproof front door so as to hear the children if they cried. I buried the second child a day or two later. I moved the family to another flat, where once again they got hopelessly behind with their rent and eventually they had to go.

But disappointments like this were rare, and were compensated for by our many other tenants who gave no trouble. Our experiences convinced me of the tremendous value to the community of a housing association like Quadrant. Its work was complementary to the housing programme that was being undertaken on a far larger scale by the Local Authority. Borough Councils, in order to be fair, have to have strict rules about length of residence, size of family, etc. before they can house people. Again and again hard cases crop up which the Local Authority is prevented by its own rules from helping. It is in these cases that the housing association can step in with immediate help. One example will illustrate the point. A mother of three children living with her husband in their own home takes the children on holiday. On her return she discovers that her husband has brought his 'fancy lady' into the home and 'doesn't want to know' the wife and children, against whom the doors are locked and bolted. They are homeless, yet they cannot qualify for Council housing because they would not have even been on the Council list. In the Borough of Greenwich every MP, every social worker, statutory and voluntary, knew if they came across a really hard case all they had to do was to pick up a telephone to Quadrant and we would try and house the family. I would like to see a 500-flat housing association in every London Borough with a large working-class population for families recommended by social workers. Once Quadrant got the breakthrough with the GLC which enabled it to expand without recourse to large sums of charitable money, the field was wide open for the Church to act on a massive scale in voluntary housing. It is sad that it has not done so. It cannot claim that it is through any lack of opportunity.

I was involved in another venture with the homeless which was much less time absorbing, but in its way as significant as Quadrant. Life had got on top of many of the

100 or so families in Plumstead's hostel for the homeless. One of the reasons was that they had had too many children too quickly. But the Supervisor of the hostel realized that family planning was not a subject that many women would be willing to discuss with him. Nor could they be expected to go three and a half miles to the nearest Family Planning Association clinic. It was decided to try and set up a clinic at the hostel—something which had never been done before in a reception centre. Admittedly it was a bit like shutting the stable door after the horse had bolted; but it might help prevent further pregnancies which would increase the strain on the already overburdened mothers. I was asked to be its chairman. The LCC gave approval and the firms that make family planning products provided them free. With a quite remarkable committee of sophisticated women from Blackheath and Dulwich acting as lay workers and a sensible and broad-minded doctor, the clinic swung into action. In spite of the fact that quite a lot of the families in the hostel were Irish Catholics and there was inevitably some suspicion and fear about this new venture, within a few months over fifty per cent of all the women of child-bearing age were attending the clinic regularly. I believe its success depended on the lay workers, who used to visit each new mother who came to the hostel, win her confidence, and if she wanted, escort her to the clinic on the premises or look after her children while she was seeing the doctor. Although there were Welfare Officers and Health Visitors looking after the residents; although they only had to go downstairs or along the corridor to get to the clinic and were visited in their rooms by a lay worker if they failed to keep an appointment, the difficulties of getting them to take the pill on the appropriate dates and preventing the children from taking them by mistake were considerable. One woman came back for a new Dutch cap because the cat got the one she had been

given the previous week. It made one realize the problems of running a birth control programme in India and why many experts are claiming that sterilization is the really only effective method. At Plumstead the advantages of sterilization were being extolled to one mother with eight children. At the end of the explanation she said she didn't fancy the idea because she didn't want to deny her husband his only hobby. The explanation started all over again and it was pointed out that the whole purpose of the operation was to enable the husband to indulge in his hobby without fear of a further pregnancy. Birth control is no cure-all, but seeing this clinic at work convinced me of the prime need of a domiciliary family planning service for those sad submerged families in our society. If there is any connection between increasing human happiness and building the Kingdom of God, the work of God was being done in that clinic.

Sixteen

THE PEOPLE OF WOOLWICH MAY NOT HAVE responded to the traditional spiritual ministry of the Church, but whenever we tried to meet other types of need, and serve and care in a way the public thought was relevant the response was encouraging. The conversion of St. Mary's church into a multi-purpose building continued to be an outstanding success.

I wrestled with what additional socially creative uses we could make of the church. It was clear that whatever we did was not going greatly to increase the regular congregation. Why not, therefore, seal off the side aisles of the nave under the galleries and make eight offices of them —four on either side? This would still leave a seating capacity of 350 to 400 in the nave and chancel—ample for our needs. In any case the side aisles were not a good place to sit for worship as one's view of the church was interrupted by pillars. By reducing the worshipping area we would also reduce the cost of heating, lighting and cleaning. But much more important, if we could attract tenants involved in the field of social concern it would even increase the use of St. Mary's as a centre of community care. There was a further point. I was very concerned to put the church on a sound financial footing and free it from financial dependence on my money-raising activities outside the parish. The building was insured for £150,000 and to set aside £750 for repairs and dilapidations was an absolute minimum figure that would ensure the building was never again allowed to get into the state it was in when I took over. My family and friends, together with the buildings we had been able to sell, had made the restoration of St. Mary's possible. I was determined that their generosity should not be squandered. Yet for the Anglican and Presbyterian congregations to set aside £750 a year from the regular church income was a virtual impossibility. If I could arrange a lease for the offices which made it legally binding upon my successors to put the money into a fabric fund, the future of the building would be safeguarded in perpetuity. All in all I thought the plan had great promise although there was the major problem of how we could pay for the work.

As these ideas were going through my mind I was discussing the future of the Youth Club which was being brilliantly run by Paul Jobson. The small room in the crypt where they were meeting was inadequate for their eighty or so members. We came up with the idea of digging out the rest of the 700 square feet of crypt under the chancel, which was only four feet high and useless except for storing furniture for homeless families, and making it into a discotheque. It was ideally suited for the purpose. We could create that cavern-like setting so popular with young people, and by building a separate entrance from outside the church we could cut it off from the rest of the building. The walls all round were eight feet thick, which would make it virtually soundproof—a very important consideration if one is not to have the neighbours complaining. And as it had only two small windows with bars on them it would be proof against raids from marauding gangs of other young people. I had long wanted to do something with this crypt and had at one time got Ford, our architect, to get out some rough plans for making it into offices, but I had dropped the idea because of the cost. However, I found the thought of having a nightclub in the church so captivating that I was determined that we should go ahead with it by some means or other. Ford was quickly summoned and asked to design the swingingest nightclub in London. I told him that if he did not know anything about nightclubs, he, Jobson and I would make a personal tour of the best clubs in London to see what we could learn.

In the meantime, Garrard as Sub-Rector was getting very enthusiastic about ripping out all the pews, close-carpeting the nave for warmth, quiet and cosiness and having chairs which would give much greater flexibility in our worship. The more we thought, the more excited we got and the grander and more expensive our ideas became.

At the same time the Borough Council were at last beginning to clear the slums round our miserable little mission hall, which they would soon be acquiring in order to redevelop the whole area. If I could show that we were reinstating the facilities of this building in St. Mary's then the sale of it would cover the cost of creating the discotheque and sealing off the side aisles. We did use the mission hall for youth work and for social services in the neighbourhood. Provided I could get tenants for the offices who were doing the same kind of things, then it seemed to me that we might have a plausible case. By a further fortunate chance the Borough Council was just about to acquire the headquarters of the Greenwich Council of Social Service, which not only co-ordinated the work of all the voluntary social organizations in the Borough but also ran the Citizens Advice Bureau, a domiciliary chiropody service and a personal counselling service. The side aisles of St. Mary's would make a superb headquarters for them and the office space available exactly met their needs.

The Council of Social Service had a very high reputation in the Borough and I knew there was concern about where it could be rehoused. Its Chairman and General Secretary thought St. Mary's would make a splendid headquarters for them. The Borough Council were relieved that they would not have themselves to find expensive alternative accommodation. It all began to look very hopeful.

For years I had consulted a Mr. W. R. Preston, the elder statesman of a highly respectable firm of surveyors and valuers in Central London, on all important property deals. He also always negotiated on my behalf. If he was not in his eighties he was certainly in his late seventies and was semi-retired. He was a man of total integrity who was trusted and respected by Valuers and Town Clerks throughout London. By temperament I like taking short cuts and find reading the small print tedious, so to counteract this I have always made a point of choosing advisers who err on the side of caution and whose honesty and goodness is transparent. Ford, our architect, was such a man. So was Preston. I was desperately keen to bring off this final coup for the church, but I had the highest regard for the Borough Council and would not have considered trying to press my case for equivalent reinstatement if it was a marginal one. Preston would not be party to anything that sailed close to the wind. Equally, if he believed we had a fair case I knew there was no more skilful negotiator in London. He would always apologize to the person with whom he was negotiating for being a 'doddery old man'; in fact he had a mind like a razor.

There were many times in Woolwich when I wondered whether God was on our side. But I am bound to admit that once or twice matters seemed to go our way. Such was the case with this new scheme, which would, I hoped, make Woolwich Parish Church the most exciting multi-purpose church centre in the country and demonstrate how an old and fine building could be adapted to meet twentieth-century needs.

The Borough Council agreed there was a case for equivalent reinstatement. The Council of Social Service agreed to become our tenants. The congregation of St. Mary's and St. Andrew's approved everything. The Presbyterians agreed to pay for carpeting the nave and providing the chairs. The diocesan committees approved the alterations to the church. And Ford surpassed himself by designing what I thought was one of the most attractive discotheques in London.

In my youth I had been to many nightclubs in many cities of the world. St. Mary's, Woolwich, I thought beat them all. Ford exploited the vaulted ceiling and the dungeon atmosphere to the full. It was strong and powerful, yet warm and welcoming. Cutting through the massive walls of the church at foundation level to make the separate entrance was like cutting a tunnel through the Alps. I was in New York when they eventually broke through and Jobson, whose enthusiasm for the whole project was, if anything, greater than mine, cabled me. I went out and celebrated. Ford's and Jobson's highly imaginative minds produced between them a superb design and décor with cosy little alcoves, revolving coloured lights and a multicoloured lit-up glass folly in the bar. We had what I wanted the youngsters of Woolwich to have—the best of everything. We had the best Coca-Cola machine, the best clean towel service and above all the best stereophonic equipment which the young people had paid for themselves. We had three or four different lighting systems which enabled us to create the right atmosphere for the various kinds of users.

I was so pleased with the discotheque that I wanted to show it off to everybody like a mother showing off a new baby. So I arranged a series of preview parties, prior to the official opening by the Duchess of Kent, who as Miss Katherine Worsley was a very old friend of my Oxford days. We had a party for the Borough Councillors and other leading citizens, another for all the clergy and ministers in the Borough, and a third for the social workers. Finally, we had a press conference. It created a lot of interest. Predictably I was attacked in a letter in *The Times* by a clergyman for 'turning the church into a social welfare supermarket', and by a clerical don from Oxford University in an article in the same paper which he had written without even bothering to see for himself or find out what we were trying to do.

We were wanting to create a centre for young people which they were able to make their own and run in their own way. We wanted it to be a place where they would not be got at or have good done to them. While drugs and sexual misbehaviour were banned—in practice it was the members themselves who enforced this—the general atmosphere would be permissive. There would be no church-going rules. Jobson had taken a great deal of trouble going round the local cafés and pubs where young people gathered to get a better understanding of their needs. He was convinced that, more than anything else, they wanted a place where they could relate freely with each other with the unobtrusive support of the adult community. Within weeks of opening, the discotheque became what the London Youth Authorities told me was one of the most successful centres for young people in London. Its remarkable success was due to Jobson. I do not understand what makes a gifted youth leader. There seem to be no rules and no common pattern. Sometimes I think it is something chemical between the leader and the young people. All I know is that Jobson was an exceptionally gifted leader. He ran the discotheque with incredible flair and guided the youngsters with enormous sensitivity. He believed that if they were given the best, they would respond. And respond they did. Why is mainly a mystery to me. Certainly they knew Jobson cared about them, understood them and would always stand by them. Certainly they were accepted as people. But the club evenings in the discotheque were so crowded that you could not move (when Princess Alexandra visited the discotheque incognito I thought she was going to get crushed to death) and the music so loud you could not hear yourself speak. Jobson explained that it was the very crush and noise which played such an important part in contributing to its success. The teenagers felt secure and safe in such an atmosphere. They could not help but relate to each other! And in relating they began to care for each other, which in turn led to helping each other, but always with the knowledge that when things got on top of them there was Paul Jobson and Miss Taylor, the headmistress of St. Mary's School, in the background, ready to pick up the bits. Whatever the reasons for its success, head teachers, probation officers, parents and employers used to tell me again and again that their youngsters were transformed by their membership of the club. They became more responsible, they took more interest in life, they stopped taking purple hearts and they settled down in their homes, their schools and their jobs. We were involved in many ventures in Woolwich. The work that was done among young people in the crypt of St. Mary's was the only work which we undertook about which parents would stop me in the street and thank me for what we had done for their children. I believe the Church exists to transform lives: if the transformation takes place through some unconscious group therapy in the semi-darkness with a noise that adults cannot physically tolerate for more than a few minutes, rather than in the quiet of a church service, I cannot feel that this greatly matters. It is the transformation that counts, the means are secondary.

The discotheque became so popular that it was necessary to enforce the strictest membership rules. This caused great disappointment to those who could not get in and we had to have security guards, with Alsatian dogs who appeared to be perpetually frothing at the mouth, patrolling outside whenever the club was open. I had little to do with the running of the club, but I used to visit it frequently, because I found the atmosphere so exhilarating. It throbbed with animal energy and vitality. It smelt of sweat and scent.

Few of the club members were regular churchgoers and I did not see how they could be expected to be. The cultural gap between the traditional church services and the average young person of Woolwich was too great. But from time to time the young people themselves put on their own service. Led by Jobson they took enormous trouble over them, and wrote their own prayers and hymns. Pop services can be embarrassingly awful and corny. The secret lies in their preparation. Jobson took as much trouble over them as is taken over the production of a television programme. This meant that they could only put on three or four services a year, but they were among the most sincere and expressive acts of worship in which I have ever taken part. In these services we got some way towards finding a liturgical form in the cultural idiom of young people. It was, therefore, a great disappointment to us when the BBC *Man Alive* programme did a feature on Paul Jobson and his work in the discotheque which made it look vulgar, cheap and gimmicky. It always seemed strange to me that at a time when few young people in London were going to youth clubs and when the London Youth Service thought sufficiently highly of our work to give generous grants, so many people wanted to scoff at this exciting and life-transforming venture. I believe that many young people who came under the care of Jobson and the atmosphere of the club already look back upon it as one of the most valuable influences in their lives.

As we expected, it attracted young people in the fifteen to eighteen age group. We wanted also to provide a club for the eighteen to twenty-one-year-olds, who had nowhere much to go except the rather sleazy cafés, with dope pedlars never far away, or the pubs. So we decided to use the discotheque on its two free nights for a folk and jazz club. But clearly if we were to meet the needs of these young adults we should want a licensed bar. While I was not the least bit ashamed of the plan to sell alcoholic drinks under strict supervision in the church crypt I thought it might cause opposition in some puritan circles so we decided to try and go ahead quietly. By chance there was a young reporter at the Magistrates Court to which we had to apply for our drinks licence. Understandably he smelled a good story. All hell broke loose. When the Japanese newspapers take an interest in what happens in the crypt of a church in South London it is not an exaggeration to say it is a worldwide story! I read in the papers that the temperance Peers and MPs held a special meeting about us at which it was agreed that they should ask the Archbishop of Canterbury to prohibit our scheme. In fact, of course, he had no authority to do so and even if he had would have been too sensible to contemplate such an action.

I agreed to do a broadcast with one of the temperance MPs. We sat together at a table in one of the small sound radio studios. There was a fixed microphone between us. It was just as well, otherwise I might not have been able to resist the temptation to pick it up and hit him over the head with it. It was the sheer unctuous hypocrisy of our critics that made me impatient. Nobody objects to eighteen-year-old students drinking in the Students Union which is run by them and for them. When it comes to providing similar facilities in a wholesome environment for builders' labourers who are helping to pay the students' grants from their taxes, the protesting Christians rise up in arms. We actually had one of our worker priests serving behind the bar. On the night we opened there were more members of the press than the public present. It was not the first time that I discovered the secular papers to be so much more perceptive, understanding and in a proper sense Christian than many of the Church ones.

While the bowels of the Church were bursting with bodies and bustle, in its different way another section of life was brought to the building upstairs by having the Council of Social Service as tenants.

For over forty years this independent charitable body had been serving the people of the Borough. One of the secrets of its success was that it gave competent, professional, yet informal and unpatronizing service without any strings attached and without any political or religious axe to grind. Many ordinary people are nervous about seeking advice from the civic authority. They feel overawed by the size and rigidity of the local bureaucracy. Similarly, some people felt shy about seeking help from the Church lest they should be subject to sermonizing.

The Council of Social Service had refused to align itself with any particular group or interest and was supported by every statutory, voluntary and religious body in the Borough. It worried me lest it should be thought that it was surrendering its independence or that the Church was trying to make a takeover bid because it was making its headquarters under the roof of an ecclesiastical building. In my sermon at the service before the official opening of the offices, I made a pledge. I said, 'We [the Church] will do everything in our power to see your independence

is always maintained. We count ourselves deeply privileged to have you here at St. Mary's and all we want to do,
together with hundreds of other bodies in this area, is to
be your servants.'

I was a little nervous that the kind of people who came
to the Citizens Advice Bureau and the other counselling
services they provided might be put off by having to come
to a church building although they had their own separate
entrance. I need not have feared. The numbers of people
attending actually increased. The Citizens Advice Bureau
office alone had nearly 5000 new callers seeking its help
each year.

I thrilled to see every square inch of the church building
being used every hour of the day. There were normally
between twenty and thirty people actually working in
the building—and there were thirty telephones.

One really felt that at last those old bricks were fully
mobilized to glorify God and serve the community. Tragically, relations between different charitable bodies are not
always very charitable, but due to the Council of Social
Service's excellent general secretary, Mrs. M. Syms, the
landlord/tenant relationship was one of total harmony.
Mrs. Syms knew that the Church would never interfere
with anything her Council was doing, but if ever she or
her staff needed any help from us we were always ready
to give it.

Voluntary agencies are often far less effective than they
might be because of their inability to work together. The
team work between the Council and the Church set a
valuable example to the rest of the Borough.

Richard Garrard's predictions about the effect of replacing the pews with chairs and carpeting the floors were
wholly accurate. It altered the entire atmosphere of the
building. Worshippers had become so accustomed to cold
and draughty churches with their hard flagstone floors

and uncomfortable pews, that they did not realize that the very furniture makes it almost impossible to generate that sense of peace and quiet which enables one to hear the 'still small voice'.

It had taken seven years unremitting toil to make Woolwich Parish Church what I believe ecclesiastical buildings in the twentieth century should be all about. The result was worth all the effort.

Seventeen

ABOUT A YEAR AFTER WE HAD COMPLETED the final alterations to St. Mary's—on my fortieth birthday—my wife and I became convinced that we should leave Woolwich. It was partly for domestic reasons, but mainly because I felt that I had given what I had to contribute. I cared deeply about the people and the place and I was determined that it should have me giving the best of what I am capable or not have me at all. It was not that I was no longer busy. My various jobs as Dean of Greenwich, Rector of Woolwich, Chief Executive of Quadrant and freelance journalist kept me fully occupied. But the new Deanery was established, the ecumenical team and church life at St. Mary's going along smoothly as well as being financially self-supporting and the foundations for Quadrant's massive expansion were laid. It had become a case of carrying on what had been started—of taking the mixture as before. There did not seem to be any more challenges. Most men in their thirties and early forties need new experiences. Indeed, I doubt if any well-managed business concern would leave a mid-executive in the same position for virtually the whole of the fourth decade of his life. I had begun to feel that if I stayed in Woolwich much longer I should get into a rut.

Dr. Stockwood's predictions that I would not be offered

another job in the Church of England proved to be only too accurate. Not the vaguest scent of any job of any kind from any source within the Church came my way. In the Church of England there is a long tradition that clergymen do not seek new spheres of work. They wait to be sought out. Personally, I think it is a silly tradition and I should like to see every job, from bishoprics downwards, advertised. I believe the whole system by which appointments are made is archaic, inefficient and bordering on the immoral. I have managed to get jobs for a number of clergymen because by chance I happened to meet a bishop in a London club or on a train and had been asked if I knew a suitable priest for such and such a parish. Nevertheless, the 'waiting to be asked' tradition is one that I have adhered to strictly, more for reasons of pride than of humility. I reckon that my work for good or ill was reasonably well known in the Church of England. It was not likely that I should be one of those clergymen who are forgotten. I should certainly have liked to have been asked to do another job in the Church of England. Whether or not I really wanted or would have accepted one is, as things have turned out, a hypothetical question. I only raise it because so many people think that I have 'left the Church'.

What, of course, they mean is that I have left the ecclesiastical structures, because as far as preaching sermons and carrying out some other traditional priestly functions are concerned I still do my share. I think a more accurate interpretation of the facts is that the ecclesiastical structures left me. I am partly sad and partly glad about this. I am sad because despite my disappointment with the Church there were one or two jobs in the Church which, if offered, I would have accepted because they would have given me an opportunity of making an effective contribution. But I am glad too. I felt it freed me to look outside the Church and seek other jobs which would

better enable me to fulfil my continuing vocation of helping to bring about individual and social change. For whatever else happened to me, I was determined not to become
one of those cynical and washed-up—even bitter—priests
who think the Church has passed them by. Certainly everything I have experienced since leaving Woolwich has convinced me that the Church organization is not the only,
nor necessarily the best, structure, for a man to fulfil his
Christian, and in my case, priestly vocation. I am now
inclined to think it would benefit both the Church and the
world if more priests transferred to and fro between the
ecclesiastical and the secular framework. I think it is a
pity that once a priest has decided to try and fulfil his
vocation outside the traditional ecclesiastical pattern he
is considered something of an outsider. But I suspect that
this attitude may change in the years to come. Indeed it
may have to. So many clergy are now working in the secular fields and so few coming forward for ordination that
if the Church is to survive in its present form some of them
may have to go back. There were a number of times when
I felt that having Mervyn Stockwood as a Bishop was a
drawback. But at least he had the moral courage to tell
me the score as far as I was concerned, so that I did not
waste time yearning and hoping.

Indeed it was not many days after I made a firm decision
to leave Woolwich that opportunities arose outside the
Church. The first was to work for BBC Television. It was
an attractive, glamorous and, by my standards, enormously remunerative proposition but a risky one. I think
my friends were right in advising me not to pursue it.

I came upon the second when I saw an advertisement
in a back number of the *Observer* which I was putting in
the dustbin. The headline of the advertisement was for
'A Deputy Director for Oxfam'. The 'blurb' said that the
post called for qualities of a good organizer, and a success-

ful sales manager. Extensive management experience and a keen eye for cost effectiveness was essential. I was not sure that I had the qualities or experience they were looking for, nor did I know a great deal about Oxfam. I had, however, assisted in a number of money-raising ventures for it. I had also heard grisly stories about the money never getting to the people for whom it was meant. But I did know that the developing world—the problem the organization was concerned about—was a crucial one. Ever since I had visited Hong Kong nearly a quarter of a century earlier, I had been conscious of the needs and aspirations of the emerging nations. The tour I had made of Africa three years earlier had further increased my interest and concern. As the advertisement was several weeks old I thought Oxfam would have probably closed its application list, but that no harm could come from applying. I explained, however, that I had to go to Canada in a few days' time to give a series of talks to prisoners doing long-term sentences in Canadian penitentiaries which I feared would coincide with the time that interviews for the post would be held.

To my surprise, the Secretary of Oxfam, Mr. Bruce Ronaldson, rang me the next morning to ask if I would come for a preliminary interview before going to Canada, but added that there had been over 330 applicants for the job. I discovered that some fifty of these were being screened by a sub-committee. I quickly started doing some homework on Oxfam, visited its dilapidated London offices off Fleet Street and collected all the publications I could lay hands on. The interviewing panel told me that Oxfam had always seen itself as more than a fund-raising charity. It liked to consider that it was a movement, even a crusade. I gathered that its Council had recently agreed on a policy paper which claimed that Oxfam had an important role in educating public opinion and bringing political pressure to bear concerning the needs of the Third World. I thought I might have a contribution to make in these fields and it was a prospect that excited me.

I also heard from a number of reliable sources that if Oxfam was to be as successful in the 1970s as it had been in the early part of the 1960s it would need to alter its emphasis and strengthen its organization. That this should be so was no criticism, indeed it was inevitable. Disillusionment about the developing countries and better understanding of the complexity of the starvation problem meant that the public's attitude was very different in the late 1960s to what it was ten years earlier. If Oxfam was not to stagnate as to some extent it had done since 1965 it would need a new look. The organization had expanded very fast and, as happens in all fast growth situations, some very key members of the staff had not been able to keep pace. Others, especially in the regional organization who had been appointed to do certain tasks, found that, through no fault of their own, the job had changed over the years and was growing beyond their capacity. There was also the problem created by the payment of small salaries, which was partly responsible for a fast turnover of staff; it was often the abler employees who left. This analysis was, I discovered later, a perceptive one. I was planning to go on to Jamaica after visiting Canada to stay with my godfather for a brief winter holiday. But I told Oxfam that if I was shortlisted and required for further interviews I would happily cut out my visit to Jamaica and return to Britain as soon as I had finished my Canadian commitments. It was left that I would be cabled if I was wanted to return direct from Canada, which, as I understood it, would mean that I was still in the race.

My engagements in Canadian prisons were a testing experience. There is a complex of federal prisons, three men's and one women's, around Kingston, Ontario, the most famous of which is Kingston Penitentiary which accommodates several hundred men serving long sentences. I was invited to give a talk in the chapel of each of these four prisons every day for five days. Attendance would be voluntary. The plan was that I should try and give the prisoners faith and hope. I felt this was a tall order as many of the inmates were doing ten years or more for murder, rape and armed bank robberies and similar crimes. I had, of course, frequently visited Woolwich parishioners in various London prisons and I had also given lectures on sport to prisoners in Britain. I had even spent three days at a borstal living under the same conditions as the borstal boys when I was at a theological college, but I was no expert on prisons or prisoners, let alone Canadian ones, and I had little idea of what I would find. I prepared the addresses with great care before I left, as my schedule in Canada was a heavy one. As well as giving four talks each day I was to have private interviews with prisoners who wanted to see me, preach at the Cathedral, address the clergy of the diocese and do various broadcasts and television interviews not to mention attending receptions.

Rarely have I been so frightened as when I stood before some 300 of the toughest men in North America at Kingston Penitentiary on the first morning of the five-day mission. I am not sure which frightened me most, the sullen, detached, almost vacant look on the sea of faces before me or the rows of he-men prison officers who stood shoulder to shoulder at the back. The officers were not in a relaxed mood as one of their number had been murdered by an inmate a few days before I arrived. I felt the officers were looking at me suspiciously and wondering what this Englishman, with long hair (by their standards), liberal views and an Oxford accent, was going to say and to do with the men under their care. I was wondering too.

Within seconds of surveying the scene it was over-whelmingly clear to me that the addresses that I had pre-pared would be unsuitable. If I was to get these men to relax, to smile, and to feel with me, I would have to do something off the cuff and with much lightness of touch. Yet I am not a good off-the-cuff speaker unless I know my audience and am confident in my subject. I did not know the audience and I was not confident about how I could make faith and hope relevant to the large numbers of deeply damaged personalities who were eyeing me. It was a ghastly moment. I realized the whole success of the mis-sion depended on the first talk. If it got over, the bush telegraph in the prison would do the rest. Should I plough ahead with the address I had prepared or take a fearful risk and ad lib? I took the risk and felt reasonably con-fident that it had worked out all right and continued to talk off-the-cuff at the other prisons during the day.

But the real test would come the following day on two counts. First, by the number of prisoners who turned up and secondly, on whether I could get them to ask ques-tions. The Chaplain, who was my host, insisted that the prisoners would not get up and ask questions in front of their fellow prisoners lest they should make fools of them-selves. He thought they would send in written questions anonymously which somebody else could then read out. He was a very experienced and greatly respected prison chaplain who was doing so much to help liberalize and hu-manize the Canadian penitentiary system and I felt it would be churlish not to accept his advice. On the other hand I was convinced that for the mission really to get off the ground a verbal interplay between the prisoners and myself was vital. I accepted that it would be asking too much for them to question me after my first talk, but once they had got the measure of me I was determined to try and elicit questions from the floor. I was warned not to be disappointed and written questions were prepared as a standby. At the end of the second talk, which I am glad to say was better attended than the first and which I had prepared in the early hours of the morning, I asked for questions. There was a ghastly hush and the prisoners eyed each other and smirked, and the officers at the back continued to look doubtful. During the silence I willed somebody to get up and say something—absolutely anything. The Chaplain sat nervously at my side fingering the slips of paper with the written questions. And then it happened —a prisoner spoke, and we were away. Had he been in the front row I would have gone and hugged him.

From then on we never looked back. We discussed everything in question time: the state of the world, war, the prison service, sexual deviations, God, free will and the life after death. One prisoner got up and said that he was inside for homosexual offences and did I think this was right. It was a brave thing to do as sexual deviants are not usually popular with their fellow prisoners. From then on after each talk I was questioned for an hour and sometimes longer, and indeed the only thing that drew the session to an end was the fact that I had to move on to the next prison for a repeat performance.

I found the women's prison the hardest nut to crack. Admittedly there is only one women's federal prison in Canada (except a specialist one for drug addicts) and it had only about fifty inmates but some of them were very gruesome. I lunched at the women's prison on my first day and sat down at a table with six of them. I thought they were men. But some, particularly the abortionists, were more normal. There was one jolly girl who looked after the chapel and who was very keen to wash my shirts. I discovered from the Governor that she had popped her last three babies into the deep freeze. I wondered whether prison was the right place for her.

My talks brought me face to face with the dilemma of prisons. I had private chats with some of the worst criminals in Canada who were household names throughout the country. They were friendly enough and one wondered, however hideous were the things they had done, whether being left to endure a rotting death in prison was any answer. Yet equally one realized that society had to be protected from such people. Moreover, so often whenever attempts are made to liberalize the prison régime, some prisoner would take advantage of it by murdering or beating up an officer. There was one man of about my age whom I found hauntingly pathetic. He was a brilliant musician and scholar, and, according to the Governor, more intelligent than any other officer or prisoner. His trouble was that he interfered with little boys; he was on an indefinite sentence, which meant that he might never be let out. The Chaplain told me that he had given up all hope in life and had really ceased to exist as a human being. He could not cope with the awful crudeness, roughness and overwhelming vulgarity of the main blocks and, partly for his own protection, had been committed to the psychiatric cells. It was thought that if I personally invited him to play the organ on my last day it might help him to spark into life again. I found a man who was physically alive but in every other respect dead. I could not persuade him.

It was in the Governor's office immediately before my last talk to the inmates of Kingston Penitentiary that I picked up the cable from Oxfam, which told me there was no need to return to Britain and urged me to enjoy my holiday in the West Indies. I thought it meant that I had not been shortlisted and was much disappointed. But I was determined not to let it affect the climax of my prison mission and I poured out what heart and soul there is within me to the prisoners with whom I was beginning to feel such a close bond. At the end of my talk, in their coarse and tuneless voices, they all sang, 'He's got the whole world in His hands'. After this one of the prisoners stepped forward and handed me an album that had been made in the prison workshop. It was inscribed with these words:

'Although we may not mention it,
We are hoping that you know.
Your visit meant far more to us,
Than words could ever show.
And as you journey on your way
Unto life's greater goals.
Remember!
You left an ember burning
In the hearts of all these souls.'

With a lump in my throat I tried to thank them and as I walked out of the chapel they all stood up and cheered. I was told it was the first time that cheering had ever been heard in the chapel of Kingston Penitentiary. I was humbled and moved.

A few hours later I was in Toronto dining with an old friend, John Worsley, whose sister had opened the discotheque and Council of Social Service offices at St. Mary's a few months earlier. I showed him the cable from Oxfam and he thought I had misunderstood it. He interpreted it as meaning there was no need to return to England as I virtually had the job in the bag. I rang Oxford the next morning for clarification and discovered I was on the shortlist of two and that the final decision would be made after a further interview when I returned from Jamaica. Within a few hours of being in one of the toughest maximum security prisons in the world in the extreme cold of a Canadian February I was lying in the sun on a private beach in Jamaica. I was grateful for a rest but overwhelmed by the contrast.

On returning to Britain and after further interviews I was offered the Deputy Directorship of Oxfam. My various jobs in Woolwich were distributed among several different people and Mervyn Stockwood appointed a successor as Rector. On Easter Day 1968 I climbed into the pulpit for the last time. I told the congregation that the events of Good Friday left the disciples in dismay, and even Easter Day, with the empty tomb and Jesus' appearances, was at the time inconclusive and bewildering. 'Anyway Thomas found it so, and so would most of us had we been there at the time.' I suggested that from the human standpoint there were many other ways that Christ could have made his tremendous claims more convincing and more easily understood by ordinary people. I went on, 'But man's ways are not God's ways, and in the broad sweep of history it is God's ways that seem to go to the heart of the matter rather than the plans of man . . . I see most clearly a parallel between this and our experience in Woolwich during the last eight years. When I came here eight years ago I made no bones about what we wanted to try and do together. Among other things we wanted to fill St. Mary's with worshippers . . . We failed and I made no bones about our failure. Of course it was a disappointment. We tried so hard. We did so many things. We hoped so much. In our small way we felt a little like what the disciples must have felt on Good Friday. But God's ways are not our ways. And as we look back at it now we can see that it was out of our "failure" that all sorts of things have sprung which would never have happened if we had succeeded in the way we wanted. Just as out of Good Friday came Easter Day, so out of our disappointments have come all sorts of things which were neither planned nor foreseen.' I then reminded them how Church history had been made by the sharing of St. Mary's with the Presbyterians, how our crypt was being used by over 500 youngsters a week, how the Quadrant Housing Association had accommodation for over 1000 people in need and how we had built up an ecumenical team of clergy and ministers. With confidence and conviction I proclaimed, 'Out of our initial defeat has come victory. Out of the failure of old ways has come more exciting and perhaps more worthwhile new ways. Out of despair has come hope—out of death has come life.'

Eighteen

AN ACCOUNT OF MY TWO YEARS AS OXFAM'S Deputy Director is not part of this tale, except where it relates to my experiences in the Church and highlights my personal dilemma. This dilemma is that I always seem to find m self in organizations which desperately need to change if they are to be effective. I have never pretended to be a theologian. I am certainly no prophet or visionary. But I do think I have the capacity to make clear and perceptive analyses of situations, and seeing what is wrong with an organization and what needs to be done to put it right. I would make the modest claim that I often seem to be able to see round the next corner. It is in no spirit of boasting that I say that so many of my predictions about the Church of England have proved accurate.

I had not been at Oxfam very long before it became abundantly clear to me that changes in direction and emphasis coupled with an increase in discipline were necessary if the organization was to recapture the dynamic it had in the middle sixties. Although inflation had disguised the fact to the casual observer, Oxfam had in fact been declining in effectiveness as a fund-raising organization since the mid-sixties. More seriously, the public's attitude to the Third World, to development and overseas aid is so very different today to what it was in the late 1950s and early sixties. The formula that had been so successful in those days would not in my opinion carry it through the 1970s.

It was equally clear to me that very few people in the organization saw the need for change, and even if they could have been persuaded I doubted whether the organization would have had the will to make the somewhat painful decisions that would have been necessary. It was a difficult situation for me. I did not want to be thought of as the kind of person who cries 'wolf' in every job he goes to. On the other hand, I had spent the fourth decade of my life in an organization whose policies I was convinced were wrong and would lead to its steady decline. The thought of being in the same situation in another organization for my fifth decade was not one that appealed to me. At least in the Church nobody expected me to have any influence over its direction at national level. In Oxfam, with which my name was widely associated in the public mind, it was assumed that as its chief salesman and spokesman, I was confident about its direction, priorities and organization. There was a further problem. Charities are very vulnerable organizations—more vulnerable than Churches because loyalties do not run so deep. Internal disagreements, if known to the public, can be particularly damaging. The one that was going on in the United Nations Association at the time I was at Oxfam was a timely reminder of what had to be avoided at all costs. Although my disagreement with Oxfam was almost entirely on policy, rather than personalities, there is always a temptation for the press to turn policy differences into personality conflicts.

For these and other reasons after I had been at Oxfam for a year I told its Chairman, Professor Charles Coulson, that I thought I ought to leave as there was little that I could effectively contribute to the organization in the present situation. In the event I stayed another year before resigning.

Unfortunately a confidential paper on possible changes in Oxfam policy and organization which I had been asked to prepare for internal circulation was leaked to the press. This was done by a few people in Oxfam, whom I thought at the time did not have the best interests of the organization at heart. Subsequent events have proved me right, and for Oxfam's sake, I am glad to say that they have now left.

The leak, which was sadly distorted, created a difficult situation both for Oxfam and for me. Perhaps particularly difficult for me as I could not defend myself without damaging Oxfam. It is something of a tribute to the good sense, coolness and charity (a rare quality in charities) of those involved that it caused no damage. I genuinely hope that my predictions for Oxfam's future, if it continues along its present path, will prove to be wrong. It is run by well-meaning and dedicated people and does good.

My experiences in the Church touch me at a much deeper level than my experiences with Oxfam. Oxfam is a man-made organization which will sink into Establishment mediocrity and safeness or slowly wither and die if it is not abreast of the mood of the times. This is sad but of little real significance. Because if Oxfam fails to measure up, a new organization with a contemporary style and ethos will inevitably spring up to take its place, and plead the cause of the Third World. The Church, however, is irreplaceable. I believe it is of God, founded by Jesus Christ to represent Him, to carry on His work, to repeat His message of hope and salvation for the human race. As long as there are human beings on earth it cannot die, although its outward form and expression may well become very different from its present one. This is why, in spite of all,

I still care so much about it. There is no substitute for it. There never can be.

When I was Chaplain to the late Bishop Leonard Wilson, I used to have long sessions with him during which I would tell him what a tragedy I thought the Church of England was. He used to say, 'I know, I know, but tell me a better hole to go to.' (He did not agree with me, however, when on one occasion I told him jokingly that any man of ability could run the Birmingham diocese while he was shaving in the morning, which would allow him time in the rest of the day to concentrate his efforts on the Church at large.) Of course, I know from the little history that I learned when I was at Oxford, that large organizations with their roots deep in British history do not change quickly.

The Church of England which is so much an expression of the British people, who have an understandable horror of tyranny, is a very democratic organization. This adds to the slowness of change, and doubly so when one realizes that when it comes to questions of religion, human beings are particularly conservative. It is trite to point out that the Church on earth is made up of sinful, insecure and muddled human beings like myself, and, therefore, is bound to be imperfect. Moreover, no one who has had the kind of experience I did in Woolwich can think there are any simple panaceas which will transform and revitalize its life. I understand why the clergy cling to their freehold (which is one of the main factors holding up reorganization in the Church of England). It is the one bit of security they have at a time when they are losing out in terms of job satisfaction, status and finance. I am even dimly aware of some of the complex theological issues raised by the secular society. I am also deeply conscious of the devoted and usually unsung work being done by the Church up and down the country. I know of some clergy who faithfully slave away for little or no reward of any kind save that of thinking that they are trying to do God's will. For the last two and a half years I have had no official job in the Church. This has enabled me to stand apart from it to some extent and look at it in a more detached way than I was able to when I was up to my eyes in it. As a result, I have become more sympathetic about its problems and less critical of its performance. When I was at Oxfam, I stumped the country addressing meetings. I discovered it was frequently the Church which was giving the lead in the local community on the challenge of world poverty.

All these things I understand with my head, yet my heart cries out that after making every allowance the Church of God ought to be very much better than it is. It seems to me that it is terribly difficult and not very convincing for the Church to speak to the world about the love of God if it shows so little of it in its own life. Let me just take one simple example. If the Church really cared about people surely it would deploy its clergy where the people live today instead of where they lived in the Middle Ages. More than that it would deploy the greatest number of men in those areas where there is the greatest suffering, underprivilege and despair. It does the opposite. Four-fifths of the clergy of the Church of England still work in areas where one-fifth of the people live, and it is the plushy suburban parishes which get the curates while too often in the sad and seedy areas a broken-down vicar carries on single-handed.

How can the Church talk to the world about reconciliation and unity when it cannot even reunite with the Methodists? How can the Church give people a wider vision and effectively challenge them to raise their sights when it spends so much of its own time on pettifogging and irrelevant details? Canon John Collins illustrates what I mean in his autobiography, *Faith Under Fire* in which he describes Chapter meetings at St. Paul's Cathedral, after the war. John Collins says, 'It was with some excitement that I went to my first Chapter meeting. Matins was over. The Dean and four Canons sat round a table in the Dean's Vestry; the door was shut, the large red minute book unlocked. With no prayer, no pause for silence we plunged into our solemn and vital conclave. The first item of business arising, I seem to remember, from the minutes of the previous meeting took up practically the whole of our time. It was a discussion about the order of precedence in Cathedral processions and at Cathedral functions, about whether the Archdeacon of London should take precedence over the senior Canon, as the Archdeacon supposed, or vice versa, as the senior Canon supposed. And this wrangle about precedence remained a major issue at subsequent Chapter meetings for months, affecting personal relationships for many years. That Chapter meetings were normally like this I soon discovered.' And so are many Church meetings.

My belief in, my love of and my commitment to the Church remain unshaken because of my belief in God. But I am bound to say that I find it very hard to reconcile this with the fact that I have found less imagination, enthusiasm and inspiration in the Church than I have found in any secular organization with which I have been associated. I do not think it is open to debate that any secular organization which was as badly and unimaginatively run as the Church of England would have gone bankrupt or been the subject of a takeover bid by now. It is about this squandering of talent and resources that my heart bleeds, and it is about this that over the years I have felt bound to speak out.

My disagreements with the leaders of the Church have not affected the good personal relationships which I have with many of them. But somehow I seem unable to get the reasons for my anguish across to them. They give me the impression that when it comes to the Church they think I am too intense, too worried and have become almost humourless. Perhaps they are right. But my problem is this: everywhere I go I see men and women needing to find some kind of faith in God which will give them the strength to cope with life on earth and the assurance of a life hereafter.

People want to be convinced that there is a God who cares about them personally, that in the end love will prevail and that there is hope for us all. To millions, and I am among them, the so-called joys of living are not always self-evident. We wonder what life is all in aid of and whether it is worth the battle.

The Church of the holy and living God, Creator and Father of us all, exists to provide this hope. Yet to the outside world, it often gives the impression of being sick people playing a sick game to keep a sick show going.

I believe the sin lies in having a relaxed, detached almost casual attitude in such a situation. God knows there should be no grounds for complacency in the Church of England. Yet this is the impression which the leadership often gives. While those of us who feel deeply about the Church's inadequacies and burn to try and put things right often find ourselves dismissed as discontented, if not disruptive, pessimists frustrated by not having fulfilled our personal ambitions. I find this sad.

I often think it is the organizational radicals such as myself who have more faith in God than our more conservative-minded colleagues. I know the Church will go on in some form. God will see to that, however blind and stubborn His followers may be. Because there is a great streak of the conservative in me, I should have liked to have seen the old familiar structures revived. I worked hard in Woolwich to do just this. But if they have outlived their usefulness as instruments for building God's Kingdom, I am not concerned to cling to them or fight a rearguard action trying to preserve them. I would rather look to find new ways for using the Church's enormous resources—resources of love and of insights, of experience and of knowledge, of loyalty and of vision, as well as resources of men —16,000 clergy—and money (the break-up value of the Church Commissioners alone is £416 million and this is by no means all the Church's capital wealth), and buildings, all 18,000 of them in England and Wales alone, mobilized effectively to bring comfort and joy to the hearts of men. If ever an institution cries out for dynamic and courageous leadership that institution is the Church of England. As someone who has worked so long in its structure, I know the difficulties but it should not be beyond the wit of churchmen to take a new and fresh look at its resources and work out 'a back to square one' strategy.

Let me illustrate what I mean by taking as an example the riverside areas of South London in the diocese of Southwark. Some 1½ million people live in the district. A survey of the Church's resources currently deployed in the area would need to be made. Let us, for the sake of example, say that this survey shows that there are salaries available for 200 full-time workers who may or may not be clergy and that by rationalizing Church property and other assets, an additional £100,000 a year of free money would become available, and that there are over 10,000 churchmen of widely varying abilities who on an average give three hours of their time each week to pastoral, social, evangelistic or community work. A further survey would be made of the area which would aim to pinpoint the most pressing pastoral and social needs both now and those likely to develop in the future. Then, in conjunction with the Local Authority, central Government and other statutory and voluntary bodies in the area, a master plan which would need to be kept flexible, would be drawn up which would ensure that the Church's resources were used to the maximum of spiritual and moral benefit of the people. My mind boggles with excitement at the contribution such a plan could make to the community, after the church workers had been given the appropriate training.

I think of the calibre of the workers such a scheme would attract. The Young Volunteer Force Foundation, which sends groups of three or four young graduates to do community service and development in deprived areas in a way that is very little different from what a team of good young curates have traditionally done, gets over fifty applicants for every vacancy. Yet the Church on the other hand is finding it increasingly hard to attract able recruits to the ordained ministry.

By its refusal to take radical measures now the Church is relentlessly being nibbled away and as economic pressures and the shortage of ordained manpower really begin to tell, it is going to be pushed more and more on the defensive, which will leave it less and less room for manœuvre. Perhaps in another ten or twenty years the seriousness of the situation will be so overwhelmingly obvious that Churchmen will be ready for drastic change, but by that time one wonders what there will be left to change. One could understand and forgive the Church's reluctance to take a completely new look at its resources and priorities if the present formula were being successful. But it is not. To say the Church is in decline is to understate the position. Poke beneath the surface and one finds it is in a state of near collapse. The actual statistics on the decline in the number of men being trained for the priesthood, in confirmations and baptisms and churchgoing all tell the same sad story. One survey on confirmations in the Southwark diocese that was taken while I was Rector of Woolwich demonstrated that if the numbers continued to decline at the same rate that they had from 1960 to 1965 there would be no confirmation candidates at all by 1975, and the biggest drop was taking place in the suburban areas of the diocese where traditionally the Church has been strongest. But what the statistics do not portray is the loss of morale among the parochial clergy and church people. Many of them have lost heart. I believe that one could go a long way to restoring their confidence and giving them renewed hope and a wider vision if they were involved in a new plan more related to man's real needs. At the moment they feel they are flogging a very tired and lame old horse to keep the traditional ecclesiastical cart moving. However optimistic and hopeful an interpretation one tries to put on the facts, the short-term prospects of the Church as we know it cannot be good. But I do not despair. Nor do I lose heart. The Church may reject me, but I cannot reject it. One must go on working, praying and pleading for vision, courage and commonsense whether one be inside or outside the ecclesiastical structures.

Of one thing I become increasingly certain as I get older. It is that the basic essentials of the Christian faith are both true and relevant. I have freely admitted in this book that my ministry as a priest in the Church of England has not always gone as I would have hoped. But I am grateful indeed that I have at least been spared a crisis of faith, such as has afflicted so many of my contemporaries. I think I do find myself believing more and more in less and less, but then I have never been much concerned about what I have considered to be the less essential doctrines of the Christian religion, which some Churchmen take so seriously. About the Virgin birth, or exactly what happened on Easter Day, I admit to being agnostic. But I find that the few things I do believe are enough to be going on with.

They do not illuminate my path as much as I should like, but they shed enough light for my faltering footsteps through life.

I take my stand that in the end God. And that ultimately He has everything under control and in the long run His love will prevail. I take my stand that God revealed Himself in Jesus Christ and that with this Christ men can have some kind of personal relationship through prayer. I take my stand that Christ comes to us and strengthens us in many ways and in diverse places, but most particularly I believe His spirit is with us when those who would try to follow Him break bread together in the manner of the Last Supper. I take my stand that our life here on earth is but the beginning of something so much better which God has prepared for us and passes our understanding. And finally, I take my stand that the gates of Hell will not prevail against His Body here on Earth—which is the Church.